D0575064

(*endpapers*) The menu for a traditional
Sichuan-style banquet which would be served in
the evening. Reading from top to bottom and
left to right the courses are: Spring in Jin Jiang –
cold plates; the Phoenix Shark's Fin; Duck
Smoked over Camphor Wood and Tea Leaves;
Pan-fried Lobster; Vegetables with Almonds;
Steamed Fillet of Fish; Sichuan Noodles; Lotus
Seed Soup – a dessert flavoured with fungus
and osmanthus blossoms.

AUTHENTIC RECIPES FROM THE CULINARY AUTHORITIES OF BEIJING, SHANGHAI, GUANGDONG AND SICHUAN

# China
## THE BEAUTIFUL COOKBOOK

中國名菜集錦節本

不懂得一個
國家的飲食，
就無法了解一個
國家的文化。

中國諺語

*"No one can understand the culture of a country without first experiencing its food and drink."*

FISHERMAN ON RHONGU LAKE IN GUILIN, GUANGXI PROVINCE

ADAM WOOLFITT

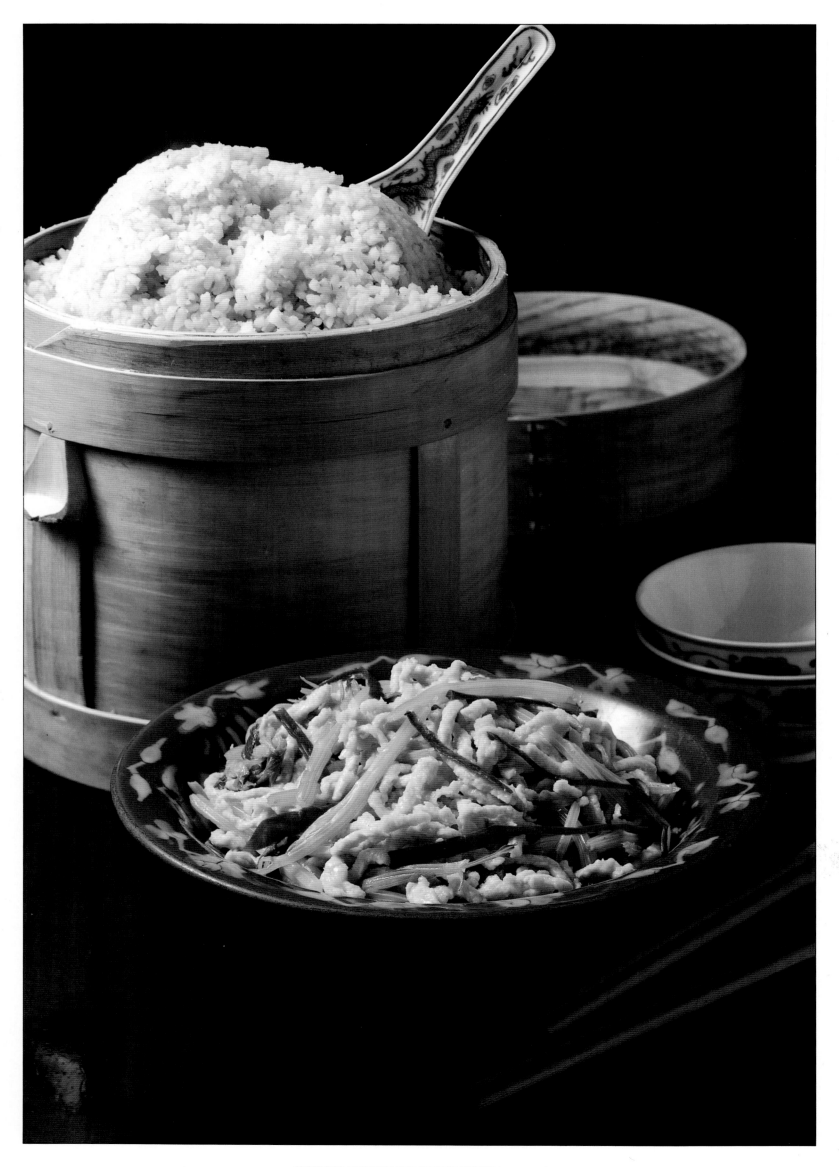

SHREDDED CHICKEN AND TENDER CELERY *(see page 54)*

AUTHENTIC RECIPES FROM THE CULINARY AUTHORITIES OF BEIJING, SHANGHAI, GUANGDONG AND SICHUAN

# *China*
## THE BEAUTIFUL
## COOKBOOK

中國名菜集錦節本

## CollinsPublishersSanFrancisco
*A Division of HarperCollinsPublishers*

Published in the U.S.A., 1991 by
Collins Publishers San Francisco, 50 Osgood Place,
San Francisco, California 94133

Produced by Weldon Owen Pty Limited
43 Victoria Street, McMahons Point NSW 2060 Australia
A member of the Weldon International
Group of Companies
Sydney ● San Francisco ● Paris ● London

© 1986 Intercontinental Publishing Corporation Limited
© 1990 Weldon Owen Pty Limited
USA © 1990 Weldon Owen Inc.
Food photographs © 1982 Shufunotomo Co. Ltd

Text: Kevin Sinclair

The recipes in this book provided by the following authorities:
Beijing Friendship Commercial Services Corporation
Shanghai Municipal Meal and Service Corporation
Guangdong Provincial Meal and Service Corporation
Sichuan Provincial Meal, Vegetable and Service Corporation

Editorial Director: Elaine Russell
Managing Editor: Julia Roles
Recipe Translators: Frances Ting Chiu Ling, Chen We Yei,
Cai You Qing, Kung Sen Wei De
Recipe Editors: Tan Lee Leng, Jacki Passmore
Picture Editor (China Landscapes): Mary-Dawn Earley
Calligraphy: Ethna Gallacher, Wong Chiu Tung
Map Illustrator: Linda Love
Designer: John Bull, Bull's Graphics

President: John Owen
General Manager: Stuart Laurence
Co-editions Editor: Derek Barton

All rights reserved. No part of this work may be reproduced or
utilised in any form by any means, electronic or mechanical,
including photocopying, recording or by any information storage
and retrieval systems, without the prior written permission of the
copyright owners.

ISBN 0-00-215999-6

Production by Mandarin Offset
Printed by Toppan Printing Co (S) Pte Ltd
Printed in Singapore

A Weldon Owen Production

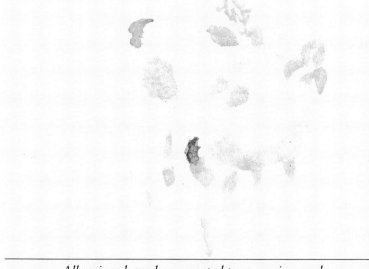

*All recipes have been created to serve six people*

THE GREAT WALL SNAKES
THROUGH MOUNTAINOUS NORTHERN CHINA
KEN DUNCAN

*(following page)* TERRACED HILLSIDES IN
THE LIPING VALLEY, GUIZHOU PROVINCE
GEORG GERSTER

APPETISERS IN A LACQUER BOX (*see page 142*)

# Contents

# The Culinary Heritage

CHINA is more than just a country. It is a culture, a civilisation, a way of life that has developed through five thousand years of recorded history. It began when the Han people, forebears of the modern Chinese nation, started their long march to destiny from their ancient homeland near the modern city of Xian. Even before these fifty chronicled centuries of settled society, food played a vital role in the developing Chinese culture.

In the misty era before the Han tribes coalesced into the beginnings of the Chinese race, the first mythical hero to emerge was Fu Hsi. The main activities of this god-like fabled figure were hunting and fishing, and to him is attributed the invention of the kitchen and cooking. The next legendary figure in early Chinese mythology was Shen Nung, the Divine Husbandman. To him goes credit for the plough, the hoe and the care of farm animals. Huang Ti, the Yellow Emperor and the patron saint of Taoism, is worshipped still for the conception of planting grain and the invention of the pestle and mortar to crush it to make flour.

The hunter, the husbandman and the farmer; it is no accident that the first three objects of worship of the ancient Chinese should all have to do with food. Emperor Yu, the founder of the Xia Dynasty (twenty-first to sixteenth century BC), the first to unify the early Chinese, has been honoured over the centuries not so much for his political role as the earliest emperor but for his development of water control. This worthy step helped to stop the floods which ruined crops and encouraged the use of irrigation to improve yields. Since the days of the Great Yu, the overwhelming priority of every ruler of China has been to fill the rice bowls of the people. So it remains today. The fact that the billion people of China enjoy a healthy, satisfying, substantial diet with no rationing of basic foodstuffs is widely regarded as the single most vital achievement of the modern government in Beijing.

Things have not always been so auspicious. Throughout its long and turbulent history, the vast wealth of China, most of it created on the solid base built by the endless toil of peasants in the fields, has been a magnet for plunderers, adventurers and invaders. Nature, likewise, has taken a savage toll with drought and flood, earthquake and landslide, tidal wave and typhoon destroying the crops and herds so patiently built up at such a cost in sweat and tears. Not for nothing is the Yellow River, once tamed by Huang Ti, referred to as "China's Sorrow". Its floods over the centuries have left generations homeless, beggared whole provinces, destroyed crops over enormous areas and sentenced untold millions to death by famine.

But Chinese ingenuity, grit, vigour and endless toil have overcome all the obstacles. And when the time comes to give thanks to their many gods and beliefs, the

MANCHURIA

INNER MONGOLIA

KOREA

*Yellow River*

SHANXI

Beijing•

HEBEI

•Tianjin

*GULF OF BOHAI*

GANSU

SHANDONG

•Qingdao (Tsingtao)

NINGXIA

*Yellow River*

SHAANXI

*Yalong River*

•Luoyang

JIANGSU

*HUANG HAI (YELLOW SEA)*

Xian•

HENAN

DABA MOUNTAINS

Chengdu•

Yang-zhou•

SICHUAN

HUBEI

ANHUI

Nanjing• •Wuxi

•Shanghai

•Suzhou

Hangzhou•

•Ningbo

*Yangtze River*

Luzhou•

*Yalong River*

*Yangtze River*

*Min River*

JIANGXI

HUNAN

GUIZHOU

*DONG HAI (EAST CHINA SEA)*

Kunming•

•Guilin

FUJIAN

YUNNAN

GUANGDONG

TAIWAN

*Mekong River*

*Xi River*

*Dong River*

Nanning•

Foshan• •Guangzhou

VIETNAM

LAOS

*GULF OF TONKIN*

*NAN HAI (SOUTH CHINA SEA)*

HAINAN

15

people of China do so while gathered around the dining table. Family feasts, celebratory banquets, birthdays, the summer and winter equinoxes, wedding anniversaries, celebrations of the birthday of Tin Hau, Goddess of Heaven, or of imported faiths like Christianity, Buddhism or Islam, the conclusion of one successful business deal or the agreement on launching a new one; all these and many more occasions call for glasses to be raised and chopsticks to be wielded. Any event can and is used as worthy excuse for a feast. It can be as simple as a home-cooked meal for an unexpected visit by friends, or as lavish as an imperial banquet that takes twenty chefs three weeks to prepare. Whatever the reason, and no matter how humble or splendid the surroundings, the way Chinese traditionally celebrate is by eating.

So food in all its aspects has, since the birth of Chinese civilisation, been a cornerstone of the national culture. In no other people has the preparation, preservation, cooking, cultivation and serving of food taken such a dominant and pervasive role. China's very history revolves around the table and the kitchen. The folk heroes of the nation, no matter who rules it, are often in some way or another connected with eating, drinking or making merry. In China today and in the homes of thirty million overseas Chinese scattered around the world, kitchen gods sit in family shrines staring amiably at housewives or chefs preparing the daily meals. Twice a year ancestral graves are swept and incense lit to pay homage to departed ancestors. Roast pork, rice wine and fruit are offered to the dead; food in Chinese culture is important even to those who have passed on.

## A DIVERSE CUISINE

Any cuisine is limited by the raw ingredients that are available. In the case of China, the range is virtually boundless. The country is vast: twice as large as Europe excluding Russia, bigger than the United States including Alaska and Hawaii, a quarter as huge again as Australia. Into this gigantic land are crowded more than a billion people. They are unfairly distributed: packed into the rich flatlands along the east and southern coasts; jammed into the great valleys of the Yellow, Yangtze and Pearl rivers; stacked by the millions in the sprawling industrial conurbations; and crammed – no less than one hundred million of them – into the rice-bowl basin of inland Sichuan. But elsewhere they are scattered lightly. The steppes of Mongolia and Xinjiang are still thinly peopled by Kazakh, Uigur and Turkic tribesmen, and the descendants of Genghiz Khan. The ice plateau of Tibet, a land of soaring peaks, precipitous caverns and frigid highland plains, is bigger than Austria, Czechoslovakia, the Netherlands, Switzerland, Belgium, Italy, Portugal, Luxembourg and Hungary combined, and has fewer than two million people. In the jumbled mountains of the southwest, a chaos of races – minority tribes of dozens of nationalities – live in steep river valleys, unaware and uncaring about those who occupy the next ravine.

This huge landscape has dictated the scores of regional cuisines that have developed in China over the centuries. Although the country produces every delicacy under the sun, much of the grain, vegetables and live-

TIBETAN NOMADS ON HORSE AND YAK, SICHUAN PROVINCE
LEO MEIER

A BAI WAITRESS AT A DALI CITY RESTAURANT, YUNNAN PROVINCE · GREGORY HEISLER

stock is available only in the locality where it is produced. Even today, with vast improvements in communications and transport, what goes into the family pot tends to be that which is grown or raised nearby. The delectable camel hump of Mongolia is a rare and costly luxury in the south. Seafood is understandably scarce in Chengdu, 3000 kilometres (1,800 miles) upriver from the mouth of the Yangtze. Fresh vegetables are unknown in the frigid Manchurian winter, although the gardens blossom all year round in semi-tropical Guangdong.

From this immense geographical diversity have developed the manifold varieties of Chinese cuisine. In the past the climate dictated what people ate and to a lesser extent in the age of efficient artificial preservation, refrigeration and dehydration, so it still does today. This is partly because of the inherited and acquired love of the favourite dishes with which people grew up from childhood. While experimentation is encouraged in every Chinese kitchen, the family favourites of childhood tend to hold a tight gastronomic rein throughout life. For Chinese, as for every other people, this is probably because of the international love for the food that mother cooked.

But intertwined with the love of good food is also the ancient basic philosophy of China, the belief in harmony, of the balance of nature, of the duality of existence, of the blending of contrasts. Yin and yang, the two elements, are as significant in the Chinese kitchen as they are in the temple. Yin is soft, yielding, dark, feminine. Yang is hard, bright, masculine, vigorous. In the wok, the hotpot or the steamer, yin and yang combine and complement each other. Sweet contrasts with sour. The two basics of stir-frying – ginger and spring

onions – are yang and yin. Crunchy sea salt goes with Sichuan peppercorns. Steamed chicken goes with stir-fried fresh greens, the yang of fiery chillies goes with the gentle yin of sugar. The contrast of taste and texture, colours and cooking methods, which results in any balanced Chinese meal is a triumph of the philosophical theory of yin and yang, the world in a happy balance. A Chinese meal, ordered correctly, should be orchestrated like a Mozart symphony: hot and cold, sweet and sour, plain and spicy, meat and pickle, fish and greens, yin and yang.

## THE NATIONAL DRINK

Tea is the drink of China and has been so since recorded history began. The preparation and sipping of tea are part of the education of a scholar and the daily life of a manual worker. Learned discussions about how best to make tea, with what implements, the source of the best water, the method of boiling it and the vital question of how long the leaves should be left to steep are matters which for thousands of years have preoccupied writers and artists, generals and merchants, mandarins and emperors. Throughout the land in almost every dialect it is called "cha". The exception is in Fujian where the word "deh" is used. Because the seafarers of Fujian exported the dried, chopped leaves of the tree, and because it was in the ports of the southeast coast that foreigners loaded it, the beverage is known in the Western world as "tea".

Tea has played a vital role in China throughout recorded history. It has been the reason for polite and learned academic discussions in teahouses; it caused social unrest and riots in China as it once did in Boston;

MARC BERNHEIM

PICKING THE FAMOUS DRAGON WELL TEA, HANGZHOU, ZHEJIANG PROVINCE

## THE TEA CEREMONY

When Lu Yu wrote his scholarly but chatty "Classics of Tea" at the time of the early Tang Dynasty (618-907 AD), tea was more than just a drink, it was a symbol and a ceremony. He discoursed on types of water to use, the twenty-four different items of equipment needed to make a cup of tea and the way in which it should be prepared. The best tea leaves, he wrote, "should curl like the dewlap of a bullock, crease like the boot of a Tartar horseman, unfold like the mist rising from a ravine and soften gently like fine earth after it is swept by rain".

Lu Yu, along with similarly minded scholars, helped to inspire centuries of poetry, arts, porcelain manufacture and an enormous range of other academic and industrial activities all concentrating on the best way of making tea. This ostentatious, quasi-religious elevation of the tea ceremony rose to a pinnacle among the idle rich and the literati during the Song Dynasty (960-1279 AD) when fortunes would be paid for a perfectly glazed teacup, and officials would sit for hours discussing different brands. This came to an abrupt end with the arrival of the less sophisticated and more direct Mongols of the Yuan Dynasty (1260-1368 AD) for whom a cup of tea was a cup of tea. The tea ceremony still flourished in Japan where it had been exported to, but in China the ceremony was never again to reach such esoteric heights. However, in modern China the teahouse remains the favoured rendezvous.

## ALCOHOLIC DRINKS

Loosely translated as wine, the Chinese expression "jiu" means any beverage containing alcohol, of which there are many in China. Like tea, wine is the fountainhead of a thousand legends, most of them affably eccentric. A chef of ancient times is said to have put some rice to soak in a covered jar, which he placed in a corner of his warm kitchen and promptly forgot. A few days later he raised the lid and was engulfed by a strong, unfamiliar aroma. He cautiously dipped in his serving spoon and tasted the contents; and again, and again. Other kitchen staff were attracted by his joyful mirth. They too tried the strange mixture. So was held the first cocktail party in China, and thus was born the Chinese tradition of drinking and making jolly.

The Chinese made a variety of jiu as far back as 2000 BC. Modern vintners would probably not award the ancient beverages any prizes, but ancient tipplers seemed partial to a glass with their meals, and for the past four thousand years Chinese imagination has run enthusiastically riot in distilling alcoholic drinks from almost anything that has come to hand. Today that tradition remains vibrantly alive with a staggering number of wines, beers, spirits and liqueurs being made in every corner of the land. Brewers, vignerons and distillers use as raw materials everything from transplanted French grapes and German hops, to rice, sorghum, wheat, maize, potatoes and fruit of all types. Beverages range from classic German-style wines, to foaming beers, to the explosive sorghum-based Mao Tai, with which Mao Zedong and Richard Nixon toasted pingpong diplomacy, to sweet but potent tipples such as the Panda brand liqueur made in Sichuan Province and based on the hirsute Chinese gooseberry.

Wine was carried into China in ancient times by Persian traders, and at least a century before Christ vines

and it has been used as a national treasure, a state currency, a government fund-raising monopoly and, in the form of pressed bricks of leaves, as cash. It is also a relaxing, captivating, sacred drink.

There are thousands of varieties of tea. It grows on flat, fertile land but thrives equally well on steep hillsides up to 2000 metres (6,000 feet) amid eternal mist where other crops fail. In its untended state the tree sprouts to 10 metres (30 feet) or more, but when clipped and pruned for cultivation it is kept to 1.2 metres (4 feet) in height so the strength goes into the leaves. The three leaves on the tip of the bud are used in top-quality teas. There are three main types of tea: red, green and black. Among the most famous of the green varieties is the astringent, pale yellow Dragon Well tea from Hangzhou. The Keemun type grown all over east China, favourite of the British breakfast table, is among the best-known of the red teas. Oolong (Black Dragon) tea includes such leaves as the Iron Goddess of Mercy type from Jiangxi, which when pressed into bars is said to be as hard as metal.

Even the most learned scholar cannot say where tea originated. According to legend a forgotten emperor (or a thirsty deity, some versions hold) was sitting contemplatively in his garden sipping a bowl of hot water when a gust of autumn wind blew some leaves off a tree. They landed in the imperial bowl and coloured the water. The monarch sipped it and liked what he tasted. Tea was born.

Since then more legends have sprouted from the teacups of China than from almost any other source. Tea is said to soothe the excited and help the restless to sleep. On the other hand, it is held to awaken the senses and rouse the drowsy. It has been used as a medicine and a placebo, to quiet the restless young, relax the tensions of the mature, and to ease the discomfort of the old.

were growing around the imperial palace. The grape had a seesaw existence throughout history, often depending on the personal inclination of the emperor. If he drank, vines flourished. If he happened to frown on the pressed and fermented fruit of the vine, imperial decrees went out ordering farmers to rip up the vines and replant their land with food crops. A fillip to the vineyards came at the end of the last century when Europeans in north China, especially missionaries, planted extensive areas of grapes. Today they still exist in vast areas of Shandong and Hebei provinces, and new plantings by French and other joint-venture partners are renewing production of first-class wines in China. With the aid of foreign expertise and modern techniques used in Europe, America and Australia, Chinese wines have won international awards.

Beer also came from foreign influences, many of them unhappy. During the rush to grab parts of China in the last century, Europeans and Japanese brought with them a demand for their native drinks. This dismal episode in China's history had at least one auspicious result because there are thousands of ales and beers in the country today, many of them drawn from brewing techniques introduced into the Treaty Ports. The most famous is the magnificent Qingdao beer which originated in the port city of that name during German occupation of parts of Shandong Province in the late nineteenth, early twentieth century.

Most Chinese drinking is done along with eating; tradition abhors drinking alone or on an empty stomach, and it is at banquets with family, friends or guests that most Chinese indulge in some of their huge range of drinks. Usually the glasses are filled with one of the countless varieties of rice wines, the most famous of which is Shaoxing wine from Zhejiang Province. This tends to be darkish in colour and is poured warm from a vessel like a teapot into small glasses and then drunk with flamboyant gusto. Also favoured at banquets, particularly during feasts or when foreigners are present, are some of the strong spirits of China. These include some truly fearsome distilled beverages like the fragrant but potent Mao Tai; the transparent Fen Chiew liquor which is used as a base for Zhu Ye Qing liqueur; and the ferocious Kaoliang of north China, designed to keep out the frigid cold of winter and which, to boot, numbs all other feelings with its 130 proof punch.

Much dinner-table drinking is associated with games. In one, the serving circle in the middle of the table is spun and the person who ends up staring into the head of the remains of a duck or chicken dish has to swallow his or her drink. Then the host toasts his guests, and the visitors toast the host, and the young raise their glasses to the old, and the aged drink to the more youthful, and everyone drinks to the person sitting next to them. As every glass is raised, everyone calls "kan pei", which in rough translation means good health.

Many of the stories associated with Chinese drinking deal with poets. Historically, poets were regarded as a rather bohemian, happy-go-lucky lot, a large number

SELLING MEDICINAL WINE IN A ZUNYI STREET MARKET, GUIZHOU PROVINCE

MICHAEL YAMASHITA

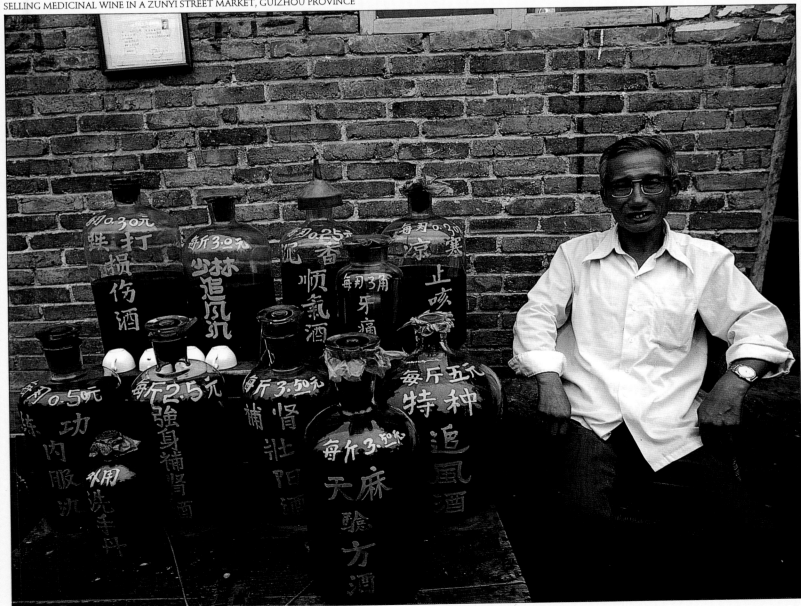

of them from wealthy or influential families, who spent their lives writing classical couplets, generally while deeply in their cups. Several of them often cited in classical tales came to bad ends because of overindulgence. One is said to have rolled to his death down a steep hill while staggering home from a wine shop. Another of these "drunken dragons", as poets were known, was Li Po who wrote with enthusiasm of "the rapture of drinking and wine's heady joy". He went everywhere accompanied by two servants whose job was to carry their literary master safely home. Li Po proclaimed during his bouts that he could not write without a drink. His end would seem to bear out this claim; he is said to have clambered into a sampan and pushed himself out on a lake on a still night to admire the reflection of the moon in the calm water. While enthusing about the view, he took another drink. Leaning over the side of the boat trying to embrace the vision of the glorious reflection, he fell into the water and drowned.

Even the stern Confucius liked a drop and noted that "there is no limit to wine drinking". One must not get drunk, he was swift to add, a lesson which was apparently not heeded by Li Po or hundreds of other poets who down the ages have sung the glories of jiu.

## THE ART OF PRESERVATION

Entering a Chinese store that sells dried foods, herbs or medicines (and sometimes it is virtually impossible to draw a line between what you take for health and what is for sustenance) is akin to going into a museum of fauna and flora. There will be fungi of incredible sizes and bizarre shapes: tiny button mushrooms from the fields, large drooping fungi from the rainforests of the southern jungles, and the strange monkey brain fungi dug from the frozen soils of Manchuria. Some stores will also have birds' nests from the cliff-side caves of Kalimantan – foul-smelling balls of grass and excrement, but a vital ingredient for the soup of the same name. There will be countless varieties of pasta, fried chillies, a mysterious selection of hundreds of herbs adorning shelf upon shelf, and dangling from the roof will be the rustling skins and skeletal shapes of octopi, jellyfish, squid, fish intestines, seaweeds and other former inhabitants of the deep; just drop them into water for a few hours and they will return to an edible reincarnation. Deers' antlers, horns of rhinoceros, gall bladders of ox and buffalo, and the dried penis of whale are also to be found at awesome prices, because a pinch of the ground powder from such potent items is widely believed to hold aphrodisiac qualities.

Just how Chinese preserves are used is a secret which many chefs guard closely. And just as only a very fine line can be drawn between the ingredients used for medicine and those for food, so can the doctor's advice merge with the recipes used in a Chinese kitchen. The saying popular among Western food faddists, "You are what you eat", was probably expressed in a score of Chinese dialects several thousand years ago, and the raw material for many of the potions mixed then and commonly in use today can still be found on the shelves of any Chinese dried food store.

A MARKET STALL IN YONGXIN, JIANGXI PROVINCE

ENRICO FERORELLI

MICHAEL YAMASHITA

THE FIERY CHILLI, AN EXPLOSIVE COMPONENT OF SICHUAN CUISINE

HARALD SUND

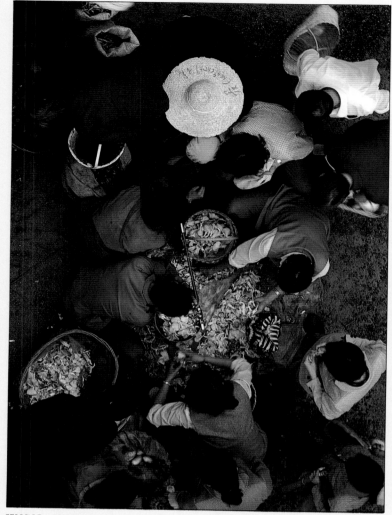

SELLING MUSHROOMS AT SHIMIAN VILLAGE MARKET, SICHUAN PROVINCE

As with everything to do with the foods of China, preserving techniques were dictated by the climate. In the south, fresh foods were almost always available (just as well, because nothing keeps for long in the torrid, humid summer). In the north, for half the year nature provided natural refrigeration. And in both regions pickling has long been a favoured technique, for reasons of taste as well as for preservation.

The average cook in China uses an extensive range of preserves, spices and seasonings every day. Hot chilli paste, biting mustard, the inescapable soy sauce, preserved plums, pickled turnips, carrots or cabbage, mushrooms in endless species and black bean sauce are among the most common accompaniments for everyday dishes. And they are the merest tip of a gastronomic iceberg of formidable proportion. Perhaps the most visible preserves in China are the pressed flocks of ducks and the salted schools of fish which hang in the streets outside restaurants throughout the land. They are edible advertisements for what is on offer inside.

Nuts of all kinds are an important and often unseen and unsung part of the Chinese culinary art. They were prominently mentioned in the gourmet recipe book of Madame Wu, printed in the eleventh century. So were many other preserved foods which can still be found today in delicatessens or dried food stores in any self-respecting Chinatown.

To preserve meat Madame Wu advised rubbing dry salt into the flesh, putting it in a clay pot with a stone on top and pressing it overnight, then hanging it up to dry in a cool, airy room. The same technique is universally in use today. Fish were kept in times of abundance by grilling them, soaking them in oil and then packing them in

jars sealed with damp clay. Similar items, perhaps marketed in more modern containers, can still be bought to be eaten either as snacks or as a course in a feast with other out-of-season foods. Preserved meat and fish and pickled fruit and vegetables are never a meal on their own, but as side dishes and accompaniments to major courses, they are indispensable and valued parts of the culinary heritage.

## A CULINARY HISTORY

Chinese culinary traditions have adapted freely and changed fluidly with time and circumstances. Five thousand years ago, at the time of the emerging Han tribes, the main crop in their arid, windblown homeland was probably a prehistoric form of millet. But archaeological digs in north China show that far before that time, Beijing Man had already developed a sophisticated caveman cuisine. Using stone weapons, he hunted down such prey as sabre-toothed tigers and roasted them over an open fire.

Steaming, that great basic kitchen technique still in very effective use today, was perfected long before the foundation of the first dynasty. Scientists testing remains outside Xian have ascertained that the inhabitants of a village named Banpo were cooking such delicacies as chicken, carp and elephant three thousand years before the birth of Christ.

Two millennia later the glorious Shang Dynasty flowered (sixteenth to eleventh century BC). In addition to art, commerce, culture and science, cuisine flourished in the rich atmosphere of the court and such delicacies as rhinoceros and elephant were consumed. Religion, closely linked with food, also developed, and as the cooking fires died down the shells of turtles and the thigh bones of oxen were thrown in the embers. From the shapes produced in the flames, soothsayers read omens and foretold the future.

There is no evidence that the prophets of Shang gave warning of the rise of Zhou (1122-256 BC), the dynasty that was to supplant them. The kings of Zhou claimed descent from a ruler of the northwestern plains named Hou Ji, which means Lord Millet, and by the time they imposed their rule over the embryonic northern kingdom that was to grow into the Chinese nation, they had learned how to grow rice, wheat, soy beans, melons, celery and squashes, and on feast days ate roast sheep and boar.

But early gastronomic development was not restricted to the north. As the Han people melded into a great and unified nation on the plains of the Yellow River, a political and culinary evolution was taking place along the fertile banks of the mighty Yangtze. Kingdoms and dukedoms rose and fell and flowered and wilted. But as armies marched, clashed, died and conquered, the peasants of China continued their eternal task of providing food for the ever-increasing population.

Thanks to modern scientific techniques, archaeologists and anthropologists can now fit together much fascinating historical evidence. The resulting jigsaw puzzles have many missing pieces, but enough have survived to tell us of a rich gastronomic feast in the vast Yangtze Valley during the ceaseless warring eras of the kingdoms of Wu, Yu and Chu. For three centuries, the warriors and lords battled for supremacy. Politically they were stalemated, but on the culinary front, seven hundred years before Christianity, chefs won magnificent victories with such outstanding dishes as noodles sautéed with honey, lamb stewed with sugarcane, braised ox tendons and bitter melon soup. The soldiers did not beat their swords into ploughshares, rather the farmers used the shoulder blades of their oxen to turn the deep, rich soils in which they grew such delicacies in the hot, damp summers as peaches and juicy melons. This gave rise to internal trade. Peaches went north to the sophisticated table of the emperor, and bear paws were dispatched south to the semi-barbarian kings of the warring states.

By the second century BC, the Yangtze Valley was the frontier of Chinese civilisation, an Oriental Wild West where the only law was the sword. But China was about to take the gastronomic and geographical shape of today, as the Qin Dynasty (221-206 BC) brought under imperial rule the blooming basin of Sichuan in the upper Yangtze and the broad plains of Guangdong. For the first time the four great branches that were to grow into modern Chinese cuisine – classical Beijing, rich Shanghai, delicate Guangzhou and hearty Sichuan – were all to come under one rule. That rule did not last long because on a tour of his new lands, the man who united China into one realm died. Legend says his body was carried back to the capital Xian amid a load of salted fish (even then a southern delicacy) which disguised the smell of death. He was buried with great honour, guarded by thousands of terracotta soldiers.

Next onto the imperial stage came a commoner from stout farming stock named Liu Bang. In blood and fire he forged the Han Dynasty (206 BC-220 AD), one of the greatest in China's history. Gastronomically the Han

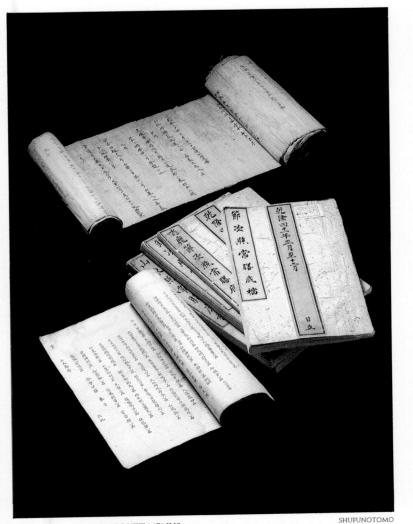

ANCIENT CHINESE BANQUET MENUS

SHUFUNOTOMO

A STREETSIDE BREAKFAST, GUIZHOU PROVINCE

MICHAEL YAMASHITA

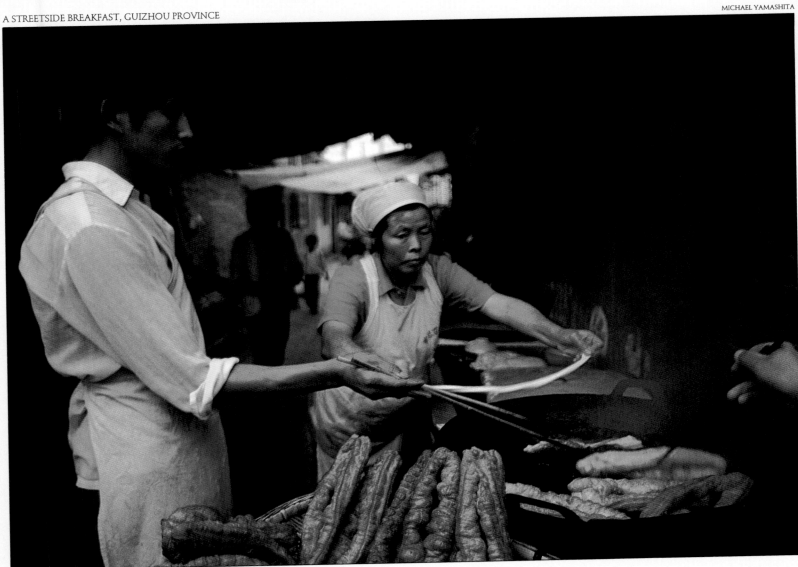

period was a vital one. There were staggering culinary achievements. Noodles were invented, so were flour mills. The ancient soy bean was made into tofu. Expeditionary forces went into central Asia (then green and fertile, now mostly arid) and brought back treasures like sesame, peas, grapes, coriander and garlic. The culinary delights of the New Territories added Sichuan peppercorn to the imperial banquets. From the tropical south horsemen galloped in relays to speed the exotic lychees of the Pearl River delta to Xian. Today the first lychees of autumn are still rushed north to gourmets, but now they go by express train or jet aircraft.

The Han had pacified, or at least kept at sword's length, the savage Hun horsemen. But when, in the third century AD the Han Dynasty toppled because of internal plots, the barbarians galloped into China and occupied the north. They brought gastronomic disaster with them as well as political terror: their favourite dishes were boiled sheep and smelly cheese. However, the culinary flame was kept burning brightly south of the Yangtze where the Wu Dynasty (222-280 AD) took what a bountiful climate, fertile soil and dedicated farmers and fishermen had to offer to raise cooking to an art. Oranges went into the cooking pots as did other southern crops such as lotus seeds and coconuts.

It took three centuries for the Huns to be thrown back from north China to their heartland on the steppes of central Asia, and then the Sui Dynasty was to rule for only four decades (581-618 AD). But what it accomplished in such a tiny span! The Grand Canal was frantically dug by armies of human bulldozers. It linked the two mighty rivers on which China's history had been written, and from Yangzhou on the Yangtze the grains of the south were towed by barge north to the Yellow River plains. Yangzhou became the capital and its chefs laboured mightily over charcoal stoves to bring forth miracles of culinary creation that are today some of the most famous manifestations of the Chinese kitchen. The fat, plump Wo noodles that make up rich winter soups came from the Sui Dynasty chefs. So did fried rice and immortal dim sum. It might not have long dominated the political throne of China, but the Sui Dynasty passed on a culinary heritage that today is still renowned.

## TRAVELLERS' BOUNTIES

And then came the Tang (618-907 AD). Their legacy is both diverse and delectable. They bequeathed us the wok and therefore that most distinctive of Chinese cooking techniques, stir-frying. Distilled spirits came during their three-century rule, during which China was the dominant power on earth. Trade flowered and with the merchants from other lands came nutmeg, saffron, eggplants, spinach and dill. Travellers brought back ideas as well as herbs, and Buddhism, with its vegetarian cuisine, had an immense and lasting influence on Chinese cuisine.

The tides of history washed the Song Dynasty (960-1279 AD) into power, mostly on the shields of barbaric nomads. The Great Wall failed to keep out the savage horsemen, and wave after wave of invaders intent on plunder swarmed into the treasure house that was China. The Song emperors retreated before this storm of uncouth aliens, and once again it was in southern China that food and farming developed. Thwarted from spreading to the north, the Song reached for the sea and their traders brought home exotica from as far afield as

India and Indonesia. More importantly, from what is now Vietnam came seeds for a rice that produced a crop much earlier in the year than existing strains. From these few sacks of seeds can be traced the vast rice-growing tradition of the humid southern provinces.

Most of the barbarians who invaded to plunder, loot and conquer soon fell under the awesome wonder of China's culture, including the cuisine. Over the centuries they were usually lulled into quiet good manners, generally after being liberally plied with gentle wine and strong spirits, soothed with tea and gorged with the incomparable delicacies of the Chinese table. This did not apply, however, to the rude Mongols of the Yuan Dynasty (1206-1368 AD). They gulped down fermented horse's milk and tore at chunks of meat, often raw, which they carried in their sheepskin jackets or stowed under the saddles where, legend has it, the meat was tenderised after being subjected to the pounding of a day's hard riding. Their contribution to culinary history is confined to the one dish that originated from the horseback-broken piece of meat, steak tartare, and an increased appetite for mutton in the north.

It was under the magnificent Ming (1368-1644 AD), the last truly Chinese imperial dynasty, that modern cuisine developed. Their traders roamed the seas to Madagascar and Arabia. Chinese culture was exported and in return foreign ingredients made their way to the kitchens – first in the court, then in the cities, and finally in the peasant homes of the nation. But once again, the

THE TERRACED HILL SIDES OF YUDU COUNTY, JIANGXI PROVINCE

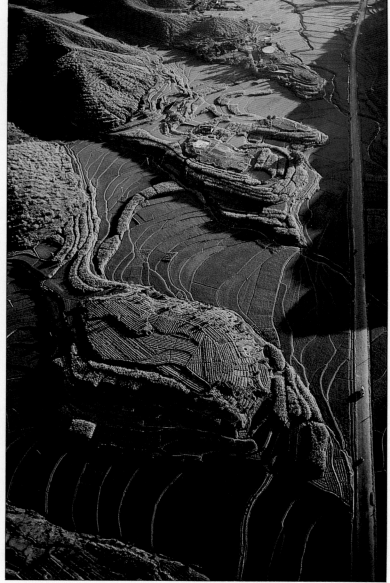

GEORG GERSTER

glory and wealth of China proved a jewel too precious to be ignored by the hungry and fierce barbarians outside the Middle Kingdom. The Ming pleaded with their fearsome neighbours the Manchus for military aid, and they answered this invitation promptly by marching into China. The Manchus threw out the invaders and just as quickly decided that as they had saved China they might as well stay and rule it. Reigning as the Qing Dynasty, the Manchus set up a regime that was to last until the early twentieth century.

The Manchus, though not as crude as the Mongols, brought few gastronomic delights with them from the frozen plains of their homeland. Winter Fire Pot, designed to warm them during the frigid six months of winter, was their major legacy, and it is still enjoyed all over China today. After the initial savage repression of their new realm, designed successfully to terrorise the population into accepting their rule, the Manchus settled down to enjoy life in the graceful civilisation that suddenly was theirs. They became, it is said, more Chinese than the Chinese. A couple of generations removed from their horses, the Manchu rulers relaxed in a life of luxury and leisure and spent much of their time concentrating on concubines and the table, while Chinese scholars and civil servants administered the realm.

It was, for two centuries, a time of peace and prosperity. As the Manchus became decadent and feasted on elephants' trunks and larks' tongues in three-day imperial banquets, the food consumed every day by gourmets

was developing into the Chinese cuisine we know and love today. Portuguese traders brought chillies to Macau from where they travelled up the branches of the Pearl River and into Hunan and Sichuan, creating the basis of the modern spicy dishes of the southwest. Fujian was gaining fame for seafood cooked with imagination. Guangdong dishes were reaching the degree of subtlety and clarity they are now noted for.

Just as important perhaps, from the point of view of culinary history, was how Chinese cooking was being taken abroad. The Western powers who grasped parts of China during the nineteenth century had little impact on the cuisine. But out of China from the mid-nineteenth century onwards flowed a steady stream of labourers to work the tin mines of Malaya, to dig for gold in Australia, New Zealand and South Africa, to hack railways across the Rocky Mountains and to take their commercial skills to every corner of the Pacific and beyond. This exodus of people, the forebears of today's thirty million overseas Chinese, came mostly from the great southern provinces of Guangdong and Fujian and with them they took Chinese cooking to every country of the world.

But the greatest Chinese cuisine on earth is still found today in the land where it developed. A combination of many centuries of love of good food, a tradition of hospitality and endless experimentation with the fruits of the good earth has gone into making the rich and vibrant feast that is the culinary heritage of China the Beautiful.

DRYING MAIZE IN THE ERLANG MOUNTAINS, SICHUAN PROVINCE

HARALD SUND

THE SUMMER PALACE IN BEIJING

THOMAS HOPKER

北京
Beijing

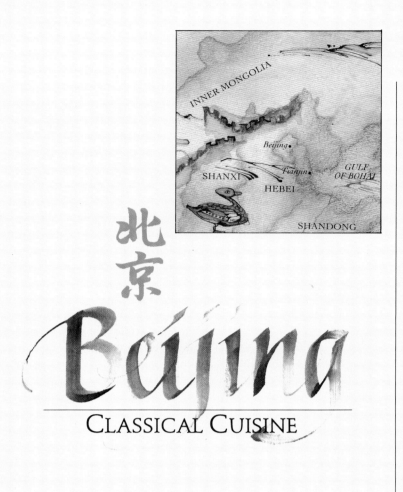

北京

# Beijing
## CLASSICAL CUISINE

THE cuisine of Beijing is a contradiction. It is a combination of two very different legacies, the magnificence of classical court cooking being a splendid but thin veneer over the honest, solid food prepared by farmers' wives in the countless tiny hamlets that dot the dusty plains of northern China.

What the world regards as Beijing food is very different from the daily diet of the peasants of Hebei, Shandong, Henan and Shanxi provinces. For this is poor country, infertile and often arid, a land where living has for centuries been precarious, balanced delicately between persuading the cruel land and bitter climate to provide sufficient millet, wheat, lentils, maize and sweet potatoes to feed the village, and all too often the threat of famine. For the peasant farmers on their tiny plots nature was as often an enemy as a friend. In November, almost overnight it seems, a chill wind begins blowing from the icy wastes of Manchuria and Siberia. The next morning the village ponds are frozen. Over the next few weeks the ground itself is gripped and for five solid months the land is one vast block of unyielding ice.

Through this austere winter, grain, turnips and cabbage provide the basis for the peasant kitchen. Often in the past there has been too little of even these basics. Before the great irrigation works began three decades ago, another unpredictable and savage enemy was that sleeping dragon which curls in bizarre muddy loops across the plains: the Huang Ho, the Yellow River, China's Sorrow. The river that brought the water to give life to the fields also brought floods that ruined crops and signalled famine. So did the many other waterways that meander over the flats towards the Gulf of Bohai or the Yellow Sea.

After the thaw turns the roads to mud and the fields suddenly awaken, the heat of summer comes like a blast from hell itself. The heat sears the plains bringing a dry wind that in autumn causes almost instant dehydration to a million ducks hanging from every home to provide the main ingredient in the most famous dish of the north, Beijing duck. But if the heavy rains of summer

THE FORBIDDEN CITY IN BEIJING
THOMAS HOPKER

29

ONE OF BEIJING'S BUSY INDOOR MARKETS                                          LEONG KA TAI

have not come, the winds from the west bring dust clouds and add to the misery of drought. Little wonder that after a wet summer when the crops are in and the cold winds begin to blow, a time when the farmers of the northern plains have sufficient food to last themselves and their families through the icy months, they bring out the explosive Mao Tai spirits and celebrate in hearty feasts and banquets.

In Beijing the glittering banquets in the Great Hall of the People present the world with a glimpse of the pinnacle of modern Chinese feasts. The capital's business community, the diplomats, the foreign journalists, all have their favourite restaurants featuring gastronomic riches unknown to the millions of peasants of the plains. The capital has people from every province in China and, in addition to the northern dishes, offers a wide range of regional restaurants providing homely provincial favourites for those in the army, government or bureaucracy who serve in Beijing, as well as local gourmets and adventurous visitors to the capital.

Like every other region, the common food of north China, away from the state banquets, is a mixture of tradition, imported outside influences and restrictions imposed on agriculture by the savage climate. During the brief hot summer the cities of north China are almost choked with a flood of vegetables. Huge tomatoes, immense zucchini, giant cauliflowers, juicy melons, succulent marrows, plump eggplants and enormous pumpkins fill the markets. Alas, it is all too brief. Soon the summer vegetables are gone and the hardy dry staples of winter make for a long and dull gastronomic season until, weather permitting, the bounty of another

growing season is harvested. Despite the harsh environment the genius of Chinese chefs over the centuries has developed a cuisine out of necessity. A rich culinary stew takes a few local ingredients (millet or wheat), adds a dash of imported Muslim custom (mutton), a hardy staple that thrives in the summer and keeps well throughout the long winter (white turnip or that superb standby of the north, Tianjin cabbage), and from such simple components comes up with a succulent, filling meal like a delicious sliced lamb hotpot.

Muslim cooking has had a strong influence on northern cuisine. Horsemen who surged over the Great Wall into the flatlands were often Muslims. They came to conquer and stayed to settle, and today the countless millions of Chinese with the family name Ma (Horse) can often trace their ancestry to the Muslim raiders. Today, however, it is only in name and culinary tastes that their heritage shows. Mongol, Manchu, Muslim – all have merged in the common Chinese sea to bring influences to modern northern food.

The influence of the Mongols lingers still, although the Yuan Dynasty held sway for less than a century (1206-1368 AD) before the "Devil's Horsemen" retreated to their wide steppes. In no other area of China have the Mongols left any notable culinary legacy.

The Manchu influence, however, is pervasive in the north, particularly around Beijing itself. Over the three centuries of the Qing Dynasty (1644-1911 AD) intermarriage was so common that many residents of the capital today, knowingly or not, carry Manchu genes. After their initial conquest of China the Manchus sat back to enjoy three hundred years of the good life. They caroused with gusto, drank with enthusiasm, had large harems and armies of concubines, and although they may not have made much of a contribution as chefs, they certainly encouraged fine cooking by their conspicuous consumption of the better things of life.

There were up to two thousand chefs at any one time in the kitchens of the Forbidden City, cooking delicacies for the emperor and his court; officials such as the army of advisors, mandarins, and generals; foreign dignitaries seeking audiences with the occupant of the Dragon Throne; the hordes of concubines, eunuchs, members of the royal family, and the rest of the imperial court. The Manchus may have ruled the empire through their corps of fast-riding Bannermen, but in the kitchens of Beijing the Chinese reigned supreme. A standing joke was that the Manchus had invaded China to get a decent meal.

Hated and scorned though they were by many Chinese in the dying decades of their long dynasty, the Manchus enthusiastically assimilated Chinese culture. They became, it is said, more Chinese than the Chinese, and in no way was this more obvious than at the dining table. They had a lust for life. One reason for the strong Muslim influence in modern Beijing is often attributed to the Manchu Emperor Qian Long. Of all his hundreds of concubines recruited from throughout the empire he was obsessed above all with a Muslim girl he named the Fragrant One. To humour her the Emperor decreed that a town for her co-religionists be erected in the Forbidden City. From this love affair can be traced the large Muslim presence in Beijing today, and items on menus throughout the northern provinces such as lamb, kid and horse meat. Inland in Shanxi, donkey meat is also a legacy of the Muslim presence.

OUTSIDE A HOME IN SUBURBAN BEIJING                    THOMAS HOPKER

EARLY MORNING BARGAINING AT A STREET MARKET

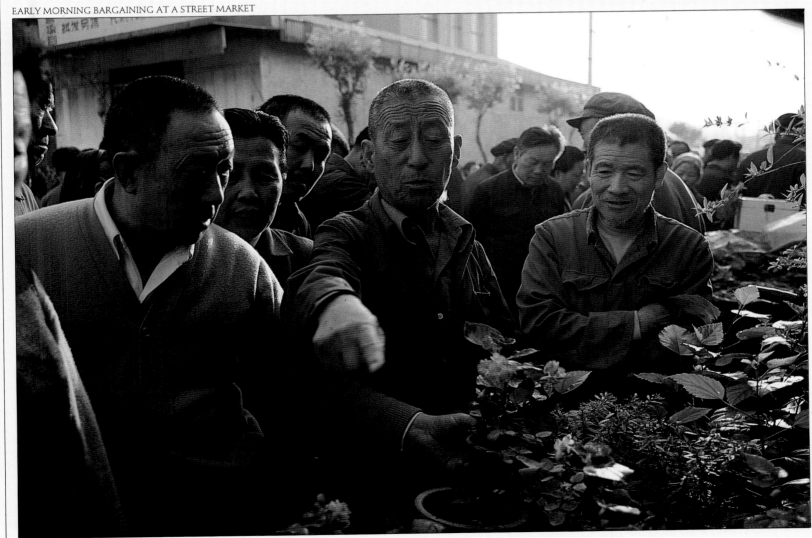

LEONG KA TAI

Despite the Yellow River slicing through the northern plain, freshwater fish does not play an important role in the diet. Some say the turgid, muddy waters that carry heavy loads of silt are too thick for a fish to breathe. In winter shallow ponds freeze solid, making fish farming a practical impossibility. Northern chefs hold that only when the Golden Carp was vigorous enough to fight the flow of the Yellow River and reach as far upstream as the town of Dragon Gate in Henan Province was it fit to eat. By reaching so far upriver the fish was held to have exhibited great courage and stamina. As such, it was classed as a dragon and therefore became worthy of the wok. Shandong is the exception in the north as far as seafood is concerned. It produces notable seafood from both coasts bordering the Gulf of Bohai and the Yellow Sea. The giant prawns of the gulf are sent by train and truck to Beijing where they have won fame in top gourmet kitchens and restaurants.

Shandong has other special claims to gastronomic fame. For thirty-five years until 1914 the area around the town of Qingdao was leased to Imperial Germany, and this brief spell gave a Teutonic flavour to the cuisine as well as to the architecture. One bequest was Qingdao beer, made to an old German recipe and now, very justifiably, the most famous beer in all of China.

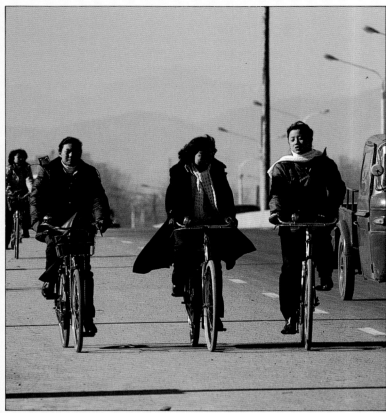

CITY DWELLERS BICYCLE TO WORK                    LEONG KA TAI

A CHINESE OPERA CHORUS

G. MONRO

32

Europeans planted large areas of grapes in Shandong, and these vines are now producing wine of international standing. Riesling, Chardonnay and other varieties are now helping Chinese vignerons and their partners from France, Germany, America and Australia to produce top quality table wines. The whites, in particular, have won awards in several international arenas. Many of the varieties of wine being produced from the grapes of Shandong are specially blended and balanced to accompany Chinese food.

Shandong food is a cuisine formed by combining a bountiful sea harvest with the richest agricultural production in northern China. The population has strong links with the outside world, and this has infused into their cuisine many culinary notions from other regions of China and overseas. It is the most vigorous of the cuisines of the north, but unfortunately is also one of the least known.

Just as wealth, power and influence flowed inexorably towards the seat of power during Beijing's years as capital of the nation, so too did many of the most talented chefs gravitate to the political centre of the Middle Kingdom. Here a young chef could make a name for himself, and with a lot of hard work and a bit of luck, catch the eye of a wealthy gourmet who would set him up in his own establishment – much the same as young French chefs head for Paris today. From all over the nation such ambitious cooks took their knowledge of China's various regional cuisines with them to the kitchens of Beijing.

A wide variety of imported foods, like the sweet potatoes of Shandong, play a vital role in what are now regarded as purely local dishes. In the hard years of this century it was common for Shandong peasants, if they were fortunate, to have three meals a day of sweet potatoes: one potato per meal. This vegetable has become such an integral part of the northern cuisine that it is easily overlooked that sweet potatoes only reached coastal China, via the Philippines from America, in the sixteenth century, about the same time as the potato reached Europe. Today, as it has been for a couple of centuries, the sweet potato is to Shandong what the spud is to Ireland. And it has played just as vital a political role.

Within the sweep of the provinces of the northern plains there is variety upon variety in the way commonplace ingredients are prepared. From one village to the next a tiny but subtle change may be made to the staple kitchen fare so that the food at one side of a province may be very different to that at the other. But everywhere such delicacies as salty soy bean sauces, spring onions and strong garlic give a distinctive tang to the taste of the north.

A FAMILY OUTING

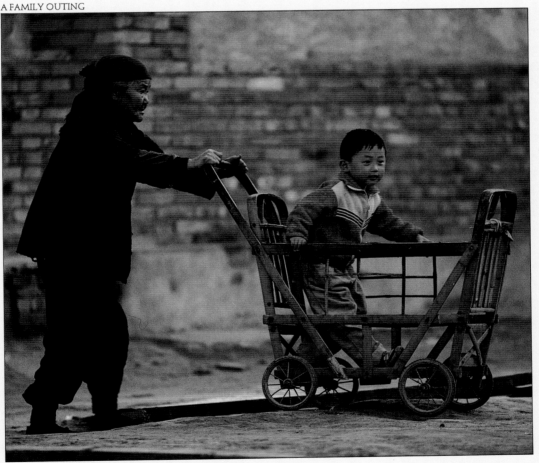

LEO MEIER

(following page)
SUBURBAN BEIJING
WELDON TRANNIES

Poultry

家禽及野味

YOUNG BOYS TEND THEIR FLOCK OF GEESE

ENRICO FERORELLI

家禽及野味

# Poultry

"FIRST, steal a chicken" is the immortal first line of the recipe for Beggar's Chicken. Nobody knows the origin of the dish, but one version often repeated in ancient Chinese texts holds that a humble peasant was sitting by a cooking fire at the side of a lake in Anhui Province when a feudal lord approached. When the poor man saw the nobleman and his armed entourage, he quickly scooped out mud from the lake side, plastering it around a chicken he had just stolen and threw the bird onto the coals. The nobleman stopped and got off his horse to warm himself by the fire. By the time he remounted and rode on, the chicken was encased in a brick-hard ball of fired clay. Frustrated, the peasant hurled a stone at the clay which promptly broke, releasing the delicious aroma still enjoyed by modern diners who order this piquant dish.

POULTRY SELLERS AT A FARM MARKET, JIANGXI PROVINCE

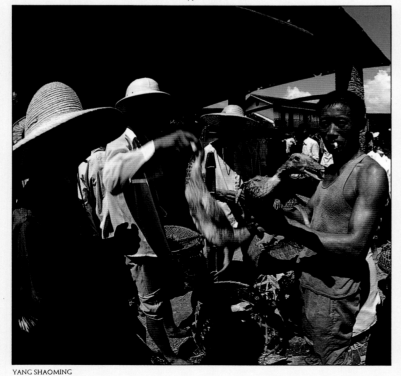

YANG SHAOMING

Every regional kitchen has its own distinctive poultry favourite. Indeed, virtually every county town in China has a special way of cooking local birds. The visitor can go into a restaurant in any corner of the country and ask for chicken confident of getting a tasty, satisfying dish. Ask how it has been cooked and the answer is likely to be: "Our way". That way differs throughout the land. In Shandong, it could mean chicken legs steamed, seasoned and then fried. If the chef is from Yunnan, the chicken could have been double-steamed in a sealed container. The bird may have been cooked in oyster sauce in Guangdong; brushed with sweet honey in Hebei; smeared with hot red bean paste in Hunan; simmered with anise in Gansu: inflamed with hot chillies in Guangxi or barbecued with white pepper in Mongolia.

Poultry of every description was a favoured dish before the first recipe was ever written. Game was always popular at imperial courts and is still eagerly sought today by keen huntsmen. Eagles, owls and other rare creatures once shot for the pot are now totally protected under international agreements honoured by China; but ducks, swans, pheasants, quail, geese and a myriad of other birds are the targets of enthusiastic shooters and archers. A prized dish in certain specialty restaurants is made from tiny rice birds caught in nets strung above the ripening grain, salted or preserved in honey and eaten whole: bones, innards and all.

In the capital, of course, pride of place goes to the glory of Beijing Duck, dried in the arid northern winds then crisply roasted and served with classical grace. But the residents of Nanjing will by no means bow to the duck of the northern plains. Their award goes to the famed pressed duck of the central Yangtze. Further up the river, the proud chefs of the Sichuan kitchen haughtily concede nothing to any poultry dish other than their own smoked duck; while in Guangdong, the subtle delicacy of steamed chicken is the most honoured dish.

Then there is the magnificent goose of the Chiu Chow kitchen with its spectacular accompaniment of plum sauce; the Yellow Chicken of Hainan Island; the plump roasted pigeons of Fujian; the wild birds of prey shot by archers in the pine forests of the remote Black Dragon River in far northern Manchuria, and the young fowls cooked in coconut juice which are a specialty of the tribal people of the steamy tropical coasts of Guangxi. In Guizhou, a pepper-blasted diced chicken is named Guardian of the Palace after the title of the Ming Dynasty Mandarin who invented the dish.

Throughout the country, and even in Beijing where duck is the dish for celebrations, chicken is the daily king of every kitchen. The bird appears in thousands of guises. Sometimes, as in a famous Guangdong recipe, the chicken is not a bird at all. A fowl is skinned and the meat cooked. The chef or housewife puts away the skin for another day when it will be stuffed with glutinous rice, mushrooms, ham, bacon, sweet wine and seasonings. With the holes sewn, baked and put on the table, it looks like a plump bird. Only when the diners try to eat it is the joke discovered; but it still tastes magnificent.

The humble chicken eaten in China is usually a more mature fowl than that cooked in the Western kitchen. Most Chinese chefs prefer a bird of about 1½-2kg (3-4lb) because of the richer flavour. Important medicinal values are attributed to the fowl; it is said to keep the five vital internal organs – the heart, liver, kidneys, lungs and spleen – active, to stimulate the stomach, to strengthen muscles and bones and improve the circulation of the blood. The stock from a boiled bird is invariably kept to make one of a million varieties of chicken soup, held by Chinese grandmothers to be the cure-all for every ailment.

WHITE GEESE ON A VILLAGE POND

LEO MEIER

CHICKEN BALL AND PEA SOUP

## Beijing 北京

# CHICKEN BALL AND PEA SOUP

155 g (5 oz) chicken breast meat
1 egg white, lightly beaten
1 tablespoon cornflour (cornstarch)
iced water
½ teaspoon salt
2 cups (500 mL/16 fl oz) lard or oil for deep-frying
4 cups (1 L/32 fl oz) chicken stock (broth)
2 teaspoons rice wine or dry sherry
1 cup (155 g/5 oz) fresh peas, cooked
1 tablespoon rendered chicken fat, melted (optional)

Reduce the chicken meat to a paste with a cleaver or in a food processor. Add the egg white, cornflour and ½ cup (125 mL/ 4 fl oz) of iced water and season with the salt. Stir in one direction only. The mixture should be so smooth and moist that the chicken paste falls from a chopstick in large droplets.

Heat the lard or oil in a wok and reduce the heat. Pour the chicken paste into a funnel and allow it to drip into the hot fat in drops about the size of green peas. Fry until just white and cooked through, then lift out on a slotted spoon and drain.

Heat the chicken stock and add the rice wine. Then add the drained peas and the chicken balls and heat through. Season with salt to taste and thicken, if preferred, with 1½ tablespoons cornflour mixed with cold water. Add the chicken fat, if used, and serve.

## Sichuan 四川

# STEAMED WHOLE CHICKEN WITH GLUTINOUS RICE AND DELICACIES

*Chicken prepared according to this recipe is one of the most delectable of the Sichuan traditional dishes. It requires skilful preparation, but the result is well worth the effort involved. The dried "eight delicacies" used are sold in packages and simply need to be soaked before adding the rice to make this unique stuffing.*

1 x 1¼ kg (2½ lb) chicken
1 carrot (garnish)
1 small cucumber (garnish)
2 eggs (garnish)
1 tomato (garnish)

STUFFING

125 g (4 oz) glutinous rice
2 tablespoons barley
20 fresh or dried lotus seeds
¼ cup (30 g/1 oz) fox nuts or gingko nuts (white nuts)
1 tablespoon dried shrimp
4 dried black mushrooms, soaked for 25 minutes
75 g (2½ oz) salty ham or bacon
1 tablespoon fresh peas
1½ teaspoons salt
OR use one pack of "eight delicacies" and glutinous rice for the stuffing

SAUCE

½ cup (125 mL/4 fl oz) chicken stock (broth)
1 tablespoon arrowroot or cornflour (cornstarch)
½ teaspoon salt
few drops sesame oil
pinch of pepper

Clean the chicken and bone it, leaving the skin intact – use a sharp knife with a long narrow blade to work around the carcass until it can be completely removed. Sever the wing and leg bones from the carcass, leaving the skin and meat in place.

To prepare the stuffing, soak the rice in water for 1 hour, then place on a rack in a wok or steamer, cover and steam for about 25 minutes until almost cooked through.

Wash fresh lotus seeds or soak dried ones with the barley and fox nuts for 2-3 hours to soften. Shell gingko nuts and soak in hot water for about 25 minutes. Use a toothpick to push out the bitter core and discard. Soak the shrimp to soften, then chop coarsely. Squeeze water from the mushrooms, remove the stems and dice the caps. Dice the ham.

If using packaged "eight delicacies", soak for one hour and steam for 10 minutes.

Mix these ingredients with the peas, steamed rice and barley and stuff into the chicken, moulding it into its original shape. Sew up the opening, then place breast downwards in a heatproof dish on a rack in a wok or a steamer. Steam, covered, over gentle heat for 50-60 minutes until completely tender.

Prepare garnishes by carving the carrot and cucumber into attractive shapes. Beat the two egg whites and the yolks together separately. Pour into separate dishes and steam until firm. Slice and cut into diamond-shaped pieces. Drop the tomato into boiling water, remove and peel. Cut into wedges, trim away the pulp and seeds leaving petal shapes. Set the garnishes aside.

When the chicken is done, lift out and place breast upwards on a serving plate.

Pour about ½ cup (125 mL/4 fl oz) of the liquid from the steaming dish into a wok and add the sauce ingredients. Bring to the boil and simmer, stirring, until it thickens. Adjust seasoning.

Add the garnishes, simmer for a few moments, then pour over the chicken and serve.

STEAMED WHOLE CHICKEN WITH GLUTINOUS RICE AND DELICACIES

BRAISED CHICKEN WITH LEMON

CHICKEN AND GINGKO NUTS

## *Shanghai* 上海

# BRAISED CHICKEN WITH LEMON

1 x 1 kg (2 lb) chicken
2 tablespoons light soy sauce
1 tablespoon rice wine or dry sherry
2 tablespoons lemon juice
1 cup (250 mL/8 fl oz) peanut oil
1 lemon, sliced

SAUCE

2 cups (500 mL/16 fl oz) chicken stock (broth), or water
3 spring onions (shallots/scallions), chopped
6 slices young fresh (root) ginger, shredded
1 tablespoon tomato sauce (ketchup)
3 tablespoons lemon juice
1 tablespoon sugar
½ teaspoon salt

Clean the chicken and wash well. Dry with paper towels, then place in a dish. Mix the soy sauce, rice wine and lemon juice together and rub over the chicken, pouring the remainder inside the cavity. Cover and leave for 1 hour, turning once, then drain, reserving the marinade, and leave to dry on a rack.
❀ Heat the peanut oil in a wok and fry the chicken over moderate heat on all sides until golden, then transfer to a casserole.
❀ Pour the remaining marinade over the chicken and add the sauce ingredients. Cover and bring to the boil, then reduce heat and simmer very gently for about 1 hour until the chicken is completely tender.
❀ Remove the chicken, drain and cut straight through the bones into serving portions. Arrange on a plate and place the sliced lemon in a line down the centre of the back.
❀ Rapidly boil the sauce until well reduced, then pour over the chicken and serve.

## *Sichuan* 四川

# CHICKEN AND GINGKO NUTS

*There are groves of gingko trees on Mount Ching Chen in Kuan Shian County. They are a popular tourist attraction, and many believe that the age-old trees will bless them with longevity.*

*In ancient China, people regarded the gingko as a fruit. Yang Wan Li, a famous poet in the Bei Song Dynasty (960-1127 AD) wrote: "Silver gingko might well keep the golden peach company".*

*The core of the gingko nut must be removed before the nut is used, as it is very bitter and is said to cause stomach pain.*

375 g (12 oz) fresh peeled or canned gingko nuts
1 x 1¼ kg (2½ lb) chicken
3 spring onions (shallots/scallions)
6 slices fresh (root) ginger
2 tablespoons rice wine or dry sherry
1 teaspoon salt
pinch of white pepper

Soak fresh gingko nuts in boiling water, then drain and scrape off the skin. Pick off the two ends, push the bitter core through with a toothpick, then soak again.
❀ Blanch the chicken in boiling water, then hold under cold running water to rinse. Drain and place breast upwards in a casserole.
❀ Add the remaining ingredients, except the gingko nuts, cover with water, bring to the boil, reduce the heat and simmer for 15 minutes. Turn the chicken over, add the gingko nuts and continue to simmer until the chicken is completely tender.
❀ Remove the chicken and cut in half lengthways. Then cut the meat diagonally from the centre into slices. Arrange in its original shape on a serving plate. Lift the gingko nuts from the stock with a slotted spoon, arrange around the chicken and serve at once.

# Beijing 北京

# CHICKEN IN A LANTERN

*The presentation of this dish is impressive. Lightly cooked chicken pieces and selected vegetables are placed in a square of clear cellophane and tied with ribbon. The parcel is held over a wok of hot oil and the oil is quickly ladled over the bag. The heat causes the air inside the bag to expand, blowing it up like a lantern.*

250 g (8 oz) chicken breast meat
2 teaspoons light soy sauce
1 egg white, lightly beaten
1 tablespoon cornflour (cornstarch)
1 spring onion (shallot/scallion)
2 slices fresh (root) ginger
1 clove garlic
3 dried black mushrooms, soaked for 25 minutes
4 canned water chestnuts, drained
2 tablespoons fresh peas
1 tablespoon blanched almonds
6 cups (1½ L/48 fl oz) oil for deep-frying
90 g (3 oz) rice vermicelli
1 tablespoon oil for stir-frying

SEASONING

1 tablespoon rice wine or dry sherry
1 tablespoon chilli sauce (or less, to taste)
2 teaspoons sugar
1 teaspoon salt

Cut the chicken into small cubes and place in a dish with the soy sauce, egg white and cornflour. Mix well and leave for 20 minutes.

❁ Trim the spring onion and cut into short lengths. Shred the ginger and chop the garlic. Drain the mushrooms, squeezing out all the water, cut off the stems and dice the caps. Dice the water chestnuts. Parboil the peas and halve the almonds.

❁ Heat the oil in a large wok over medium heat and deep-fry the chicken in a wire ladle or frying basket for about 2 minutes, shaking frequently to cook evenly. Lift out and drain well. Deep-fry the almonds briefly and set aside to drain.

❁ Increase the heat under the oil, and when very hot deep-fry the vermicelli quickly. They will expand to several times their original volume and turn white. Lift out and drain – do not allow them to colour. Place on a serving plate.

❁ In another wok heat about 1 tablespoon of oil and briefly stir-fry the spring onion, garlic, ginger and mushrooms. Add the seasoning ingredients and stir-fry briefly, then add the chicken, water chestnuts, peas and almonds. Mix together thoroughly.

❁ Spoon the mixture into the centre of a square of clear cellophane, bring the corners together to enclose it and tie a ribbon round the centre. Reheat the oil, hold the parcel over the wok and quickly ladle oil over until it blows up. Drain and place in the centre of a serving dish. Untie the bag at the table and tip the contents over the vermicelli.

CHICKEN IN A LANTERN

PHOENIX BREAST WITH SOUR SAUCE

## Sichuan 四川

# PHOENIX BREAST WITH SOUR SAUCE

*According to legend, the phoenix is the king of birds, symbolising nobility, respect and glory. The emperor's residence used to be called the phoenix residence, the emperor's carriage the phoenix carriage and the queen's head-dress the phoenix crown. Chicken breast, being the best part of the chicken, is known as phoenix breast in China, and in this dish is deliciously sour and tasty.*

185 g (6 oz) chicken breast meat
1 tablespoon rice wine or dry sherry
½ teaspoon salt
1 egg white, well beaten
2 tablespoons soy bean powder or cornflour (cornstarch)
375 g (12 oz) lard or oil for frying

### SAUCE

1½ tablespoons red vinegar
1 tablespoon sugar
1 tablespoon light soy sauce
2 slices fresh (root) ginger, finely chopped
2 cloves garlic, finely chopped
1 pickled red chilli, finely chopped
1 spring onion (shallot/scallion), minced (ground)
30 g (1 oz) fresh or canned bamboo shoots, very finely chopped

Cut the chicken into very small dice and place in a dish with the wine, salt, egg white and soy bean powder or cornflour. Mix well and leave for 20 minutes. Heat the lard or oil in a wok to smoking point, then lower the heat and fry the chicken, stirring with chopsticks to separate the pieces. When it turns white, lift out and drain well.

✄ Drain the wok and wipe out. Add 1 tablespoon of the lard or oil and stir-fry the chopped sauce ingredients for 1 minute, then add the remaining ingredients and return the chicken. Toss together over high heat until well mixed and the sugar dissolved, then serve.

# FRIED CHICKEN LEGS

8 chicken drumsticks, about 750 g (1½ lb)
2 pieces pork fat net (caul lining), cut into triangle shapes
1 egg, well beaten
1 cup (125 g/4 oz) dry breadcrumbs
oil for deep-frying
hot soy sauce
tomato or chilli sauce

### SEASONING

1 tablespoon rice wine or dry sherry
2 tablespoons light soy sauce
3 tablespoons water
1 tablespoon finely chopped fresh coriander
1 tablespoon finely chopped spring onion (shallot/scallion)
¾ teaspoon finely chopped fresh (root) ginger
1 cinnamon stick
1 piece dried orange peel
1 teaspoon Sichuan peppercorns (Fagara or Sansho)
1 star anise
½ teaspoon salt
1 tablespoon sugar

Mix the seasoning ingredients together in a large, shallow heatproof dish and put in the chicken drumsticks. Cover with plastic wrap and leave for 3 hours, turning several times. Then uncover and place the dish on a rack in a wok or in a steamer, cover and steam over gently simmering water for about 30 minutes. Remove and leave to drain.

✄ Wrap each drumstick in a triangle of the pork fat net, then dip into beaten egg. Coat with dry breadcrumbs then refrigerate for about 30 minutes for the breadcrumbs to "set".

✄ Heat the oil in a wok to smoking point and deep-fry the drumsticks until crisp and golden on the surface. Drain and arrange on a serving place. Serve with small dips of hot soy sauce and tomato or chilli sauce.

✄ The drumsticks can also be served straight from the steamer, omitting the crisp-frying, and are excellent with a plain bowl of rice and a little of the sauce.

FRIED CHICKEN LEGS

## Shanghai 上海

# BRAISED CHICKEN LEGS IN A LOTUS SHAPE

12 chicken drumsticks
3 tomatoes
1 cup (250 mL/8 fl oz) fresh milk
1 egg
1 egg white
lard or vegetable oil
12 vegetable hearts (miniature Chinese white cabbage)
   or bok choy
pinch of salt
grated lemon rind (optional)

SEASONING/STOCK

2 cups (500 mL/16 fl oz) chicken stock (broth)
2 tablespoons dark soy sauce
1 tablespoon sugar
3 slices fresh (root) ginger
2 tablespoons vegetable oil

Use a sharp knife to cut around the chicken bones to where the meat begins to be fleshy. Scrape the skin completely away from the lower part of the bone, leaving it exposed.

Arrange the chicken drumsticks in a wide flat saucepan. Mix the seasoning/stock ingredients together and pour over the drumsticks. Bring almost to the boil, then simmer gently for about 45 minutes until the drumsticks are very tender and the sauce reduced to a syrupy glaze.

Blanch the tomatoes in boiling water, then skin. Cut each into large wedges and trim away the pulp and seeds to leave pointed petal shapes. Set aside.

Lightly beat the milk and eggs together. Stir-fry in a wok in a little lard or vegetable oil over gentle heat until thickened. Set aside, keeping warm.

In another wok, stir-fry the vegetable hearts in a little oil or lard, adding a pinch of salt. Pour in 1 tablespoon of water, cover and steam until tender. Lift out and arrange on a round serving plate, placing the drumsticks between each piece of vegetable.

In the centre of the platter, mound the fried egg, and then place the tomato "petals" in a lotus flower shape in the egg and sprinkle the centre of the "flower" with a little grated lemon rind.

Spoon any remaining sauce over the drumsticks and serve.

CHICKEN ROLLS WITH SESAME SEEDS

MANDARIN DICED CHICKEN

## Beijing 北京

# CHICKEN ROLLS WITH SESAME SEEDS

*The best chicken for this dish is a special breed of Beijing chicken that is large and strong and said to have high nutritional value. The coating of sesame seeds gives it a delightfully nutty taste.*

375 g (12 oz) chicken meat, cooked
1 spring onion (shallot/scallion)
2 slices fresh (root) ginger
125 g (4 oz) canned bamboo shoots, drained
1 tablespoon rice wine or dry sherry
1 teaspoon salt
4 eggs
oil for deep-frying
60 g (2 oz) white sesame seeds

GLAZE

1 egg, beaten
2 tablespoons flour

Finely chop the chicken, spring onion, ginger and bamboo shoots, add the rice wine and salt and mix well.

🔥 Beat the eggs with a pinch of salt. Rub out a wok with an oiled cloth and pour in one-sixth of the beaten eggs. Tilt and slowly move the pan so that the egg spreads out into a thin round omelet. Fry gently on both sides. Cook the remaining egg to give six omelets.

🔥 Divide the filling between the omelets, spreading one-sixth across the centre of each. Fold 3 sides over and roll up.

🔥 Coat each roll with the pre-mixed glaze, then roll in sesame seeds.

🔥 Heat the oil and fry the rolls over moderate heat until golden brown. Drain well and serve.

## Sichuan 四川

# MANDARIN DICED CHICKEN

*This is one of the most famous traditional Sichuan dishes and its creation is connected with an interesting anecdote.*

*A few years before the downfall of the Qing Dynasty (1644-1911 AD), a new governor, Ting Pao Ts'en, was assigned to Sichuan. Upon his arrival a banquet was given in his honour. The cooks created a special dish for this old mandarin using spring chicken cut into tiny pieces and flavoured with local spices. They named it Kung Pao, or Mandarin Diced Chicken after him.*

*Kung Pao has since become a technical term in Sichuan cooking, referring to a dish containing dried chillies and Sichuan pepper (the seed of the prickly ash tree), with a tart, hot, slightly vinegary taste.*

315 g (10 oz) chicken breasts
2-3 dried red chillies
1 teaspoon Sichuan peppercorns (Fagara or Sansho)
90 g (3 oz) raw peanuts
2 spring onions (shallots/scallions)
3-4 slices fresh (root) ginger
2 cloves garlic
2 cups (500 mL/16 fl oz) oil for deep-frying

MARINADE

1 tablespoon rice wine or dry sherry
1 tablespoon superior or other light soy sauce
1/2 teaspoon salt
1 1/2 teaspoons cornflour (cornstarch)

SEASONING/SAUCE

2/3 cup (150 mL/5 fl oz) chicken stock (broth)
1 tablespoon superior or other light soy sauce
1 teaspoon sugar
1 teaspoon brown vinegar
1 1/2 teaspoons cornflour (cornstarch)

Cut the chicken into small dice, place in a dish with the marinade ingredients, mix well and leave for 20 minutes.

🔥 Chop the chillies into short lengths and lightly crush the peppercorns. Drop the peanuts into boiling water, leave for a few minutes, then drain and peel off the skins. Cut the spring onion and ginger into shreds and thinly slice the garlic.

🔥 Heat the oil in a wok to smoking point. Deep-fry the chillies and peppercorns in a frying basket or wire strainer until crisp, remove and set aside. Add the chicken to the wok and fry until it turns white and firm. Remove, then fry the peanuts until lightly coloured, lift out and drain on paper towels.

🔥 Pour off all but about 2 1/2 tablespoons of the oil, then reheat and stir-fry the spring onions, ginger and garlic briefly. Return the chicken with the chillies and peppercorns and stir-fry together briefly over high heat. Add the pre-mixed seasoning/sauce ingredients and bring to the boil. Simmer, stirring, for about 1 minute, then stir in the peanuts and serve.

SLICED CHICKEN AND SEASONAL VEGETABLES

STEAMED WHOLE LANTERN-SHAPED CHICKEN

## *Sichuan* 四川

# SLICED CHICKEN AND SEASONAL VEGETABLES

*This simple dish is typical of home-style Sichuan cooking, light and delicate ingredients contrasted by a hint of hot spice.*

250 g (8 oz) chicken breasts
1-3 pickled red chillies
2 spring onions (shallots/scallions)
90 g (3 oz) marrow, choko (chayote) or winter melon
2½ tablespoons oil for frying
2 teaspoons brown vinegar

SEASONING/SAUCE

1 clove garlic, crushed
½ teaspoon grated fresh (root) ginger
1 tablespoon light soy sauce
2 teaspoons rice wine or dry sherry
1 teaspoon sugar
3 tablespoons chicken stock (broth)
pinch each of salt and Sichuan pepper (Fagara or Sansho)
1 teaspoon cornflour (cornstarch)

Skin and slice the chicken very thinly, then stack the slices and cut them into fine shreds. Shred the pickled chillies and spring onions. Peel the marrow, slice thinly, then cut into matchstick pieces and set aside.

❈Heat the oil in a wok and stir-fry the chicken until it turns white, then remove and set aside. Add the chilli, spring onions and marrow sticks and stir-fry over moderate heat for about 2 minutes. Add the garlic and ginger from the seasoning/sauce ingredients and stir-fry briefly, then return the chicken and add the vinegar. Stir-fry together for 1 minute over moderate heat, then add the remaining premixed seasoning/sauce ingredients, simmer until thickened and serve.

## *Sichuan* 四川

# STEAMED WHOLE LANTERN-SHAPED CHICKEN

*Lanterns are used on many occasions to symbolise happiness. This particular dish is meant to bring that happiness to the table. The chicken is bright red and looks like an elegant lantern on the plate.*

*The red colour is obtained from chilli powder, so the chicken is quite hot, aromatic and very tasty. Only a tender young chicken will give good results.*

1 x 1¼ kg (2½ lb) chicken
1 teaspoon chilli powder
carrot slices (garnish)
lemon peel (garnish)
steamed carrot (garnish)
salted cabbage (garnish)

MARINADE/SEASONING

2 tablespoons rice wine or dry sherry
1 tablespoon grated fresh (root) ginger
1 tablespoon minced (ground) spring onion (shallot/scallion)
1½ teaspoons salt
1 teaspoon Sichuan peppercorns (Fagara or Sansho)*

Clean and wash the chicken, then wipe dry inside and out.
❈Mix the marinade/seasoning ingredients together, rub on the chicken both inside and out, and pour any remaining liquid into the cavity. Place on a rack and leave for at least 12 hours.
❈Place the chicken in a pot and cover with cold water. Remove the chicken and bring the water to the boil, then return the chicken, reduce the heat, cover and simmer gently for about 30 minutes, turning once.
❈Lift out, drain, retain the stock and put the chicken on a rack to dry, then rub the chilli powder in the skin to make it bright red. Set the rack in a wok or steamer over simmering water, cover and steam for 30 minutes.
❈In the meantime briskly boil the retained stock until reduced to about 1 cup (250 mL/8 fl oz) and adjust the seasoning.
❈When the chicken is done, add the liquid from the cavity of the chicken to the stock and simmer briskly until well reduced. Spoon over the chicken and serve.
❈The simple but effective garnishing in the above photograph comprises carrot slices carved into Chinese characters and symbols. The two lanterns are carved from lemon peel with tassels of shredded steamed carrot, and the cord is made from shreds of salted cabbage.

*Dry-fry the peppercorns to bring out their full flavour, then grind to a powder.*

DICED TOMATO AMIDST CHICKEN SNOW

## Sichuan 四川

# DICED TOMATO AMIDST CHICKEN SNOW

*The chicken paste cooked according to this recipe is white and soft as snow. The chef adds contrasting taste, colour and texture with diced tomato. A dish typical of Sichuan to serve in early spring.*

1 large ripe tomato
250 g (8 oz) chicken breasts
¾ cup (175 mL/6 fl oz) chicken stock
2 egg whites
¾ teaspoon salt
1 tablespoon soy bean powder or cornflour (cornstarch)
pinch of white pepper
1½ tablespoons lard

Place the tomato in a pot of boiling water, leave for eight seconds, then remove on a slotted spoon and peel. Cut the flesh into dice, discarding the seeds.

Use either two cleavers simultaneously or a food processor to pound the chicken to a smooth paste. Pull away any tough tendons. Mix with one-third of the stock, the lightly beaten egg whites, salt, soy bean powder and pepper, and stir until the mixture is smooth and creamy.

Heat the lard in a wok and stir-fry the chicken gently over moderate heat until it turns white and is cooked through. Pour in the remaining stock and simmer for 1½ minutes.

Spoon onto a serving plate, carefully stir in the diced tomato, and serve at once.

## Sichuan 四川

# CHICKEN SHREDS AND GARLIC CHIVES

*Bright green, tender and aromatic, garlic chives are one of the vegetables of early spring. They have a subtle flavour of onion and garlic, and are often cooked with pork and chicken.*

12-18 garlic chives or small spring onions (shallots/scallions)
185 g (6 oz) chicken breasts
2 tablespoons oil for frying

### SEASONING

1 egg white, lightly beaten
1 tablespoon cornflour (cornstarch)
½ teaspoon salt
pinch of white pepper

CHICKEN SHREDS AND GARLIC CHIVES

### SAUCE

½ cup (125 mL/4 fl oz) chicken stock (broth)
2 tablespoons rice wine or dry sherry
pinch of salt
1½ teaspoons soy bean powder or cornflour (cornstarch)

Rinse the garlic chives in cold water, shake well, then cut into 5 cm (2 in) lengths and set aside.

Slice the chicken very thinly, discarding skin and any bone fragments. Stack the slices and cut into fine shreds. Place in a dish, add the pre-mixed seasoning ingredients and set aside for 20 minutes.

Heat the oil in a wok and stir-fry the chicken over moderate heat until white. Push to one side of the pan and add the chives. Stir-fry over higher heat for about 1 minute.

Pour in the pre-mixed sauce ingredients, mix with the chicken and chives and simmer until thickened and clear, stirring occasionally, then serve.

## Shanghai 上海

# CHRYSANTHEMUM FIRE POT

*Chrysanthemum dishes are a speciality of Chinese cuisine. Over two thousand years ago poets wrote of the beauty and edibility of the chrysanthemum flower. The great medicinal expert Le She Zhen of the Ming Dynasty (1368-1644 AD) praised chrysanthemums for their ability to brighten the eyes and relieve internal heat, and today they are still used as a medicine and served as tea.*

*Chrysanthemum Fire Pot is a famous dish, served in autumn and winter. The uncooked ingredients are arranged in an attractive design on plates around a stove on the table and cooked by the diners.*

24 prawns (shrimps)
1 x 315 g (10 oz) carp or other meaty white fish, filleted
2 duck gizzards or duck or chicken hearts
185 g (6 oz) chicken breasts
250 g (8 oz) spinach leaves
6 eggs
oil for deep-frying
125 g (4 oz) dried bean thread vermicelli
125 g (4 oz) dried egg noodles
assorted meat*

### STOCK

6 cups (1½ L/48 fl oz) chicken stock (broth)
2-3 slices fresh (root) ginger
2 spring onions (shallots/scallions)
2 teaspoons salt
½ teaspoon white pepper
1 white chrysanthemum flower

## DIP

1 cup (250 mL/8 fl oz) superior or other light soy sauce
½ cup (125 mL/4 fl oz) sesame oil
1-2 tablespoons toasted white sesame seeds (optional)

Peel and de-vein the prawns, leaving the tail section intact. Thinly slice the fish, duck gizzards and chicken breasts and arrange on small plates.

❀ Wash the spinach under running cold water and trim, discarding stems. In a wok, heat the oil to smoking point, then reduce the heat slightly. Deep-fry the vermicelli for a few seconds. They will expand dramatically, but should not be allowed to colour. Drain on paper towels, then place on a large serving plate. Soak the egg noodles to soften, then drain and place in a dish.

❀ Combine the dip ingredients and divide between six small bowls. Beat one egg in each of six rice or soup bowls.

❀ Place all the stock ingredients except the flower petals in a hotpot or large saucepan over a portable cooker in the centre of the table, and bring to the boil. When gently bubbling, pull the chrysanthemum flower apart and scatter the petals over the stock.

❀ Each diner can choose the ingredients he likes, hold them in the hot stock until lightly poached, and then dip into the beaten egg and the dip before eating. Take care to use wooden or bamboo chopsticks and not plastic ones.

❀ The noodles and fried vermicelli are cooked after the other ingredients have been eaten, and consumed with the rich stock at the end of the meal.

*Additional plates of very thinly sliced lean pork, ham, pork liver, beef, squid or tripe can be added to the above assortment.*

CHRYSANTHEMUM FIRE POT

CHICKEN BRAISED IN SOY SAUCE WITH TWO KINDS OF MEATBALLS

## Guangzhou 广州

# CHICKEN BRAISED IN SOY SAUCE WITH TWO KINDS OF MEATBALLS

*The soy sauce used in this recipe is a special product of Guangdong's Pu Ling county and has a distinctive flavour not found in other soy sauces. It is smooth, strong and golden coloured. The meatballs are optional additions to the basic recipe, which transform it into an elegant banquet dish.*

1 x 1 kg (2 lb) spring chicken
2 teaspoons cornflour (cornstarch)
SEASONING
2 tablespoons Pu-Ling or other light soy sauce
2 tablespoons rice wine or dry sherry
1 teaspoon sesame oil
1 teaspoon sugar
1 tablespoon finely chopped spring onion (shallot/scallion)
1 teaspoon grated fresh (root) ginger
1 tablespoon chopped fresh coriander

Clean the chicken, rinse with cold water, dry thoroughly inside and out and place in a dish. Mix the seasoning ingredients together and rub over the chicken, pouring the remainder into the cavity. Leave for at least 2 hours to absorb the flavours.

※ Prepare the meatballs as described in the following recipes.

※ Place the chicken in a heatproof dish on a rack in a wok or steamer, cover and steam over rapidly boiling water for at least 30 minutes until tender. Remove and leave to cool.

※ Chop the chicken into serving slices, cutting straight through the bones in the Chinese style and arrange on a serving plate.

※ Pour the sauce from the dish in which the chicken was steamed into a wok and add the cornflour mixed with a little cold water. Bring to the boil and simmer, stirring, until thickened. Pour over the chicken, arrange the meatballs on the side and serve.

## PRAWN BALLS

185 g (6 oz) fresh prawn (shrimp) meat
60 g (2 oz) finely minced (ground) pork fat
salt and pepper
1 egg, well beaten
1 cup (125 g/4 oz) flour, seasoned with salt and pepper
dry breadcrumbs
oil for deep-frying

Place the prawn meat on a board and bat with the side of the cleaver until reduced to a pulp, or use a food processor. Mix to a smooth paste with the pork fat, season with salt and pepper and roll into balls. Coat lightly with the seasoned flour, dip into the beaten egg, then coat with breadcrumbs.

※ Heat the oil in a wok to smoking point, lower the heat slightly and deep-fry the balls for about 2 minutes until cooked through and golden brown. Remove, drain well and keep warm.

## DUCK GIZZARD "FLOWERS"

3 duck gizzards or duck or chicken hearts
1 tablespoon Pu-Ling or other light soy sauce
1 teaspoon sugar
salt and pepper
oil for deep-frying

Score the duck gizzards very deeply from the inside, cutting almost through them in a criss-cross pattern so that the finished gizzard has the appearance of a chrysanthemum. Cut each into several pieces. Place in a dish with the soy sauce, sugar, salt and pepper and leave for 5-6 minutes.

※ Heat the oil in a wok to smoking point and deep-fry the duck gizzards for about 45 seconds in a frying basket until they curl up and change colour. Drain well and serve.

## Shanghai 上海

# ASSORTED EARTHEN POT DISH

*This recipe shows a delicious way to use leftover roast chicken and duck. Combined with the typical Chinese ingredients of simmered sea cucumber, fried pig's skin and fresh bamboo shoots it has a wonderfully rich flavour.*

1 cooked dried or fresh sea cucumber*
185 g (6 oz) pig's skin (from the belly or leg)
oil for deep-frying
250 g (8 oz) cooked roast chicken
250 g (8 oz) cooked roast duck
125-250 g (4-8 oz) lean cooked ham
185 g (6 oz) cooked fresh or canned bamboo shoots
12 fresh or canned straw mushrooms
2 freshwater prawns (yabbies/crayfish)
2 tablespoons Shaoxing rice wine or dry sherry
6 cups (1½ L/48 fl oz) chicken or superior stock (see page 124)
1¾ teaspoons salt
2 tablespoons lard

Deep-fry the pig's skin in a wok in heated oil until bubbles appear on the surface, then place in water or stock and simmer for several hours until tender.

※ Cut the sea cucumber, pig's skin, chicken, duck, ham, bamboo shoots and mushrooms into thin slices and arrange separately in a wide shallow casserole. Sprinkle with the wine and add the stock and salt.

※ Set the pot on a rack in a wok or steamer, cover and steam over simmering water for at least 30 minutes until the flavours are well mingled and the stock full of flavour. Add the lard and place the prawns, still in their shells, on top. Return to the steamer for another 5-10 minutes. Serve in the pot.

*To cook the sea cucumber, soak in cold water until softened, then drain, cut open and clean. Simmer in water with spring onion, ginger, salt and wine for several hours until completely tender.*

ASSORTED EARTHEN POT DISH

WENCHANG CHICKEN, GUANGZHOU STYLE

## Guangzhou 广州

# WENCHANG CHICKEN, GUANGZHOU STYLE

*More than forty years ago, the chef of the Guangzhou Restaurant heard that chickens reared in Wenchang County on Hainan Island were particularly plump and tender. Journeying there to investigate, he found it was indeed true, the only setback being that the bones were rather hard, making it difficult to serve the chicken in the traditional ways. After much experimenting, he perfected this recipe.*

1 x 1 kg (2 lb) tender young chicken
2 teaspoons salt
6 slices salted ham
4 chicken livers
1 angled luffa, or 10 stalks kale or broccoli
1 tablespoon vegetable oil
1 teaspoon sesame oil

SAUCE

1½ cups (375 mL/12 fl oz) chicken stock (broth)
1 tablespoon light soy sauce
½ teaspoon salt
pinch of white pepper
1½ tablespoons cornflour (cornstarch)

Clean the chicken, wipe dry and rub inside and out with the salt. Set aside for 30 minutes.

※ Cut the ham and chicken livers into pieces about 6 x 4 cm (2½ x 1½ in).

※ Using a sharp knife or vegetable peeler, remove the sharp ridges of the angled luffa, but do not peel the sections in between unless they are tough. Cut into pieces the same size as the ham. Plunge into boiling water with the vegetable oil and simmer until tender, then refresh under cold water. If using broccoli or kale, cut into short lengths and boil for 3-4 minutes in lightly salted water, refresh and drain.

※ Oil a large heatproof plate, cut the chicken in half down the centre back and spread out on the plate. Place on a rack in a wok or steamer, steam over briskly simmering water for about 25 minutes. Brush with sesame oil and leave to cool. Pour off the liquid to use in the sauce.

※ Bone the chicken and cut the meat into slices. Place a slice of chicken liver on each piece of chicken and top with a piece of ham. Arrange on a heatproof plate in a chicken shape with the head, wings and drumsticks. Return to the steamer and steam until the ham and chicken livers are tender and the dish hot and moist, for about 6 minutes. Surround with the vegetables and heat through briefly in the steam.

※ Pour the sauce ingredients into a wok and boil until the sauce clears. Pour over the dish and serve at once.

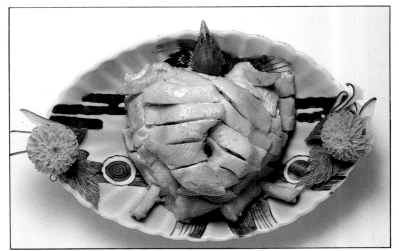

SLICED CHICKEN WITH SCALLION OIL

## Guangzhou 广州

# SLICED CHICKEN WITH SCALLION OIL

*In Guangdong this dish features frequently in family meals and feasts. It is simple to prepare and has a pleasant, distinctive flavour.*

1 x 1 kg (2 lb) spring chicken
1 tablespoon grated fresh (root) ginger
1 teaspoon salt
3 tablespoons peanut oil
4 spring onions (shallots/scallions)
cucumber slices (garnish)
carrot (garnish)

Wash the chicken, drain well and dry with a paper towel. Rub thoroughly inside and out with the ginger and salt and leave for 1 hour to absorb the flavours.

※ Heat the peanut oil in a wok and add the roughly chopped spring onions. Fry until light brown, then remove the onions with a slotted spoon and pour the scallion oil into a dish.

※ In a large saucepan, boil enough water to cover the chicken, adding a pinch of salt. Put in the chicken and then reduce the heat and simmer gently for about 25 minutes. Remove the chicken and cover with cold water. This shrinks the skin and gives it a better texture.

※ Return the chicken to the boiling water and simmer gently for another 10-15 minutes.

※ Lift out and drain well. Brush with the scallion oil and leave to cool. Cut into slices and arrange on a plate with a garnish of cucumber slices and carrot.

## Guangzhou 广州

# DONG JIANG SALT-BAKED CHICKEN

*Historical records of the area of Dong Jiang in Guangdong state that cooked chickens wrapped in tissue paper were preserved in salt mounds in local salt fields. Their golden colour and moist, delicious taste were much appreciated by businessmen and bureaucrats of the area.*

*In the late Qing Dynasty (1644-1911 AD) the area became the collection and distribution centre for salt merchants who often served their guests the Dong Jiang style of salt-preserved chicken. Eventually they turned to baking fresh chickens in coarse salt for immediate consumption, thus retaining the unique salty flavour, while making the chickens even more tender and tasty.*

DONG JIANG SALT-BAKED CHICKEN

BONED CHICKEN WINGS WITH CRAB ROE

1 x 1½ kg (3 lb) plump young chicken
1 teaspoon salt
¼ teaspoon ground star anise
6 slices fresh (root) ginger
2 spring onions (shallots/scallions)
3-4 large sheets tissue or greaseproof paper
4-5 kg (8-10 lb) rock or coarse salt
sesame oil (optional)

DIPPING SAUCE

1 tablespoon grated fresh (root) ginger or powdered galangal
1 tablespoon table salt
3 tablespoons melted lard or vegetable oil

Clean the chicken, rinse with boiling water and hang in an airy place for several hours to allow the skin to dry.

✹ Using a sharp knife or cleaver, slash through the skin on either side of the wings and legs to allow the flavours to penetrate the meat more thoroughly. Dust the cavity with the salt mixed with the star anise and place the ginger slices and spring onions inside. Brush the chicken skin sparingly with lard to prevent the paper sticking, then wrap the chicken with the paper.

✹ In a very large wok heat the rock salt until almost smoking. Stir with a ladle, then make a large well in the centre. Put in the chicken and mound the hot salt evenly over it.

✹ Maintain a steady moderate temperature under the wok and cook for about 25 minutes, then turn the chicken and cook the other side for about 30 minutes or until cooked through. It should be slightly pink around the bones but the juices should be clear when the bird is pierced near the thigh. Remove from the salt, unwrap carefully and discard the paper.

✹ Skin and bone the chicken, then cut the meat into strips. Place the head, wings and drumsticks in position on the serving plate and pile the bones in the centre. Mound the chicken over the bones to resemble its original shape. Brush sparingly with sesame oil if desired.

✹ Divide the ginger or galangal powder between three or four small dishes and add the table salt. Cover each dish with the melted lard, stir lightly and serve with the chicken.

## Guangzhou 广州

# BONED CHICKEN WINGS WITH CRAB ROE

*This recipe is a good example of the Chinese approach to the balance of flavour, presentation and aroma in cooking.*

*Chicken wings are selected as the smoothest, most tender part of the chicken, especially when deep-fried. The bones are removed to enhance the diners' pleasure, and the chicken is complemented by a bright green vegetable, the coral red of crab roe with its unique flavour*

*and texture, and the fresh tang of ginger and spring onions. The result is a unique dish with the colours of jade, coral and pearl.*

8 chicken wings, central sections only
2 tablespoons superior or other light soy sauce
500 g (1 lb) choy sum or other Chinese green vegetable
3 small dried black mushrooms, soaked for 25 minutes
2 cloves garlic
2 slices fresh (root) ginger
5 slices canned or cooked fresh bamboo shoots
1 spring onion (shallot/scallion)
90 g (3 oz) crab roe from a female crab
oil for deep-frying

SAUCE

¾ cup (175 mL/6 fl oz) chicken stock (broth)
1 tablespoon superior or other light soy sauce
¼ teaspoon dark soy sauce
¼ teaspoon sesame oil
¼ teaspoon salt
¼ teaspoon sugar

Using a sharp knife with a long thin blade, remove the bones from the wings. Place in a dish and add the soy sauce. Rub well into the chicken and leave for 20 minutes.

✹ Trim the choy sum, cutting off the thick ends of the stems, rinse and drain well. Squeeze water from the mushrooms. Finely chop the garlic and shred the ginger. Cut the bamboo shoot slices into decorative shapes and the spring onion into 2.5 cm (1 in) diagonal slices.

✹ Heat the oil to quite hot. Place the choy sum in a wire sieve and lower into the oil. As soon as it changes colour, remove and place under cold running water, then set aside.

✹ Reheat the oil and deep-fry the chicken wings until lightly coloured, then remove and drain on a paper towel.

✹ Drain off the oil, reserving about 3 tablespoons. Stir-fry the garlic briefly. Add the mushrooms, ginger and bamboo shoots and stir-fry for 1 minute, then pour in the sauce ingredients and bring to the boil, stirring continually.

✹ Push a stalk of choy sum into the cavity of each chicken wing. Place in the sauce and simmer gently until the wings and vegetables are tender.

✹ Place the crab roe on a plate over a saucepan or wok of gently simmering water and steam until bright red and firm.

✹ Arrange the wings and vegetables on a plate and top with the roe. Serve at once.

STEAMED CHICKEN WINGS WITH FILLING

## Shanghai 上海

# STEAMED CHICKEN WINGS WITH FILLING

12-15 chicken wings, central sections only
75 g (2½ oz) lean ham
75 g (2½ oz) fresh or canned bamboo shoots
3 dried black mushrooms, soaked for 25 minutes
2-3 fresh Chinese long-leaf lettuces
pinch of salt
1 tablespoon vegetable oil
1 egg
oil for frying
1 tablespoon chopped ham

### SAUCE

1 cup (250 mL/8 fl oz) stock (broth)*
1 tablespoon Shaoxing rice wine or dry sherry
1 teaspoon dark soy sauce
2 teaspoons superior or other light soy sauce
2 teaspoons vegetable oil
½ teaspoon salt
2 teaspoons cornflour (cornstarch)

Use a long, thin-bladed knife to remove the bones from the chicken wings.

🍴 Cut the ham, bamboo shoots and drained mushrooms into matchstick lengths and insert several of each into the cavities in the chicken wings.

🍴 Lightly oil a heatproof plate and arrange the stuffed chicken wings on it. Set on a rack in a wok or steamer, and steam, covered, over simmering water for about 30 minutes.

🍴 Cut the lettuces in halves lengthways and drop into a saucepan of boiling water to which a pinch of salt and 1 tablespoon vegetable oil has been added. Blanch for 2 minutes, then remove and drain well. Arrange around the chicken wings.

🍴 Beat the egg lightly. Heat the frying oil in a wok and stir-fry the egg, breaking it up with a fork into fine drops (or fry the egg in a thin flat sheet without stirring, and cut into fine shreds). Arrange over the chicken.

🍴 In another wok, bring the pre-mixed sauce ingredients to the boil and stir until thickened. Pour over the dish and serve at once.

*An excellent stock can be made with the water in which the mushrooms were soaked and the wing tips, removed from the chicken wings. Simmer for 20 minutes.

## Sichuan 四川

# SHREDDED CHICKEN AND TENDER CELERY

*Celery is said to strengthen vigour, calm the nerves and release summer heat. In this dish, tender stems of celery are cooked with shredded chicken. The contrasting greenish yellow of the celery, white of the chicken and the deep red of the pickled chilli complement each other perfectly.*

250 g (8 oz) young celery stems
185 g (6 oz) chicken breasts
1 egg white
1 tablespoon cornflour (cornstarch)
125 g (4 oz) lard
2 spring onions (shallots/scallions), shredded
3 slices fresh (root) ginger, shredded
1 pickled red chilli, shredded

### SEASONING

2 teaspoons rice wine or dry sherry
½ teaspoon sesame oil
3 tablespoons chicken stock (broth)
½ teaspoon salt

Cut the celery into 7.5 cm (3 in) lengths. Very thinly slice the chicken breast, cut into narrow strips, place in a dish and mix with the lightly beaten egg white and cornflour.

🍴 Heat the lard in a wok and stir-fry the chicken over moderate heat until it turns white, then remove. Drain off all but 1½ tablespoons of lard and stir-fry the celery over higher heat with the spring onions, ginger and chilli until the celery begins to soften.

🍴 Return the chicken and add the pre-mixed seasoning ingredients. Stir-fry together over high heat for 1 minute, then serve at once.

SHREDDED CHICKEN AND TENDER CELERY

STEWED CHICKEN, LI KOU FU STYLE

## Guangzhou 广州

# STEWED CHICKEN, LI KOU FU STYLE

*During the 1930s, all restaurants in Guangzhou competed with each other in creating their own chicken specialities. When the Li Kou Fu Restaurant was newly established, the owner devised this chicken dish which he named after his restaurant, and only he and his wife knew the seasoning ingredients. The distinctive flavour is now known to come mainly from the Zhu Hou soy sauce and the mellow Mei Gui Lu wine. Both are famous for their exquisite fragrance.*

1 x 750 g (1½ lb) spring chicken
4 spring onions (shallots/scallions)
fresh coriander

SEASONING

⅔ cup (150 mL/5 fl oz) Zhu Hou or other dark/mushroom soy sauce
⅓ cup (75 mL/2½ fl oz) Mei Gui Lu wine (rose-scented Chinese rice wine)
2 teaspoons sugar
2 teaspoons sesame oil
pinch of salt

Clean the chicken and wipe dry. Place the spring onions in the cavity and put into a deep, small casserole. Mix the seasoning ingredients together. Pour a little into the cavity, then pour the remainder over the chicken.

※ Cover the pot tightly and simmer the chicken very gently until tender, for about 1¼ hours, turning once or twice. Stand the casserole in a dish of boiling water to prevent the chicken coming into direct contact with the heat and burning.

※ Lift out the chicken, cut into serving pieces and arrange on a plate. Pour over the sauce and garnish with fresh coriander.

STEAMED SPRING CHICKEN WITH STRAW MUSHROOMS

## Beijing 北京

# STEAMED SPRING CHICKEN WITH STRAW MUSHROOMS

12-18 dried or canned small straw mushrooms
1 x 1 kg (2 lb) spring chicken
2 spring onions (shallots/scallions)
2 slices fresh (root) ginger
2 teaspoons cornflour (cornstarch)

### SEASONING

2 teaspoons rice wine or dry sherry
2 tablespoons light soy sauce
¼ teaspoon salt
1 teaspoon sugar
2 tablespoons rendered chicken fat

Cover dried straw mushrooms with lukewarm water and soak for about 30 minutes. Drain, reserving the liquid, then trim the mushrooms removing the stems. Wash the caps thoroughly in clean cold water, squeeze out and set aside.

Cut the chicken into cubes, discarding all bones. Dice the spring onions and shred the ginger.

Arrange the chicken in a heatproof dish with the mushroom caps and place the spring onion and ginger on top. Pour on the reserved mushroom water (or use the liquid from the can if using canned mushrooms). Add pre-mixed seasoning ingredients and place on a rack in a wok or steamer. Cover and steam over gently simmering water for at least 15 minutes until the chicken is tender and the dish very aromatic.

Discard the spring onion and ginger, pour the liquid into a wok and thicken with cornflour mixed with a little cold water. Simmer, stirring until the sauce clears, then pour over the dish and serve at once.

## Shanghai 上海

# DICED CHICKEN STIR-FRIED WITH SESAME SAUCE

*This style of cooking was originally the speciality of Sichuan Province, but the chef in the Green Willow Village Restaurant in Shanghai modified the original recipe and added a local speciality – wine-pickled egg yolk.*

375 g (12 oz) chicken breasts
90 g (3 oz) raw peanuts
oil for frying
2 spring onions (shallots/scallions), chopped
½ cup (125 mL/4 fl oz) chicken stock (broth)

DICED CHICKEN STIR-FRIED WITH SESAME SAUCE

### SEASONING/SAUCE

2 tablespoons sesame seed paste (tahini)
3 tablespoons light soy sauce
1 tablespoon brown vinegar
1-3 teaspoons chilli oil or chilli sauce
1 tablespoon sugar
½ teaspoon Sichuan peppercorns (Fagara or Sansho), ground
1 teaspoon grated fresh (root) ginger
1 teaspoon crushed garlic
1 wine-pickled egg yolk, mashed

Cut the chicken into small cubes, discarding any skin and slivers of bone. Drop the peanuts into boiling water to loosen the skins, then drain and peel.

Mix the seasoning/sauce ingredients together, mix with the chicken meat and leave for 20 minutes.

Heat about 2½ tablespoons of oil in a wok and stir-fry the peanuts for about 1 minute. Add the chicken and spring onions and stir-fry over fairly high heat until the chicken is done. Pour in the stock and simmer for about 1½ minutes until absorbed.

Spoon into a serving dish and serve at once.

## Guangzhou 广州

# SAUTÉED CHICKEN BREASTS WITH TOMATO SAUCE

375 g (12 oz) chicken breasts
1 tablespoon Shuang Huang or other light soy sauce
2 egg whites
½ cup (60 g/2 oz) cornflour (cornstarch)
12-18 dried prawn crackers
oil for deep-frying

### SEASONING/SAUCE

1 tablespoon rice wine or dry sherry
2 tablespoons tomato sauce (ketchup)
1½ tablespoons vinegar
2 tablespoons sugar
½ teaspoon salt
½ teaspoon grated fresh (root) ginger

Skin the chicken breasts and cut into thin slices, cutting diagonally across the grain to improve tenderness. Place in a dish, add the soy sauce and leave for 20 minutes.

Beat the egg whites lightly and make into a thick batter with the cornflour. Heat the oil to quite hot and fry the prawn crackers until well puffed and crisp. Drain and set aside.

Dip the chicken pieces one by one into the batter, then place in the oil. Fry, turning twice, until cooked through and golden. Remove and drain well.

SAUTÉED CHICKEN BREASTS WITH TOMATO SAUCE

STEAMED CHICKEN WITH EGG WHITE

🦐 Pour off the oil, reserving about 1 tablespoon. Add the sauce ingredients and bring to the boil, stirring. Put in the chicken pieces and cook gently, stirring carefully from time to time until the liquid has been absorbed.

🦐 Arrange the chicken in the centre of a serving plate, pour a little of the hot frying oil over the chicken to give it a gloss and surround with the prawn crackers.

## Beijing 北京

# WHITE DEW CHICKEN

250 g (8 oz) chicken breast meat, steamed
185 g (6 oz) white fish fillets
5 egg whites
2 tablespoons rendered chicken fat, melted
red capsicum (bell pepper) or carrot shreds
fresh coriander

SEASONING

½ cup (125 mL/4 fl oz) milk
2 teaspoons rice wine or dry sherry
1 teaspoon ginger juice
¾ teaspoon salt
1½ tablespoons cornflour (cornstarch)

SAUCE

¾ cup (175 mL/6 fl oz) chicken stock (broth)
½ teaspoon salt
1 teaspoon rice wine or dry sherry
1 teaspoon ginger juice
1½ teaspoons cornflour (cornstarch)

Cut the chicken into thin slices and arrange evenly in the bottom of a shallow casserole. Sprinkle lightly with a little flour.

WHITE DEW CHICKEN

🦐 Finely mince (grind) the fish and mix with the pre-mixed seasoning ingredients. Beat the egg whites until fluffy but not stiff and fold in with the fish and chicken fat.

🦐 Spread over the chicken slices and garnish with the shredded capsicum or carrot and the fresh coriander.

🦐 Place on a rack in a wok or steamer, cover and steam for about 18 minutes until just firm.

🦐 Mix the sauce ingredients together and boil them in another wok, stirring until the sauce thickens and clears. Pour over the dish and serve.

## Shanghai 上海

# STEAMED CHICKEN WITH EGG WHITE

*This is a meticulously prepared dish. The three layers of ingredients are subjected to three separate steaming procedures. The lower layer consists of very thinly sliced chicken breast; the central layer of minced prawn and pork fat mixed with wine; and the upper layer of whipped egg white. When the dish is completely assembled and cooked for the second time, it is cut into diamond-shaped sections and garnished with pea leaves and ham before its final steaming.*

*The elegant appearance of this dish enhances its delicious flavour.*

125 g (4 oz) chicken breasts
250 g (8 oz) peeled fresh prawns (shrimps)
90 g (3 oz) pork fat
2 teaspoons rice wine or dry sherry
1 teaspoon salt
1 tablespoon cornflour (cornstarch)
4 egg whites, well beaten
fresh pea or young spinach leaves (garnish)
1 slice salted ham (garnish)
1 tablespoon rendered chicken fat, melted

Very thinly slice the chicken breasts, which should be skinless and without bones, and arrange in the bottom of an oiled, 20 cm (8 in) square baking tray.

🦐 Mince (grind) the prawns and pork fat and mix with the wine, salt and cornflour. Spread this over the chicken. Place on a rack in a wok or steamer and steam, covered, over high heat for about 20 minutes until cooked through.

🦐 While the tray is still hot, pour on the beaten egg whites, cover and steam gently until the egg is just set. Remove from the steamer and leave to cool.

🦐 Cut into diamond-shaped pieces and place a double pea leaf and a tiny piece of ham, cut into the shape of a flower, on each piece. Transfer them to a flat heatproof plate, then return to the steamer for about 5 minutes until heated through. Sprinkle over the chicken fat just before serving to give the dish a gloss.

QUICK-FRIED CHICKEN CUBES IN BROWN BEAN SAUCE

## Beijing 北京

# QUICK-FRIED CHICKEN CUBES IN BROWN BEAN SAUCE

*Brown bean sauce is a special sauce from Beijing made from soy beans, flour and salt. It is light brown, and as fine and smooth as a paste, with a sweet and salty smell. It is used for quick-frying and to season stuffings.*

*This well-known Shandong dish is rated as one of the best quick-fried dishes seasoned with brown bean·sauce. The sauce should adhere to the chicken pieces when cooked, and not remain in the bottom of the wok.*

315 g (10 oz) chicken breast meat
1 egg white, lightly beaten
2 tablespoons cornflour (cornstarch)
125 g (4 oz) lard
1 teaspoon sesame oil

SEASONING

1 tablespoon brown bean sauce
2 teaspoons sugar
2 teaspoons rice wine or dry sherry
1 teaspoon ginger juice

Cut the chicken breast into small cubes and dip into a mixture of beaten egg white and cornflour, coating evenly.
✖ Heat the lard in a wok and quick-fry the chicken until white and almost cooked through. Remove and pour off all but 1½ tablespoons of the lard. Add the sesame oil and heat well, then fry the brown bean sauce briefly before adding the remaining seasoning ingredients. Mix well, then return the chicken and stir-fry until the seasoning ingredients coat the chicken cubes. Transfer to a serving plate and serve immediately.

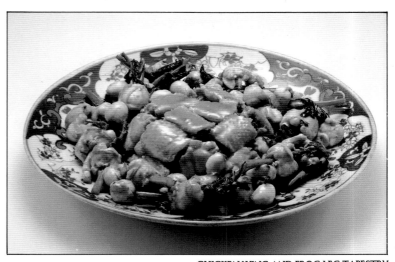

CHICKEN WING AND FROG LEG TAPESTRY

## Guangzhou 广州

# CHICKEN WING AND FROG LEG TAPESTRY

*The wings are golden yellow, the frogs' legs are pale, the ham is pink and the vegetables green. This dish is as colourful as a tapestry, hence its name.*

12 chicken wings, central joint only
3 slices lean ham
12 frogs' legs
6 stems choy sum or other Chinese green vegetable
oil for deep-frying
¾ cup (175 mL/6 fl oz) chicken stock (broth)
2 teaspoons cornflour (cornstarch)

SEASONING A

1 tablespoon rice wine or dry sherry
½ teaspoon sesame oil
¼ teaspoon salt
pinch of white pepper

SEASONING B

1 tablespoon rice wine or dry sherry
2 teaspoons cornflour (cornstarch)
½ teaspoon salt
pinch of white pepper

Cut the wings in halves and use a sharp knife to remove the small bones. Cut the ham into shreds the length of the chicken pieces, and place several ham shreds in the cavity of each chicken wing. Arrange side by side in a dish, add the seasoning A ingredients and set aside for 20 minutes.
✖ Bone the frogs' legs. Cut the vegetable stems in halves and place a portion in the cavity of each frog's leg. Arrange in a heatproof dish, add the seasoning B ingredients and set aside for 20 minutes.
✖ Set the dish of chicken wings on a rack in a wok, or in a steamer, over simmering water. Cover tightly and steam for about 35 minutes until tender.
✖ Heat the oil and deep-fry the frogs' legs until golden and cooked through. Drain well.
✖ Pour the liquid from the wings into a wok, add the stock mixed with the cornflour and bring to the boil. Simmer, stirring, until the sauce clears.
✖ Pile the chicken wings in the centre of a serving plate and surround with the frogs' legs. Pour over the sauce and serve.

## Beijing 北京

# VELVET CHICKEN WITH SHARKS' FINS

*This classic dish is often served as the first course of an elaborate ten-course dinner banquet.*

60 g (2 oz) dried shredded sharks' fins
5 cups (1¼ L/40 fl oz) superior stock (*see page 124*)
315 g (10 oz) chicken breasts
3 tablespoons ice cold water
4 egg whites, well beaten
1½ tablespoons cornflour (cornstarch)
¾ teaspoon salt
2 teaspoons rice wine or dry sherry
3 cups (750 mL/24 fl oz) chicken stock (broth)
½ cup (125 mL/4 fl oz) milk
2 spring onions (shallots/scallions)
3 slices fresh (root) ginger

Prepare the sharks' fins by soaking for one hour in cold water, then bring to the boil, simmer for 10 minutes and drain. Soak again in cold water for about 30 minutes, then bring to the boil and simmer for 30 minutes. Repeat the second soaking and boiling process, then drain well and cover with the superior stock. Simmer for about 1 hour until the fins are tender.

Very finely mince (grind) the chicken, mixing in the ice cold water. Add the egg whites and cornflour and season with salt and wine.

Set aside a small portion of the sharks' fins for decoration and stir the remainder into the chicken paste. Form this mixture into lotus flower petal shapes and arrange on a bamboo rack. Place the rack in a wok and pour in the chicken stock and milk. Add the whole spring onions and the sliced ginger. Cover and simmer over very low heat until most of the stock has evaporated or been absorbed. Lift out, transfer to a serving plate and garnish with the remaining sharks' fins shreds before serving.

VELVET CHICKEN WITH SHARKS' FINS

SWEET AND SOUR CHICKEN SHREDS

## Shanghai 上海

# SWEET AND SOUR CHICKEN SHREDS

*This is the Shanghai version of a traditional Sichuan dish. Tender chicken breasts are cut into fine shreds, stir-fried and then flavoured with a spicy, sweet and sour mixture of condiments and seasonings.*

250 g (8 oz) chicken breasts, skinned
1 tablespoon Shaoxing rice wine or dry sherry
1 small egg white, lightly beaten
1 teaspoon salt
2 teaspoons cornflour (cornstarch)
2 slices fresh (root) ginger
½ red capsicum (bell pepper)
1 spring onion (shallot/scallion)
250 g (8 oz) fresh spinach leaves
oil for frying

SEASONING

1 teaspoon black bean paste
2 teaspoons chilli oil or chilli sauce
1 teaspoon sugar

Very thinly slice the chicken breasts, then cut into shreds. Place in a dish and add the wine, egg white, salt and cornflour. Mix well and leave for 20 minutes to marinate.

Shred the ginger and the trimmed capsicum. Cut the spring onion into 4 cm (2 in) lengths, then lengthways into shreds. Rinse the spinach leaves thoroughly, remove stems and drain well.

Heat 2 tablespoons of the oil in a wok and stir-fry the spinach over high heat until wilted. Transfer to a serving plate.

Add about 2 tablespoons oil to the wok and stir-fry the ginger briefly, then add the capsicum and spring onion shreds and stir-fry for about 1 minute, adding the pre-mixed seasoning ingredients. Push to one side of the pan and add the chicken shreds. Stir-fry over high heat until cooked through and white, then mix thoroughly with the capsicum, spring onion and the sauce.

Lift onto the serving plate beside the spinach and serve.

DICED QUAIL STIR-FRIED IN CHICKEN FAT

## Guangzhou 广州

# DICED QUAIL STIR-FRIED IN CHICKEN FAT

*Wild quails breed in northeast China and migrate to the southeast in winter. A type of turtledove, they eat grains and grass seeds which gives them a plump and tender breast. Nowadays they are bred commercially all over China for their delicious meat and tiny eggs, the latter a favourite in Guangdong.*

4 quails, 185 g (6 oz) each
1 tablespoon light soy sauce
1 egg white, well beaten
3 tablespoons cornflour (cornstarch)
60 g (2 oz) fresh or canned winter bamboo shoots
3 dried black mushrooms, soaked for 25 minutes
peanut oil
3 tablespoons rendered chicken fat

SEASONING/SAUCE

1 clove garlic, finely chopped
2 slices fresh (root) ginger, finely chopped
2 spring onions (shallots/scallions), finely chopped
2 teaspoons rice wine or dry sherry
1 teaspoon sugar
½ teaspoon salt
pinch of white pepper
2 teaspoons oyster sauce

Cut the heads, necks, wings and legs off the quails. Reserve one lot for the presentation of the dish, place in a bowl and marinate with the soy sauce until required.

✺ Remove the meat from the quail carcasses and cut into very fine dice. Mix with the egg white and 2 tablespoons cornflour.

✺ Drop the fresh bamboo shoots into a saucepan of boiling water, simmer for 2 minutes, then drain well. Drain and trim the mushrooms, then dice them and the bamboo shoots finely.

✺ Coat the marinated quail's head, neck, wings and legs thickly with cornflour. Heat the peanut oil in a wok and deep-fry these parts until crisp and golden, then arrange on a serving plate.

✺ Drain the wok, reheat it with the chicken fat and stir-fry the mushrooms and bamboo shoots for 1½ minutes. Push to one side and add the diced quail meat. Stir-fry until just cooked, for about 2 minutes, then add the garlic, ginger and spring onions. Stir in the bamboo shoots and mushrooms and add the remaining seasoning/sauce ingredients, tossing together over high heat until well mixed. Place the mixture on the plate with the fried head, wings and legs, then serve.

✺ Traditionally diced quail is served sandwich-style, wrapped in fresh lettuce leaves.

FRIED GOOSE LIVERS WRAPPED IN PORK FAT NET

## Shanghai 上海

# FRIED GOOSE LIVERS WRAPPED IN PORK FAT NET

*This delicate dish is a speciality of the Ningbo area in Zhejiang Province, where the wrap and fry method of cooking is often used. Goose livers are said to be better than those of other poultry because they are large, soft and flavourful. Wrapping the livers in pork fat net, and then frying, preserves the tasty juices of the liver.*

315 g (10 oz) fresh goose or duck livers
1 piece pork fat net (caul lining)
1 small egg
½ cup (60 g/2 oz) flour
salt and pepper
2 tablespoons cornflour (cornstarch)
oil for deep-frying

SEASONING

1 tablespoon Shaoxing rice wine or dry sherry
2½ tablespoons finely chopped spring onions
   (shallots/scallions)
pepper

HOT SOY SAUCE DIP

3 tablespoons dark soy sauce
1 fresh red chilli, finely chopped

SICHUAN PEPPER-SALT DIP

3 tablespoons fine table salt
1 tablespoon Sichuan peppercorns (Fagara or Sansho)

Trim the livers and cut into slices. Place in a dish and add the seasoning ingredients, mix well and leave for 30 minutes.

✺ Rinse the caul fat and dry well, place on a dry paper towel.

✺ Beat the egg and flour to make a smooth batter, adding salt and pepper. Cut the caul into long wide strips and brush with the batter. Place liver mixture in a thick line down the centre and roll up in a sausage shape, tucking the ends in. Repeat with the remaining caul fat and liver.

✺ Grease a heatproof plate and place the liver rolls on it. Set on a rack in a wok or steamer, cover and steam for about 25 minutes until cooked, remove and leave to cool.

✺ When cool, brush the outside with the remaining batter and coat lightly with cornflour. Heat the oil in a wok and deep-fry until golden and crisp on the surface. Drain well and arrange on a serving plate.

✺ Mix the soy sauce dip ingredients and divide between several small dishes.

✺ To prepare the pepper-salt dip, dry-fry the peppercorns in a wok for about 1 minute, then remove and grind finely. Heat the salt in the dry wok, stirring constantly, and remove from the heat just before it begins to colour.

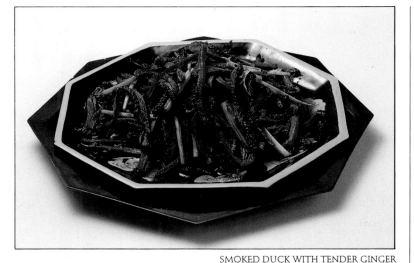

DICED DUCK MEAT WITH GREEN CAPSICUMS

SMOKED DUCK WITH TENDER GINGER

## Beijing 北京

# DICED DUCK MEAT WITH GREEN CAPSICUMS

*The large, dark green capsicums which grow in and around Beijing are characterised by their thick layers of pulp. Sweet and crisp, they are especially good for frying. In this recipe they are combined with very tender duck meat. For those who like it hot, some chilli oil can be added.*

375 g (12 oz) boneless duck meat, preferably from the breast
1 egg white, well beaten
2 tablespoons cornflour (cornstarch)
¾ teaspoon salt
500 g (1 lb) lard, oil or rendered duck fat for frying
1 large green capsicum (bell pepper)
2 teaspoons cornflour (cornstarch)

SEASONING

2 tablespoons light soy sauce
2 teaspoons rice wine or dry sherry
1½ teaspoons sugar
½ cup (125 mL/4 fl oz) duck or chicken stock (broth)
1 teaspoon sesame oil
pinch of salt and pepper

Cut the duck meat into small cubes and place in a dish with the egg white, cornflour and salt. Mix well and leave for 15 minutes.

Cut the capsicum in half, trim away the seed core and inner white ribs and discard the stem. Cut into squares.

Heat the oil or fat in a wok until smoking, then reduce the heat to moderate. Fry the duck for about 3 minutes until cooked through, then remove and set aside. Add the capsicum and fry until slightly coloured, remove and drain. Pour off all but 2 tablespoons of the oil, add the seasoning ingredients and bring to the boil, stirring constantly.

Return the duck and capsicum and stir together for a few moments over high heat. Thicken slightly with a thin mixture of cornflour and cold water and then serve.

## Sichuan 四川

# SMOKED DUCK WITH TENDER GINGER

*"Before going to bed, take some radish, after getting up take some ginger" is an old Chinese saying derived from the belief that the radish aids digestion, while ginger increases the appetite.*

*Ginger was first brought to China from Indonesia at least two thousand years ago. Poets and herbalists have written in praise of it, and chefs have created many delicious dishes using its fine flavour.*

1 complete breast of a camphor and tea smoked duck*
12 slices fresh (root) ginger
1-2 fresh red chillies
2 spring onions (shallots/scallions) or garlic chives
3 cloves garlic
2 tablespoons oil for frying
1 teaspoon brown vinegar

SEASONING

2 tablespoons light soy sauce
2 teaspoons rice vinegar
1 tablespoon hot bean paste
2½ teaspoons sugar

Do not skin the duck, but cut through the breast into thin slices, then stack several slices on top of each other and cut into narrow shreds.

Cut the ginger, chillies and spring onions or garlic chives into shreds and slice the garlic.

Heat the oil in a wok to smoking point and stir-fry the duck until crisp on the edges, remove and set aside.

Stir-fry the vegetables and garlic together for about 1½ minutes, then add the seasoning ingredients and stir-fry together for another 30 seconds.

Return the duck meat and continue to stir-fry over high heat until the ingredients are all well mixed. Stir in the brown vinegar and serve.

*Duck smoked over chips of camphor wood and Chinese black tea leaves to give a strong, smoky flavour and rich deep colour.*

FRIED SESAME DUCK LIVER

## Beijing 北京

# FRIED SESAME DUCK LIVER

*Duck livers offer a good source of protein and vitamins. They are said to be good for the liver and eyes, and able to cure night blindness and anaemia. Sesame seeds, a major source of rich cooking and flavouring oil, are said to replenish strength and help muscle and brain development. Thus the combination of duck livers and sesame in this recipe makes an extremely beneficial and nutritious dish.*

10 duck or chicken livers
2 teaspoons rice wine or dry sherry
½ teaspoon salt
1 cup (125 g/4 oz) flour
2 egg whites
¾ cup (90 g/3 oz) white sesame seeds
peanut oil for frying

Blanch the livers in boiling water, drain well, then cut open without cutting right through, and flatten out butterfly-style. Place in a dish, season with the rice wine and salt and leave for 20 minutes.
※ Pour the flour into a dish and break the eggs into another, beating until frothy. Spread sesame seeds on a plate.
※ Coat each piece of liver with flour, then dip into the beaten egg. Dip one side of each liver into the sesame seeds, coating thickly. Heat about 2.5 cm (1 in) of oil in a wide pan or wok and gently fry the livers for about 3 minutes until golden on the surface and tender inside. Serve immediately.

## Beijing 北京

# BEIJING DUCK

Records of the famed Beijing duck actually date back as far as the Song Dynasty (960-1279 AD) but the dish became a favourite of the imperial kitchen only during the Ming Dynasty (1368-1644 AD). The ducks used then were the small, black-feathered ducks from the Nanjing lakes, quite different to the plump-breasted white Beijing ducks used today.

At the beginning of the fifteenth century the capital of China was moved from Nanjing to Beijing, and rice had to be transported from Nanjing to Beijing to meet the extravagant demands of the imperial court. Canals were dug to transport the rice, but much was lost in the canals, and subsequently the ducks bred in this area became extremely well fed. A new breed of Beijing duck thus emerged, and duck breeding became a prosperous business.

Beijing ducks are now artificially fed, and sixty to seventy days after hatching their weight can be as much as 3½ kilograms (7 pounds). Their distinctive features are white feathers, short wings, a long back and strong healthy body, with the thin skin that is best for roasting.

There are different ways of roasting the duck, although this is not usually done at home. At the famous Quan Ju De Restaurant in Beijing the ducks are hung inside a special brick oven suspended on steel rods over the fire. Just beyond the front opening is a small platform where aromatic fruit tree wood is burnt, and its specially fragrant smoke penetrates the ducks during the cooking process.

The method used by the equally famous Bian Yi Fang Beijing Duck Restaurant does not allow the flame to touch the ducks directly. The walls of the oven are first heated to the right temperature, then the oven door is tightly closed and the ducks roasted in the heat from glowing charcoal underneath. Gas and electric ovens used in other restaurants also give excellent results. The correct temperature results in minimal loss of oil and juice, a light crisp skin and the characteristic bright colour of Beijing duck.

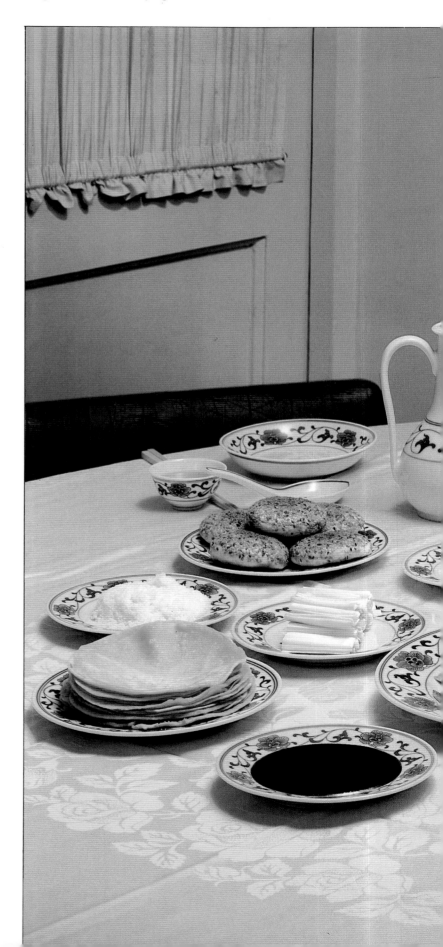

Regardless of the roasting method, the ducks are always given a standard pre-roasting treatment. After the ducks have been killed and plucked, air is pumped beneath the skin to make it balloon. The internal organs are removed and the cavity is washed well. The ducks are then hung on a hook and scalded with boiling water. A syrupy mixture made from diluted malt sugar is poured over the skin and the ducks are left to dry. Finally, before hanging in the oven to roast, the bodies are filled with water which boils the meat from the inside as it roasts outside. This gives the duck its famed crisp dry skin and succulent tender meat.

Beijing Duck should be eaten immediately. The duck is taken to the table and the brightly coloured skin, resembling brilliantly lacquered wood (giving it the name of lacquered duck) is quickly sliced off in squares. While diners enjoy the slivers of skin dipped into sweet bean paste and eaten with thin, soft wheat-flour pancakes, sticks of cucumber and fresh spring onion, the meat is carved and arranged on a serving plate.

The meat is the second course of Beijing Duck, and it is sometimes served with lotus leaf cakes and sesame buns instead of pancakes. The leftover bones and fragments of meat are boiled with white cabbage and winter melon to make a soup which is brought to the table towards the end of the banquet.

BONED DUCK SIMMERED WITH LEMON JUICE

## Guangzhou 广州

# BONED DUCK SIMMERED WITH LEMON JUICE

375 g (12 oz) boned duck meat
2 eggs, well beaten
1 cup (125 g/4 oz) cornflour (cornstarch)
3 cups (750 mL/24 fl oz) oil for deep-frying
1 teaspoon sesame oil
1 tablespoon peanut oil (optional)
sliced tomatoes, fried

SEASONING

2 tablespoons water
1 tablespoon rice wine or dry sherry
1 teaspoon grated fresh (root) ginger
2 tablespoons finely chopped spring onion (shallot/scallion)
1 teaspoon salt
1/3 teaspoon bicarbonate of soda (baking soda)

SAUCE

1½ cups (375 mL/12 fl oz) chicken or duck stock (broth)
2 tablespoons rice wine or dry sherry
3 tablespoons lemon juice
1½ tablespoons sugar

Cut the duck meat into finger-sized pieces and place in a dish. Pour on the pre-mixed seasoning ingredients and mix well, cover and leave for 1-2 hours.
※ Drain and pat dry. Dip each piece into the beaten egg, then coat thickly with cornflour. Heat the deep-frying oil in a wok to smoking point, then reduce the heat slightly and deep-fry the duck pieces, several at a time, until golden on both sides. Lift out, drain well and place in a clay pot or casserole.
※ Add the sauce ingredients and bring just to the boil, then reduce the heat and simmer, partially covered, for about 40 minutes until the duck is very tender and the liquid almost absorbed.
※ Sprinkle on the sesame oil and peanut oil, if used, transfer to a serving plate and surround with fried sliced tomato.

## Beijing 北京

# SUNFLOWER DUCK

1 x 1½ kg (3 lb) duck
16 small dried black mushrooms, soaked for 25 minutes
12 small slices Yunnan or other salty ham
3/4 cup (175 mL/6 fl oz) chicken stock (broth)
1 tablespoon rendered chicken fat
1 teaspoon sugar
1 tablespoon cornflour (cornstarch)
carrot sticks, parboiled (garnish)

SEASONING

2 teaspoons rice wine or dry sherry
1 tablespoon light soy sauce
2 tablespoons finely chopped spring onion (shallot/scallion)
½ teaspoon finely chopped fresh (root) ginger
pinch of salt

Clean and dry the duck inside and out and place in a dish. Mix the seasoning ingredients together, spoon into the cavity and marinate for 1 hour, turning the duck from time to time.
※ Set the duck on a rack in a wok or in a steamer, cover and steam over gently simmering water for about 1 hour until tender. Three-quarters of the way through cooking the duck add the mushrooms and ham to the steamer. Remove, allow to cool, then bone and cut off 16 slices of the most tender part of the duck, breast and upper thighs. Cut off the mushroom stems and arrange the caps, together with the ham and slices of duck, skin downwards, alternately in several rows on a heatproof plate.
※ Mix the chicken stock, chicken fat and sugar together and pour over the dish. Steam for a further 10-12 minutes. Drain the liquid into a wok, then place a plate over the dish and upturn so that the duck meat now has the skin facing upwards.
※ Add the cornflour mixed with a little cold water to the liquid in the wok. Bring to the boil and pour over the dish. Arrange the carrot sticks around the dish and serve at once.

SUNFLOWER DUCK

FLAMED DUCK HEARTS

## Beijing 北京

# FLAMED DUCK HEARTS

*It takes just three seconds to cook this dish! The marinated duck hearts are tossed into a very hot wok where the moisture from the marinade, contacting the hot fat, bursts into flames. This dramatic spectacle illustrates the versatility of the Chinese wok and the creative genius of the Chinese chef.*

185 g (6 oz) duck hearts
3 tablespoons rendered duck fat
4 spring onions (shallots/scallions), shredded
8 sprigs fresh coriander

SEASONING

1 tablespoon Mao Tai wine or dry sherry
2 tablespoons light soy sauce
1 teaspoon sesame oil
1 teaspoon sugar
⅓ teaspoon salt
pinch of pepper

Cut open each heart, place cut side upwards on a cutting board and bat several times with the side of the cleaver to flatten and tenderise. Make criss-cross scores across the cut side of each heart. Place in a dish, add the pre-mixed seasoning ingredients and leave for 20 minutes to marinate.

❊ In a large wok heat the duck fat to smoking point. Quickly drop in the hearts and allow the fat to catch fire. Stir the hearts once and remove from the wok in a strainer.

❊ Have the shredded spring onion and fresh coriander spread over a serving plate, pile the hearts onto the plate and serve immediately.

SHREDDED DUCK MEAT WITH BEAN SPROUTS

## Beijing 北京

# SHREDDED DUCK MEAT WITH BEAN SPROUTS

*It is an old Chinese custom to eat spring rolls filled with fresh bean sprouts at the beginning of springtime every year. This dish of shredded duck with bean sprouts is quite similar to a traditional spring-roll filling and could be used as such.*

315 g (10 oz) roast duck breast meat
125 g (4 oz) fresh mung or soy bean sprouts
1 spring onion (shallot/scallion), sliced
3 slices fresh (root) ginger, shredded
2½ tablespoons oil for frying
2 teaspoons Sichuan pepper (Fagara or Sansho) oil*

SEASONING/SAUCE

½ cup (125 mL/4 fl oz) chicken or duck stock (broth)
2 teaspoons rice wine or dry sherry
1½ teaspoons brown vinegar
3 cloves garlic, finely chopped

Cut the duck into thin slices, then into fine shreds. Blanch the sprouts in boiling water for a few seconds, then drain very well and leave to cool.

🍲 Place the spring onion and ginger in a wok with the frying oil and heat to smoking point, then turn off the heat and leave to stand for 5 minutes. Remove and discard the onion and ginger and reheat the oil.

🍲 Mix the seasoning/sauce ingredients together.

🍲 When the oil is at smoking point, very quickly put the sprouts in and stir-fry for a few seconds, then add the duck meat and stir quickly. Pour in the sauce mixture and heat through very quickly. Transfer to a serving plate and sprinkle on the Sichuan pepper oil.

*Heat 2-3 tablespoons of peanut or other vegetable oil in a wok to smoking point. Add 2 teaspoons of lightly crushed Sichuan peppercorns and fry for 1 minute, then turn off the heat and leave to stand in the oil until cool. Drain off the oil and store in a jar.*

## Beijing 北京

# DUCK WING LANTERNS

*Frills made from coloured cellophane are used to decorate the bones of these crisp-fried duck wings. If the lighting on the banquet table is correct, the brightly coloured paper causes a rainbow of coloured lights.*

12 duck wings, central joint only
¾ cup (90 g/3 oz) cornflour (cornstarch)
oil or rendered duck fat for deep-frying
cellophane frills

SEASONING

1 tablespoon rice wine or dry sherry
1 tablespoon light soy sauce
2 teaspoons dark soy sauce
2 teaspoons sugar
¼ teaspoon salt
pinch of white pepper
2 tablespoons finely chopped spring onion (shallot/scallion)
1 teaspoon grated fresh (root) ginger

Use a small sharp knife to cut around one end of each wing bone and push the meat along to form a ball at one end. Leave only one bone in each wing. Place in a dish, add the pre-mixed seasoning and marinate for 1 hour, turning several times.

🍲 Place the duck wings on a heatproof dish on a rack in a wok or steamer, cover and steam over gently simmering water for 20-25 minutes until the wings are very tender. Remove and drain well, leave to dry for a few minutes, then coat thickly with cornflour, shaking off the excess.

🍲 Heat the oil in a wok and deep-fry the wings over high heat for about 1½ minutes until the surface is crisp and well coloured. Drain well, decorate the tips of the bones with cellophane frills and serve immediately.

DUCK WING LANTERNS

## Shanghai 上海

# STIR-FRIED PHEASANT MEAT WITH BEAN SPROUTS

*Pheasant is sometimes called wild chicken. The texture of its meat is tight and fine-grained, as well as very tender and full of flavour, its breast meat being especially delicious and firm.*

*Bean sprouts, picked clean of their seed pods and tapering roots, are called silver sprouts. The colour of these two ingredients together is subtle and the texture smooth and crisp.*

185 g (6 oz) pheasant breast meat, skinned
1 small egg white
2 tablespoons lard
250 g (8 oz) fresh silver sprouts
pinch of salt
2 tablespoons Shaoxing rice wine or dry sherry
¾ cup (175 mL/6 fl oz) stock (broth) made from the pheasant bones
1 tablespoon cornflour (cornstarch)

Very thinly slice the breast meat, then cut into fine, even shreds. Lightly beat the egg white, mix with the pheasant meat and set aside for 20 minutes.

🍲 Heat the wok, add half the lard and stir-fry the silver sprouts until softened, adding a pinch of salt. Arrange around the edge of a serving dish.

🍲 Add the remaining lard and stir-fry the pheasant meat over high heat for 2-3 minutes until it changes colour and is just cooked through.

🍲 Add the wine and cook briefly, then add the stock and cornflour mixed together and boil until the sauce thickens. Check the seasoning and then pile the pheasant shreds in the centre of the dish and serve at once.

上海
Shanghai

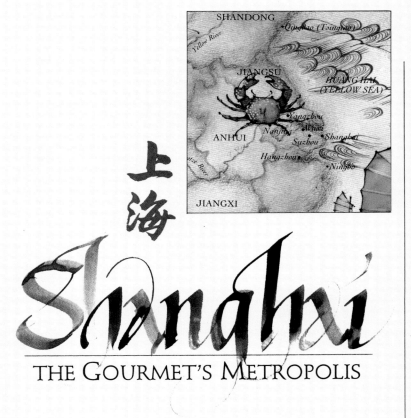

上海

# Shanghai
## THE GOURMET'S METROPOLIS

WHERE the mighty flood of the Yangtze River rushes 32 kilometres (20 miles) wide into the East China Sea, an astonishing maze of tributaries, creeks, rivers, lakes, ponds and marshlands twist, shimmering, between endless fields of rice and vegetables. On the river itself, and in the countless waterways stretching in all directions, nets are cast to harvest fish such as the Yangtze catfish, which grows up to 2 metres (6 feet) in length. A rich crop of freshwater carp and other table fish is raised to tender plumpness in a million ponds. At sea the sails of junks and sampans spread to the horizon as their crews await the flood tides to help carry them upriver to the biggest city in the world, where the twelve million inhabitants of Shanghai await their daily catch. To the north of the river lies the province of Jiangsu, now the richest in China, where more than sixty million people proudly refer to their lake-studded home as the Land of Fish and Rice. To the south, equally rich and proud of its culinary heritage, is Zhejiang Province which has made its own vital contribution to China's gastronomic heritage. As the Western world calls an area of bounteous plenty a Land of Milk and Honey, so to the Chinese a place where generous nature opens its heart and bestows all the good things of life is known as a Land of Fish and Rice. Hence the reason for joy in the bounteous harvest lands of the Yangtze delta.

And in the middle is the jewel, the immense industrial powerhouse of Shanghai. Sprawling around a river of its own, the Huangpu, with its endless wharves and berths and cranes and ferries, it is a city of superlatives. Shanghai works hard, and to keep its enormous workforce productive and churning out a third of China's industrial wealth, it supports a stunning range of restaurants. Shanghai is a working city and much of the eating is done on the run. The steaming hot buns stuffed with pork and vegetables are the Chinese equivalent of the American hamburger, the Australian meat pie or the British fish and chips. Crowds of thousands cram the hundreds of hot bun shops yelling orders.

THE GRAND CANAL IN WUXI, JIANGSU PROVINCE
TOM NEBBIA

But Shanghai is just one of the cities clustered in the fertile plain and studded on the waterways of the central coast of China. Historic and fabled places such as Suzhou, Wuxi, Hangzhou, Nanjing, Ningbo and a score of other cities all boast their own culinary traditions and local delicacies. And, above all, Yangzhou. Over the centuries this ancient city has given to the national table such dishes as the big, tender meatball known as Lion's Head, as well as fried rice, noodles and many others. In the gastronomic wealth of this region every city has a claim to culinary fame, every district has given some twist to the immense variety of dishes which originate in the Land of Fish and Rice. The busy port city of Ningbo bequeathed salted fish and other preserved foods designed to stock the galleys of its roaming fleet. Hangzhou gave a tradition of juicy carp from its West Lake, the famed Dragon Well tea, and of course its gentle but potent spiced rice wine. Little wonder Marco Polo called it the finest and most splendid city in the world, and for the rest of his life was to speak glowingly of its gastronomic glory. Some of Suzhou's specialities are so famous that gourmets from Shanghai will drive up for the day to sample the local crab, mandarin fish or eel. Spare ribs are said to have first been sizzled in Wuxi, and Nanjing claims the best pressed ducks in the land – producing a staggering fifty million birds every year. Zhejiang Province is proud of its vinegar, rightfully claimed to be the best in China and, therefore, the world.

The Shanghai region has one dish that is justifiably acclaimed as being supreme throughout the whole of China. No matter how ardent a culinary nationalist from another area of the country may be, he will concede that nothing can ever equal the freshwater delicacy known as Shanghai hairy crab. The very name of the creature that makes up this dish is misleading, because the most famous hairy crabs do not come from Shanghai but from Yangcheng Lake, halfway up the river to Nanjing. But it is as Shanghai hairy crab that they are known to the world, and the devotees who pay up to a hundred dollars for a 13 centimetre (5 inch) wide crab are certain that it is money well spent.

Those not familiar with the fame of this crustacean may look askance at such sums being paid for what appears to be an undistinguished creature which glares balefully out of two enraged tiny eyes and is covered with unsightly blackish fur. But come the autumn Yangcheng Lake delivers up its harvest, and gourmets flock from around the world to partake of the delicacy. Every day during the season two express trains leave Shanghai and rumble south to Hong Kong to deliver baskets of fresh crabs to specialist chefs in the city. The crabs are steamed alive and placed in front of eager diners. Those who throng to the tables to eat the delicacies are not only Chinese; in recent years Japanese gourmets have flown to Hong Kong by the hundreds merely to enjoy a meal of the small freshwater crabs.

The four-gilled carp is another freshwater delicacy. In all the world, the tiny fish, which averages about 15 centimetres (6 inches) in length, lives only in one small stretch of one river. The Chinese government permits only a limited number to be caught every year, and because the four-gilled carp is said to have numerous healthy benefits for those who eat it, the price paid for it is correspondingly high.

CHINA'S MAIN FILM-MAKING CENTRE, SHANGHAI HAS MANY CINEMAS

LEONG KA TAI

WATERWAYS DISSECT THE CENTRAL COAST OF CHINA                                    PAUL LAU

ONE OF SHANGHAI'S BUSY THOROUGHFARES

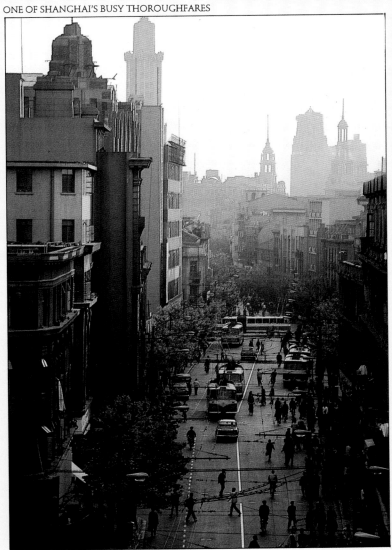

The lower Yangtze Valley is the area generally considered to be the centre of the Shanghai cuisine. Shanghai, however, became a city only in the nineteenth century when China was forced at gunpoint to open the series of coastal and river settlements known as Treaty Ports. So there is no such thing as a historical Shanghai cuisine. The city, as it swelled to its present immense size, first as an international settlement and then as China's premier port and industrial complex, borrowed the cuisines from the surrounding provinces. Into the conurbation on the banks of the Huangpu poured the genius of the people of Jiangsu, Zhejiang, Anhui and Hubei. They went to Shanghai to make their fortunes, and when they had made them they wanted to spend some of their money on eating their native foods. So up sprang thousands of provincial restaurants serving the countless delicacies of the central coast of China and the Yangtze Valley. Over the years these specialties merged into what is now known as the Shanghai kitchen.

What makes Shanghai food distinctive? Gourmets will tell you that it is more oily than that of other regions. Gentle, slow braising rather than vigorous stir-frying is a favoured cooking technique, making dishes more succulent and highly flavoured. To give balance a pinch of sugar is often added to meat recipes. Many dishes are spiced with the wine of Shaoxing, famous in all China and used so lavishly in dishes from this area that the gourmet will know immediately that he is being served Shanghai delicacies. China's favourite fish and seafood are found here in abundance, and the fish recipes from this eastern region are as good or better than those of any other part of the country. Meat and poultry are also excellent, the favourite choices being pork and chicken.

WELDON TRANNIES

The region is also famous for its beautifully arranged cold platters. The bountiful supplies of vegetables add colour and variety to the diet which, with its heavy reliance on fresh fish and fresh vegetables, is one of the healthiest and most balanced in the world.

The slower braising and stewing, and the natural delta ingredients, make for wonderful dishes in which the bounty of the canals, ponds and gardens combine their varying flavours with wine, soy and vinegar. The combination proved irresistible to one gourmet. The Manchu emperor who reigned under the name Chien Lung was noted for his love of art and literature as well as for his keen palate and enthusiastic eye for the ladies. But he was no idle dilettante. Dressing up in the clothes of a merchant, Chien Lung made it a practice to roam his realm to see for himself how people lived, to discover their problems, to uncover the mysteries of his vast domain. As a devoted student of fine food he took notes on what he ate. During one of these anonymous sojourns along the Yangtze he made lengthy notes on some of the dishes, and after his incognito trip was over he enthusiastically incorporated many of them into the menu of the imperial court.

The range is so extensive and its origins so diverse that it is impossible to generalise about the school of cooking now known as Shanghai cuisine. It has borrowed dishes, techniques, raw materials and traditions from an area as large as western Europe, with a similar population, and combined them all into the specialities of one vast metropolis. The cooking of the lower Yangtze Valley is the splendid result.

THE HUANGSHAN MOUNTAINS IN SOUTHERN ANHUI PROVINCE    PAUL LAU
LEONG KA TAI

THE PORT OF SHANGHAI

(following page) THE SERENITY OF THE HUANGSHAN MOUNTAINS, ANHUI PROVINCE

PAUL LAU

PINES CLING TO A DRAMATIC GRANITE PEAK IN
THE HUANGSHAN MOUNTAINS, ANHUI PROVINCE
PAUL LAU

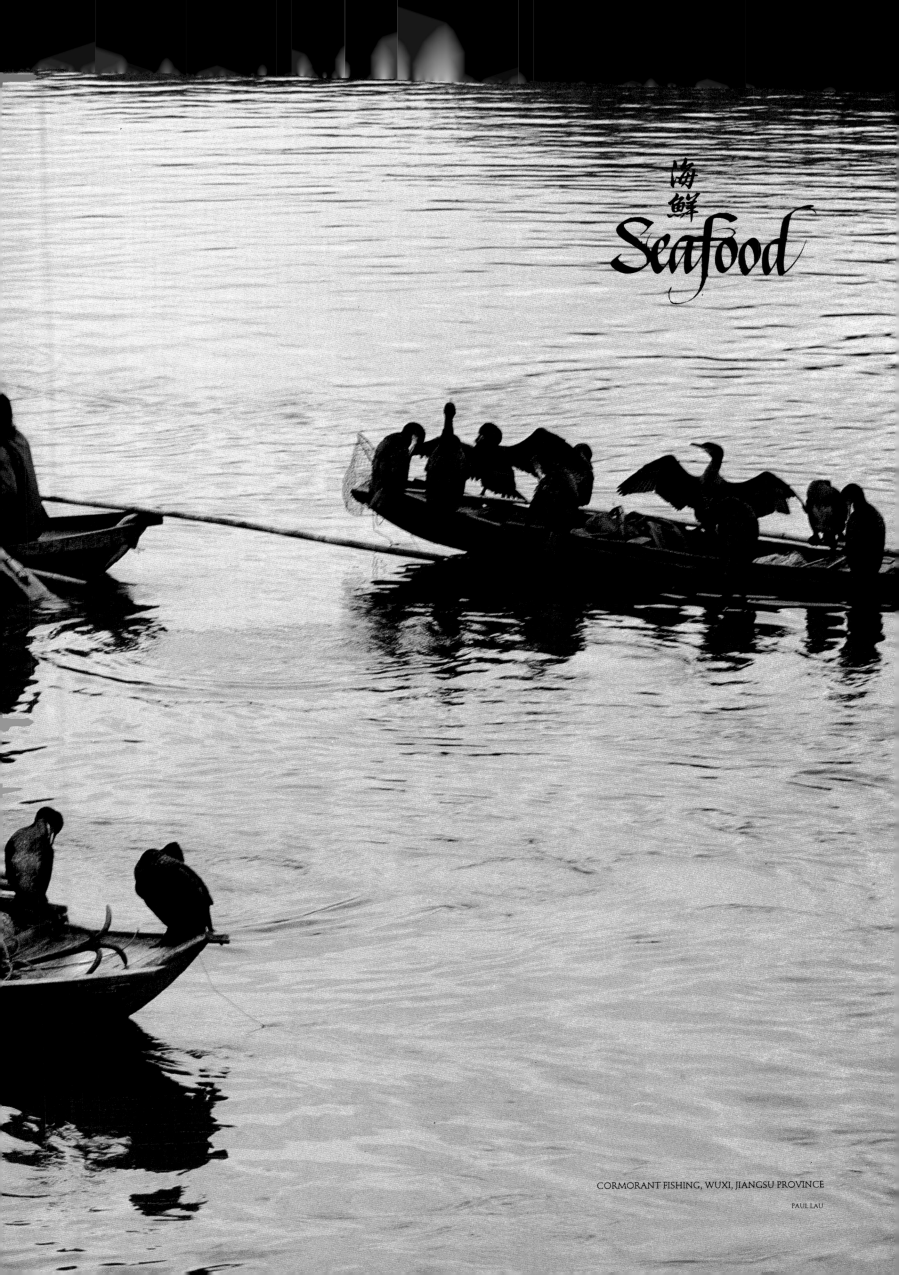

海鮮
*Seafood*

CORMORANT FISHING, WUXI, JIANGSU PROVINCE

PAUL LAU

# 海鮮 Seafood

IN CHINESE the sound for fish is "yu". Pronounced with a slightly different inflexion, "yu" also means abundance. So a whole steamed or baked fish is the traditional final dish at a formal dinner banquet, signifying to the guests that although twelve courses of rich culinary delights have already been consumed, there is plenty more to eat if they are still hungry. Fish are abundant throughout China, in the enormous landlocked interior as well as along its jagged coastline. And in almost every provincial cuisine, fish, crabs, eels, frogs and other food from the rivers, streams, canals, ponds and swamps feature on the menu.

Nature has distributed seafood and freshwater fish generously but unevenly. The fishermen who ply their craft along the banks of the Black Dragon River in the frigid north of Manchuria have a life as harsh as the climate: most of the year the river is frozen. Much easier is the lot of those who sail the warm waters of the Gulf of Tonkin and the South China Sea. If they can avoid the great winds of the typhoons they can reap one of the richest marine harvests that any of the seven seas can offer. In the bitter winter the waters of the Gulf of Bohai freeze into an iceshelf reaching far out from shore. Huddled in their padded clothes, fishermen dangle hooks for their prey through holes cut in the thick ice. Life is much easier for the crab catchers of Suzhou who can sip tea on the banks of the Yangtze lakes as they await the hairy crabs – worth literally their weight in gold – to scamper up the mud to be trapped. And what an idyllic life for shore-based fishermen in the thousands of southern bays relaxing under a sunshade as they wait for their catch to swim into the big scoop nets dangling on long bamboo poles from a cliff face.

Chinese chefs have been conducting a love affair with fish for longer than history can record. It is a feeling

NETTING RED CARP

YANG SHAOMING

still ardently expressed in every province of the land. Over 3000 kilometres (2,000 miles) up the Yangtze fish is a daily feature on Yunnan menus, and fish, albeit salted, is a treasured item even in the remote Gobi. In southern coastal ports dwell the Hoklo people, bound to their junks and frail sampans with emotional ropes as strong as those that hold their nets. The Hoklo are born, grow up, marry, give birth and die on their boats. Some can trace their family back thirty generations on the water. Seldom, apart from selling their catch, do they venture ashore.

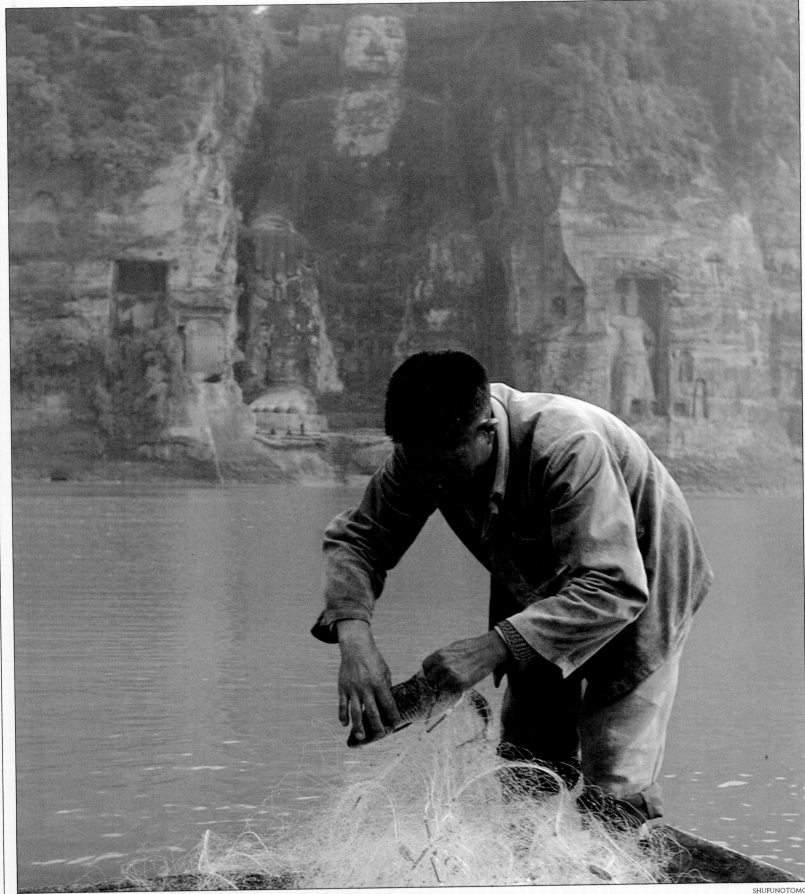

FISHING FOR CARP BY THE GIANT BUDDHA IN LESHAN, SICHUAN PROVINCE

SHUFUNOTOMO

When the catch is landed, from sea, river or pond, it must be cooked immediately. It is vital to catch the freshness of the fish in the wok – a maxim firmly held by chefs from every Chinese kitchen. A visit to a fishmarket anywhere in the country is a memorable experience: fish from sea and river swim and splash, tanks of eels squirm, live crabs, their nippers tied to safeguard the customers, crawl in huge rattan baskets, frogs hop, turtles crawl, toads squat, octopi and squid glare, and bucket after bucket holds different types of shellfish from tiny mussels to hulking whelks. If it swims, crawls, scrambles, has gills or lives in the water, it is guaranteed a pride of place on the Chinese menu. Even a creature as unattractive as the sea cucumber, difficult to define as animal or vegetable, is considered a delicacy; as indeed is seaweed, packed with vital minerals. Jellyfish is prized because it adds an unusual textural experience to a meal: chewy yet crunchy. The fin of a shark, tough as the horn of an elderly buffalo, and less attractive in appearance, is surely as indigestible an item as can be devised by nature, but it becomes the prime ingredient in one of the most famed dishes in Chinese cooking.

PRAWNS BRAISED IN SAUCE

## Shanghai 上海

# PRAWNS BRAISED IN SAUCE

*Prawns curl when they are cooked, but the chefs at the Dong Feng Restaurant in Shanghai wanted to create something different. The result is this dish, in which seven large prawns are aligned in swimming postures and bathed in a strong, sweet–sour sauce.*

7 large fresh prawns (shrimps) in their shells, weighing
    about 750 g (1½ lb)
3 tablespoons peanut oil
1 spring onion (shallot/scallion), chopped
3 slices fresh (root) ginger, shredded

SAUCE

2 tablespoons tomato sauce (ketchup)
2 teaspoons Shaoxing rice wine or dry sherry
1 tablespoon light soy sauce
1½ teaspoons sugar
½ teaspoon brown vinegar
¼ teaspoon salt

Cut the legs and antennae from the prawns and devein. Make several cuts across and along the underside to prevent them curling during cooking.

🔅 Heat the oil in a wok and stir-fry the prawns until they turn red-pink. Remove and drain off all but 1½ tablespoons of the oil.

🔅 Add the spring onion and ginger and stir-fry briefly, then pour in the pre-mixed sauce ingredients. Bring to the boil and simmer for 1 minute, then return the prawns and simmer gently in the sauce until well glazed.

🔅 Arrange on a serving plate with all the heads in the same direction, pour the rest of the sauce on and serve immediately.

## Guangzhou 广州

# FRIED PRAWN OMELET

*Like all cuisines, Chinese cooking has evolved and expanded over the years until it is now among the most diverse in the world. This recipe has evolved from two traditional dishes: Smooth Fried Eggs and Oil-fried Fresh Prawns. The former is smooth and highlights the natural taste of egg; the latter is crisp yet tender, with the delicious aroma of fresh prawns.*

250 g (8 oz) peeled fresh prawns (shrimps)
½ teaspoon salt
1 tablespoon cornflour (cornstarch)
2 spring onions (shallots/scallions)
6 eggs
¾ teaspoon salt
pinch of white pepper
⅓ teaspoon sesame oil
250 g (8 oz) lard

Devein the prawns and place in a dish with ½ teaspoon salt and the cornflour. Add a little cold water and rub the prawns gently to whiten them. Rinse thoroughly, then drain well.

🔅 Finely chop the white parts of the spring onions. The green tops may be kept to use as a garnish. Beat the eggs with the salt, pepper and sesame oil.

🔅 Heat the lard in a wok and fry the prawns quickly until they turn bright pink – about 2 minutes. Remove and drain. Pour off all but 2 tablespoons of the lard and fry the spring onions briefly, then add the eggs. Cook gently, stirring slowly, until the eggs begin to set. Add the prawns and continue to cook over gentle heat until the eggs are just firm.

🔅 Transfer to a serving plate and serve at once.

FRIED PRAWN OMELET

## Guangzhou 广州

# SCALDED PRAWNS

*Prawns scalded in their shells retain all their flavour and are easy to prepare. The prawns are eaten by hand, being first shelled and then dipped into an accompanying sauce of soy, chopped chillies and oil.*

24 large fresh prawns (shrimps)
3-4 slices fresh (root) ginger
3 tablespoons Shuang Huang or other light soy sauce
1-2 green chillies, finely chopped
3 tablespoons oil for frying
spring onions (shallots/scallions), finely chopped

Rinse the prawns and drain. Boil a large wok or saucepan of lightly salted water and add the ginger. Place the prawns in a basket, lower into the water and simmer for about 5 minutes. When ready the shells will be bright pink and the prawns will feel firm. Test one by removing the segment of shell below the head – the meat should be white and firm, no longer transparent or gelatinous looking. Drain, pile onto a plate and garnish with spring onion.

🌟 Mix the soy sauce, chillies and oil together and pour into several dishes. Serve immediately.

## Beijing 北京

# TWO-COLOUR PRAWNS

8 large prawns (shrimps) in their shells
1½ tablespoons rice wine or dry sherry
1 teaspoon grated fresh (root) ginger
1 teaspoon sugar
½ teaspoon salt
oil for deep-frying
2½ tablespoons oil for frying
cornflour (cornstarch)
1 teaspoon black sesame seeds

FILLING

30g (1 oz) pork fat, finely minced (ground)
2 water chestnuts, finely chopped
1 small egg white, lightly beaten
pinch of salt and pepper

Cut the prawns in halves, separating heads and tails. Peel the tail sections, leaving the tail shell in place. Cut deeply down the back without cutting through, then beat with the side of a cleaver to flatten. Pick out the vein. Sprinkle with ½ tablespoon of rice wine, and salt and pepper and set aside.

🌟 Cut through the head sections of the prawns just above the eyes. Cut down the centre back through the shell and pull away the vein. Place in a dish and marinate with the grated ginger, sugar, salt and 1 tablespoon of rice wine for 20 minutes.

🌟 Mix the filling ingredients together, working with your fingers until smooth and sticky. Place a portion of the filling on the cut part of each prawn tail, smoothing with a wet spoon. Sprinkle a few black sesame seeds over each, pressing in lightly, then coat lightly with cornflour.

🌟 Heat a wok with deep-frying oil and when almost at smoking-point heat another wok with about 2½ tablespoons of oil.

🌟 Place the prawn tails carefully in the deep-frying oil and leave to cook, while stir-frying the heads in the other wok. Turn the tails at least once to fry evenly. When the heads are bright red and cooked through, remove to the centre of a serving plate. Drain the fried tails and arrange around the edge of the dish then serve at once.

# Beijing 北京

## LANTERN PRAWNS

*This dish is particularly well presented: the bright red prawns are piled in the centre of a platter with a tassle of yellow egg shreds, giving the appearance of a traditional red paper lantern trimmed with gold.*

10-12 large fresh prawns (shrimps) in their shells, weighing about 1 kg (2 lb)
2½ tablespoons lard or vegetable oil
½ teaspoon sesame oil
2 eggs
1 strip dried beef (optional)
1 strip dried beancurd or carrot (optional)
1 medium cucumber (optional)

SEASONING/SAUCE

1½ tablespoons rice wine or dry sherry
2 tablespoons finely chopped spring onions
    (shallots/scallions)
1 teaspoon grated fresh (root) ginger
½ cup (125 mL/4 fl oz) chicken stock (broth)
½ teaspoon salt
1½ teaspoons sugar
pinch of white pepper

Cut off the tips of the prawn heads, then cut along the centre back through the shells and remove the intestinal vein. Rinse the prawns under cold running water, then dry well.

Heat the lard in a wok and stir-fry the prawns for about 3 minutes, until they are pink and almost cooked through.

Add the wine and cook for a few seconds before adding the remaining pre-mixed seasoning/sauce ingredients. Simmer until the prawns are coated with a rich red glaze, then pile them onto a serving plate with their heads pointing towards the top of the plate.

Rinse the wok and oil it very lightly. Beat the eggs together and pour half of the batter into the wok. Tilt the pan until the egg spreads into a thin and very wide omelet. When firm on the underside, turn over and cook the other side, then remove from the pan. Cook the other omelet and cool before rolling them up and cutting into shreds to form the tassle of the lantern.

Arrange the dried beef like the branches of a pine tree the lantern is hanging in, and very thinly slice and shape the cucumber to resemble its leaves. Form a handle for the lantern from the beancurd strip or carve a carrot in a chain shape. The decorations should be prepared before cooking the dish so that it can be served piping hot.

Sprinkle the sesame oil over the prawns immediately before serving.

SCALDED PRAWN SLICES

## Shanghai 上海

# SCALDED PRAWN SLICES

500 g (1 lb) fresh prawns (shrimps) in their shells
½ teaspoon salt
2 tablespoons cornflour (cornstarch)
1 egg white, well beaten
1½ tablespoons lard
2 spring onions (shallots/scallions), white part only, chopped
2 slices fresh young (root) ginger, shredded
2 teaspoons rice wine or dry sherry
2 tablespoons chicken stock (broth)

Peel and devein the prawns. Cut in halves lengthways, then cut each prawn into several pieces. Rinse well in cold water, rubbing with a little cornflour and salt to whiten them and remove the fishy smell. Drain and place in a dish with the salt, cornflour and egg white, mixing well.

※ Heat a wok, add the lard and stir-fry the spring onion and ginger until softened, then add the rice wine and stock and bring to the boil. Remove from the heat.

※ Boil a saucepan of water, slide in the prawns to cook for about 40 seconds, just until they change colour. Lift out and drain well, stir in the wok with the spring onions and ginger, spoon onto a serving plate and serve immediately.

## Shanghai 上海

# PRAWNS SERVED IN TWO WAYS

1½ kg (3 lb) fresh prawns (shrimps) in their shells
4 cups (1 L/32 fl oz) oil for deep-frying
¾ cup (90 g/3 oz) cornflour (cornstarch)
2 spring onions (shallots/scallions), chopped
2 slices fresh (root) ginger, shredded
90 g (3 oz) thin rice noodles

### SEASONING

1 tablespoon rice wine or dry sherry
1 teaspoon ginger juice
½ teaspoon salt
pinch of white pepper

### SAUCE

2 teaspoons rice wine or dry sherry
2 teaspoons light soy sauce
2 teaspoons white vinegar
2 tablespoons tomato sauce (ketchup)
1 tablespoon sugar
pinch of salt
2 tablespoons chicken stock (broth)
2 teaspoons cornflour (cornstarch)

Peel and devein the prawns. Place two-thirds of the prawns in a dish and add the pre-mixed seasoning ingredients. Heat the oil in a wok. Coat the seasoned prawns with cornflour and deep-fry in the oil until pink and just cooked through. Remove, drain well and keep warm.

※ Divide the noodles into six even portions and cook separately. Spread each in a small frying basket or perforated ladle, top with another basket or ladle and fry in the oil until crisp and golden. Remove the "nests" and set aside.

※ Drain the wok, retaining about 1½ tablespoons of the oil and stir-fry the spring onions and ginger. Remove and mix with the stir-fried prawns.

※ Add the uncooked prawns to the wok and stir-fry until they change colour, then add the pre-mixed sauce ingredients and simmer until the sauce thickens and clears.

※ Pile the stir-fried prawns in the centre of a large serving platter and surround with the "nests". Fill each nest with a portion of the prawns in sauce and serve at once.

PRAWNS SERVED IN TWO WAYS

PRAWNS WITH RAPE HEARTS

## Beijing 北京

# PRAWNS WITH RAPE HEARTS

500 g (1 lb) fresh prawns (shrimps) in their shells
1 egg white, well beaten
2 tablespoons cornflour (cornstarch)
¼ teaspoon bicarbonate of soda (baking soda)
¾ teaspoon salt
pinch of white pepper
2 spring onions (shallots/scallions), white parts only
8-10 young rape hearts or other fresh Chinese vegetable
2 tablespoons lard
2 thin slices fresh (root) ginger, shredded

### SAUCE

½ cup (125 mL/4 fl oz) chicken stock (broth)
1 teaspoon rice wine or dry sherry
¾ teaspoon sugar
pinch of salt and pepper
¼ teaspoon sesame oil
1½ teaspoons cornflour (cornstarch)

Peel and devein the prawns, rinse thoroughly in cold water and drain well. Place in a dish with the egg white, cornflour, bicarbonate of soda, salt and pepper. Mix well and leave for 20 minutes.

Shred the spring onion and set aside. Trim and rinse the vegetables. Heat half the lard in a wok and put in the drained vegetables to stir-fry for 2 minutes over moderate heat. Splash in 2 tablespoons of cold water, cover and cook until the vegetables are tender and the liquid absorbed. Remove and set aside.

Heat the remaining lard in the wok and stir-fry the prawns over high heat, stirring briskly until they turn white. Push to one side of the pan, add the spring onion and ginger and fry for a few moments, then pour in the pre-mixed sauce ingredients and bring to the boil until the sauce thickens. Add the vegetables, heat through, then transfer to a serving plate.

## Beijing 北京

# ZHUA CHAO YU FRIED PRAWNS

375 g (12 oz) fresh prawns (shrimps) in their shells
¾ cup (90 g/3 oz) cornflour (cornstarch)
oil, preferably peanut oil, for deep-frying

### SAUCE

1 spring onion (shallot/scallion), white part only
3 slices fresh (root) ginger
2 tablespoons lard
1 tablespoon light soy sauce
1 teaspoon rice wine or dry sherry
1 teaspoon sugar
2 teaspoons brown vinegar
pinch each of salt and pepper

Peel and devein the prawns. Rinse thoroughly and dry on paper towels. Mix the cornflour with water to make a thin paste. Coat the prawns with the paste, then deep-fry in a wok with the hot peanut oil for about 1½ minutes until cooked through and golden on the surface. Drain well.

Finely chop the spring onion and ginger and stir-fry in the lard in another wok for about 45 seconds. Add the pre-mixed remaining sauce ingredients and bring to the boil. Add the prawns, turn carefully in the sauce until it has been completely absorbed and serve.

ZHUA CHAO YU FRIED PRAWNS

YUNLUO PRAWNS

## Beijing 北京

# YUNLUO PRAWNS

*This dish of large golden prawns with their prominent red tails "swimming" through a cloud of white vermicelli makes an attractive appetiser or main course.*

375 g (12 oz) fresh prawns (shrimps)
4 egg whites
1¼ tablespoons flour
2 tablespoons cornflour (cornstarch)
oil for deep-frying
45 g (1½ oz) rice vermicelli
fresh coriander or parsley (garnish)
slivers of coloured pickled radish (garnish)

SEASONING

2 teaspoons rice wine or dry sherry
½ teaspoon salt
large pinch of white pepper

Peel and devein the prawns, then rinse under running cold water and drain well. Dry on paper towels, then mix in a dish with the seasoning ingredients and leave for 10 minutes.

❈ Beat the egg whites until frothy, mix in the flour and cornflour. Do not overstir, but leave the batter slightly lumpy.

❈ Heat the oil in a wok to smoking point, then reduce the heat slightly and put in the vermicelli. They will immediately expand and turn white. Turn and cook the other side briefly without allowing to colour. Lift out and drain well, then place on a serving plate and break up lightly.

❈ Dip the prawns into the batter and deep-fry them in a wok for about 1¼ minutes until the surface is golden. Remove from the oil and leave for 5 minutes, then reheat the oil to very hot and deep-fry the prawns briefly for a second time to make the batter very crisp. Drain and arrange over the vermicelli, adding fresh coriander or parsley and slivers of coloured pickled radish to garnish.

## Beijing 北京

# PHOENIX-TAILED PRAWNS

*In Chinese legend the phoenix is portrayed as a five-coloured creature with the head of a chicken, neck of a snake, chin of a swallow, back of a turtle and the tail of a fish. It signifies dignity and good luck.*

*The following dish received its name because the tails of the prawns bear some resemblance to the flared tail of the phoenix.*

8 large fresh prawns (shrimps)
½ teaspoon salt
2 egg whites
½ cup (60 g/2 oz) cornflour (cornstarch)
oil for deep-frying

SAUCE

4 tomatoes
1 teaspoon sugar
1 teaspoon sesame oil
½ teaspoon salt

Peel and devein the prawns, leaving the tails in place. Rinse in cold water and dry well. Place the cut side down on a cutting board and beat with the side of a cleaver to flatten. Sprinkle with the salt.

❈ Beat the egg whites until stiff and fold in the cornflour to make a batter. Add a few drops of water if necessary.

❈ Heat the deep-frying oil in a wok to smoking point, then lower the heat slightly. Coat each prawn thickly with the batter and deep-fry, in batches of four, for about 1½ minutes each, then remove and drain well.

❈ Drop the tomatoes into boiling water, remove after about 8 seconds and peel, discarding the soft centres and seeds. Finely dice the flesh and stir-fry in another wok with the sugar, sesame oil and salt until tender.

❈ Reheat the deep-frying oil and return all of the prawns to fry briefly for a second time to make the batter very crisp. Drain and arrange in a circle on a serving plate with the tomato sauce placed in the centre.

PHOENIX-TAILED PRAWNS

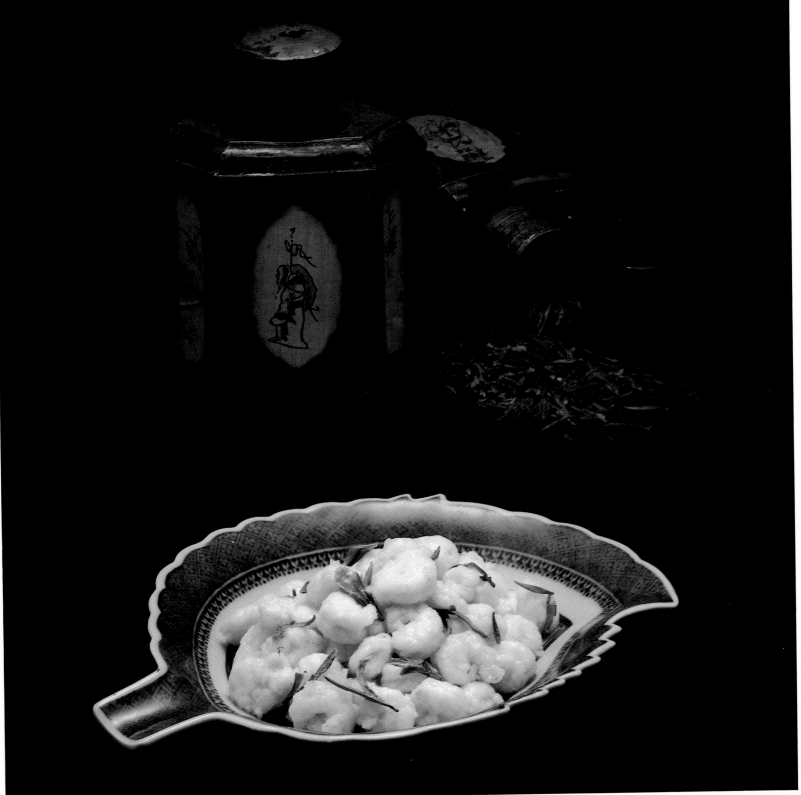

STIR-FRIED PRAWNS WITH LONGJING TEA

## Shanghai 上海

# STIR-FRIED PRAWNS WITH LONGJING TEA

*Longjing tea is named after the Dragon Well, China's famous tea growing region. After picking, the leaves are processed until they are neat and smooth, flat as a sparrow's tongue and as green as an orchid's stem. The tea's four famous qualities are its green colour, fragrant lingering aroma, sweet taste and pleasant appearance.*

*Prawns of the highest grade must be used for this dish. They are first stir-fried and then covered with the green tea leaves taken from a pot of freshly brewed Longjing tea before serving.*

2 tablespoons Longjing or other green tea leaves
1 kg (2 lb) fresh prawns (shrimps) in their shells
1 tablespoon Shaoxing rice wine or dry sherry
¾ teaspoon salt
1 egg white, well beaten
1 tablespoon cornflour (cornstarch)
2 tablespoons lard

Brew the tea leaves with 1½ cups (375 mL/12 fl oz) of boiling water, cover and set aside.

❈ Peel and devein the prawns, rinse under cold running water and rub with a little salt and cornflour to make them very white and remove the fishy smell.

❈ Place in a dish and season with the wine and salt, then mix in the egg white and cornflour and set aside for a few minutes.

❈ Heat the wok over high heat and add the lard. Stir-fry the prawns quickly until cooked through and lightly pink in colour, then remove and set aside.

❈ Rinse the wok and return to the heat. Return the prawns and pour in half a cup (125 mL/4 fl oz) of the tea, plus a spoonful of the brewed leaves. Heat through briefly, mix well and serve.

TOMATO PRAWN CAKES

DEEP-FRIED SNOW-WHITE PRAWNS

## Beijing 北京

# TOMATO PRAWN CAKES

500 g (1 lb) fresh prawns (shrimps)
2 egg whites
1 tablespoon cornflour (cornstarch)
1 teaspoon ginger juice
oil for deep-frying

SWEET AND SOUR SAUCE

½ cup (125 mL/4 fl oz) chicken stock (broth)
3 tablespoons tomato sauce (ketchup)
4 tablespoons vinegar
2 tablespoons rice wine or dry sherry
½ cup (125 g/4 oz) sugar
¾ teaspoon salt
1 tablespoon cornflour (cornstarch)

Peel and devein the prawns. Rinse in cold water, drain and pat dry with paper towels. Beat to a pulp with the side of a cleaver or use a food processor.

❊ Beat the egg whites until frothy and add the cornflour and ginger juice. Mix with the prawns and stir the mixture in one direction only until thoroughly amalgamated.

❊ Heat the oil in a wok, form spoonfuls of the prawn mixture into coin-shaped pieces and deep-fry over moderate heat until golden. Remove, place in a strainer and drain well.

❊ In another wok or a saucepan, mix the sauce ingredients and bring to the boil, stirring constantly until it thickens, then simmer for another minute.

❊ Arrange the prawn cakes on a plate and pour the sauce over them before serving.

## Guangzhou 广州

# DEEP-FRIED SNOW-WHITE PRAWNS

250 g (8 oz) peeled fresh prawns (shrimps)
2 tablespoons cornflour (cornstarch)
½ teaspoon salt
2 cups (500 mL/16 fl oz) milk
6 egg whites
1 slice lean ham, very finely diced
2 tablespoons lard
vegetable flowers and cucumber fans (garnish)

SEASONING

½ teaspoon sesame oil
1 teaspoon salt
pinch of white pepper

Devein the prawns and rub with half the cornflour and the salt, then rinse under cold running water. This helps to whiten the prawns and remove any fishy taste.

❊ Pour the milk into a mixing bowl, add the lightly beaten egg whites and the ham. Add the seasoning ingredients and mix well.

❊ Heat the lard in a wok over moderate heat. Fry the prawns gently until they just colour, then remove with a slotted spoon and set aside.

❊ Pour the milk batter into the wok and cook gently, stirring until it begins to firm up. Return the prawns and continue to cook, stirring gently, until the milk batter is cooked through and the prawns are tender.

❊ Transfer to a serving plate and garnish with brightly dyed vegetable flowers and cucumber fans. The finished dish is said to resemble "treasures buried beneath the snow".

## Guangzhou 广州

# STRAW MUSHROOMS WITH PRAWN FILLING TOPPED WITH CRAB ROE

15 fresh or canned straw mushrooms
90 g (3 oz) fresh prawn (shrimp) meat
90 g (3 oz) white fish fillets
½ egg white
2 teaspoons rice wine or dry sherry
½ teaspoon salt
pinch of pepper
4 fresh crab pincers*

SAUCE

125 g (4 oz) fresh crab roe
vegetable oil
½ cup (125 mL/4 fl oz) fish stock (broth)
2 teaspoons cornflour (cornstarch)
salt and white pepper
sesame oil

Rinse the fresh mushrooms after trimming the bases off, leaving only the darker rounded tops. Pound the prawn meat and fish on a board with the flat side of a cleaver until thick and pastelike, then add the egg white, wine, salt and pepper, mixing well with the fingers.

❊ Use a wet spoon to mound a portion of the filling over the cut side of each mushroom, smoothing the top. Stand the mushrooms on a heatproof plate and set on a rack in a wok, or in a steamer, over simmering water. Cover and steam for about 7 minutes if using canned mushrooms, 8-10 minutes if the mushrooms are fresh. (Canned mushrooms may be smaller than the fresh variety. If so, simply cut from the top almost through to the bottom, spread open and stuff the slit with the filling.)

�In a wok, sauté the crab roe in very little vegetable oil for 20-30 seconds, then add the remaining sauce ingredients, mixed together. Simmer, stirring, until the sauce thickens and the roe is brightly coloured and firm.

✖Simmer the crab pincers in boiling, lightly salted water for about 5 minutes, then remove, crack the shells and extract the meat.

✖Transfer the mushrooms to a serving plate, arrange the crab pincer meat around the edge and pour over the sauce.

*Fresh crab meat can be substituted, or the pincers may be omitted.*

STRAW MUSHROOMS WITH PRAWN FILLING TOPPED WITH CRAB ROE

## Sichuan 四川

# JADEITE PRAWNS

*This delicately textured and subtly flavoured dish is often served at banquets. The jadeite refers to the bright green peas dotted amongst the pearl white of the prawns.*

250 g (8 oz) fresh peeled prawns (shrimps)
2 egg whites, lightly beaten
1 tablespoon soy bean powder or cornflour (cornstarch)
pinch of salt
3 tablespoons oil for frying
½ cup (60 g/2 oz) frozen peas, or parboiled fresh peas
1 spring onion (shallot/scallion), finely chopped
1 pickled red chilli, finely chopped

SAUCE

1 cup (250 mL/8 fl oz) chicken or fish stock (broth)
1 teaspoon rice wine or dry sherry
¾ teaspoon salt
pinch of white pepper
1 tablespoon cornflour (cornstarch)

Devein the prawns. Rinse in cold running water after rubbing with a little cornflour and salt. Dry on paper towels and place in a dish, adding the egg whites, soy bean powder or cornflour and the pinch of salt. Mix well and leave for 20 minutes.

✖Heat the oil in a wok and stir-fry the prawns over high heat until cooked through, then remove. Add the peas, spring onion and chilli to the wok and stir-fry for 1 minute, then add the sauce ingredients, except the cornflour and a little of the stock. Cover and simmer until the peas are tender, then return the prawns.

✖Mix the cornflour with the retained stock, pour into the sauce and simmer, stirring, until thickened and clear, then serve at once.

JADEITE PRAWNS

## Guangzhou 广州

# CRISPY CRAB PINCERS

*River crabs are caught throughout the year, but in greatest quantity during autumn, the season of orange fragrance and blooming chrysanthemums. Some are found in the rivers flowing towards the sea, but they lay their eggs only in shallow water near the river mouths. Fu Zuan of the Song Dynasty (960-1127 AD) described their reproductive pattern and noted that during the change of seasons from autumn to winter, the crabs follow the river currents and swim to the sea. Hence if a net is cast during this period, you are sure of a catch.*

*The chef of the Ban Xi Restaurant removes the hard shell from the foremost section of the crab pincer, extracts the meat in one piece and supplements it with prawn and pork meat before returning it to the shell to be steamed. Alternatively, the tip of the pincer can be covered with a ball of prawn and pork meat, as in this recipe. The mock crab claw is then coated with a light crisp batter and deep-fried.*

*The very large oysters gathered along the coast of this region are also cooked in this way.*

12 crab pincers
315 g (10 oz) fresh prawn (shrimp) meat
75 g (2½ oz) fatty pork
1 teaspoon salt
pinch of white pepper
pinch of sugar
cornflour (cornstarch)
oil for deep-frying
light soy sauce or spiced salt dip

CRISP BATTER

1 cup (125 g/4 oz) flour
1 teaspoon baking powder
⅓ cup (45 g/1½ oz) cornflour (cornstarch)
2 large egg whites

Break away the main part of the crab pincer shell, leaving just the points attached to the meat.

※ Place the prawns on a cutting board and crush to a smooth paste with the flat side of a cleaver, or in a food processor. Finely mince (grind) the pork until smooth and sticky and mix with the prawn, adding the salt, pepper and sugar.

※ Divide the mixture into 12 equal portions. Dust the crab claws lightly with cornflour and mould a portion of the prawn and pork mixture around each, forming a ball shape. Coat lightly with cornflour and set aside.

※ Sift the flour and baking powder together and add the cornflour. Beat the egg whites lightly and fold into the batter, adding enough cold water to give a coating consistency.

※ Heat the oil in a large wok. Dip the crab claws into the batter, holding onto the pincers so that they remain uncoated. Deep-fry over moderate to high heat, turning several times, until golden and crisp – about 5 minutes.

※ Remove, drain well and arrange on a napkin on a serving plate. Serve with soy sauce or spiced salt dip (a mixture of ground Sichuan pepper, or Chinese five spices, and salt).

## Beijing 北京

# SUANSHAZI CRABS

6 female hairy river crabs, or small mud crabs
½ cup (125 mL/4 fl oz) rice wine or dry sherry
¼ small green capsicum (bell pepper)
¼ small red capsicum (bell pepper)
5 cm (2 in) piece giant white radish
6-8 slices young fresh (root) ginger

SAUCE

½ cup (125 mL/4 fl oz) chicken stock (broth)
2 tablespoons rendered chicken fat
½ teaspoon salt
2-3 teaspoons red vinegar
1 tablespoon sugar
2 teaspoons cornflour (cornstarch)

Rinse the crabs well in cold water and remove the undershell. Discard the inedible parts, cut the bodies in halves then put the halves back together, placing them in a wide, heatproof dish. Sprinkle on the rice wine and set the dish on a rack in a wok or in a steamer, cover and steam for 15 minutes. Transfer to a serving plate.

※ Cut the capsicum, radish and ginger into fine shreds. Simmer the radish briefly in the stock for the sauce, then arrange the shredded vegetables in groups over the crabs.

※ Bring the stock and remaining pre-mixed sauce ingredients to the boil, stirring until it thickens and clears. Pour over the crabs and serve hot.

CRISPY CRAB PINCERS

STIR-FRIED CRABS AND EGG

## Shanghai 上海

# STIR-FRIED CRABS AND EGG

*The green crab differs in shape and taste from other common crabs found in clear water, their shell being rhombus shaped and their meat very tender. The green crabs from Xiangshan, Zhejiang Province, are known for their full, rich meat.*

*This dish, combining green crabs with beaten egg, is a traditional meal from Xiangshan and was introduced to Shanghai by the cooks in the Ningbo Restaurant.*

4 medium-sized green crabs, or sand crabs
1 cup (125 g/4 oz) cornflour (cornstarch)
⅓ cup (75 mL/2½ fl oz) oil for frying
3 spring onions (shallots/scallions), sliced
5 slices fresh (root) ginger
1 tablespoon Shaoxing rice wine or dry sherry
1 teaspoon salt
3 large eggs, well beaten
1 tablespoon lard, melted

Kill the crabs by piercing them through the head and into the stomach with a sharpened chopstick or bamboo stick. Wash well in cold water, cut off the tips of the claws and discard. Remove the pincers and crack the shells with the back of a cleaver. Pull the crab shells away from the bodies, remove the inedible parts and chop each body into quarters. Then coat with cornflour.
❀ Heat the wok over high heat and put in the oil. Stir-fry the crab for about 2 minutes, add the spring onion and ginger and continue stir-frying for another 2-3 minutes until the crabs are bright red and cooked through.
❀ Pour off most of the oil and add the rice wine and salt, then pour in the beaten egg and cook gently, stirring only occasionally until the egg is just set. Pour on the lard and serve.

## Shanghai 上海

# STEAMED HAIRY CRABS

*Freshwater crab is a highly regarded delicacy in China. In all the coastal areas, from Liaoning Province in the north to Guangdong Province in the south, the rivers and lakes yield freshwater crabs, although the best by far come from the Shanghai region. Because the Shanghai lakes are inhabited by millions of minute organisms, the crabs harvested in them are fat and delicious.*

*The female crab is considered to be at its best during the ninth lunar month when it is full of roe; the male's peak season is during the tenth lunar month. The most delicate part of the crab is the roe, and the most tender part is the flesh inside the two front claws. Crab tastes best when steamed alive. The Chinese of ancient times loved to nibble on chrysanthemum flowers while eating crabs.*

*As it is cold in nature, crab is said to be bad for the health if too much is eaten. People with weak stomachs should be particularly careful not to overindulge themselves.*

*The Shanghai hairy crab is an expensive delicacy which should be served with shreds of young tender ginger, a dip of red vinegar and a glass of wine.*

6 Shanghai freshwater hairy crabs, or small mud crabs
2 spring onions (shallots/scallions)
fresh (root) ginger
red vinegar

Wash the crabs thoroughly, then tie the claws and legs together with string before steaming. This prevents them struggling during cooking, releasing their roe and juices and making them dry and tasteless. Place the crabs upside down on a bamboo rack in a wok or in a steamer and put the spring onion and several slices of ginger on top. Cover and steam for about 8 minutes until the crabs are cooked through. Untie before serving.

STEAMED HAIRY CRABS

## Beijing 北京

# CRABS WITH CHRYSANTHEMUM

6-8 fresh Shanghai river crabs, or small mud crabs
1 large chrysanthemum blossom (garnish)

SEASONING

1 tablespoon finely chopped spring onion (shallot/scallion)
½ teaspoon finely chopped fresh (root) ginger
1 teaspoon rice wine or dry sherry
1½ teaspoons red vinegar
1 teaspoon sugar
¾ teaspoon salt

Wash the crabs, open them from the underside and remove the inedible parts. Take out as much meat as possible without breaking the shell. Mix the meat with the seasoning ingredients, fill the shells with the mixture and tie with string to prevent the filling escaping during cooking.
❀ Set on a rack in a wok or in a steamer, cover and steam for about 15 minutes, then arrange in a circle on a serving plate and garnish with a single large chrysanthemum blossom.

CRABS WITH CHRYSANTHEMUM

## Shanghai 上海

# FRIED AND BRAISED RIVER CRABS

*River crabs captured in June are full of roe which is therefore called June gold. The shell is bright red after cooking and the sauce prepared according to this recipe is thick and golden, while the crabmeat remains tender and tasty. Only the choicest live crabs should be used for this dish.*

3-4 x 250 g (8 oz) freshwater crabs
3 tablespoons tapioca flour or cornflour (cornstarch)
250 g (8 oz) lard
1 tablespoon finely chopped spring onion (shallot/scallion)
2 teaspoons grated fresh (root) ginger

SEASONING/SAUCE

1 tablespoon rice wine or dry sherry
2 tablespoons superior or other light soy sauce
½ cup (125 mL/4 fl oz) chicken or fish stock (broth)
¼ teaspoon salt
1½ teaspoons sugar
1 teaspoon cornflour (cornstarch)

Clean the crabs thoroughly to remove mud and sand, then halve each crab, cutting straight through the centre of the shell from head to rear. Remove part of the soft undershell and scrape out the inedible parts. Use a cleaver to cut off the tips of the claws.

※ Dip the cut edges of the crab into the tapioca flour, coating thickly.

※ Heat the lard in a large wok and stir-fry the crabs until they turn bright red. Add the spring onion and ginger and stir-fry briefly, then pour in the pre-mixed seasoning/sauce ingredients, except the cornflour. Cover and braise over moderate heat for about 8 minutes until the crabs are completely tender. The pan should be tightly covered during braising so that the crab is steamed and braised at the same time and the cooking liquid is not reduced. If it begins to dry up, add a little extra stock or water.

※ Mix the cornflour with a little cold water, stir into the sauce and boil gently until the sauce clears, then serve at once.

## Beijing 北京

# ABALONE SLICES WITH DUCK MEAT

*Connoisseurs of Chinese cooking are traditionally rather partial to abalone, an expensive mollusc. In this recipe the duck meat is used as a filling between two slices of abalone, and the sandwich is topped with green peas. It is then steamed to perfection.*

1 x 425 g (13½ oz) can of abalone
250 g (8 oz) duck breast meat
8 water chestnuts
2 spring onions (shallots/scallions), white parts only
2 slices fresh (root) ginger
1½ teaspoons rice wine or dry sherry
½ teaspoon salt
½ teaspoon sesame oil
1 tablespoon green peas

### SAUCE
¾ cup (175 mL/6 fl oz) duck stock (broth)
1½ tablespoons rendered duck fat
2 teaspoons rice wine or dry sherry
¾ teaspoon salt
1 tablespoon cornflour (cornstarch)

Drain the abalone and cut each piece into thin horizontal slices, discarding the frilly outer edges.

Very finely mince (grind) the duck meat with the water chestnuts, spring onions and ginger. Add the rice wine, salt and sesame oil and mix to a smooth paste.

Spread half of the abalone slices with the duck paste and top with the remaining abalone slices, pressing them gently together. Arrange on a wide, heatproof plate and place on a rack in a wok or in a steamer, cover and steam for about 20 minutes over gently simmering water.

Bring the sauce ingredients to the boil, omitting the cornflour, add the peas and simmer until tender. Mix the cornflour with a little cold water and stir into the sauce. Simmer until thickened, then remove the abalone slices from the steamer and drain the plate.

Pour on the sauce and serve at once.

RAZOR CLAMS BOILED WITH SALT

## Shanghai 上海

# RAZOR CLAMS BOILED WITH SALT

20 razor clams in their shells
1 cup (250 mL/8 fl oz) water
1 teaspoon salt
1 spring onion (shallot/scallion), roughly chopped
2 slices fresh (root) ginger, chopped
1 tablespoon rice wine or dry sherry
2 tablespoons vinegar
curls of spring onion or sprigs of fresh coriander (garnish)

Wash the clams thoroughly with cold water, then put them in a pot of lightly salted water for several hours so they will empty the contents of their intestines. Wash thoroughly in cold water again and cut loose the black tendon on the back of each clam.

In a wok, bring the water to boil, adding salt, onion, ginger and wine. Put in the clams, cover and shake the pan over high heat until the shells open, then remove immediately from the heat. Do not overcook or they will become tough. Use a slotted spoon to transfer them to a serving plate.

Boil up the cooking liquid, add the vinegar and spoon over the clams. Decorate the dish with curls of spring onion or fresh coriander and serve.

ABALONE SLICES WITH DUCK MEAT

BOILED CLAMS WITH SOY SAUCE AND SESAME OIL

## Shanghai 上海

# BOILED CLAMS WITH SOY SAUCE AND SESAME OIL

625 g (1¼ lb) clams in their shells
1 teaspoon salt
2 tablespoons finely chopped fresh (root) ginger
2 tablespoons finely chopped chives or spring onions
   (shallots/scallions)

DIP

3 tablespoons dark soy sauce
2 tablespoons sesame oil

Wash the clams thoroughly, brushing off all the grit and mud. Soak for 20 minutes in cold salted water, then drain.
❀ Boil a large pot of water and put in the clams, stirring for about 2 minutes until the clams open.
❀ Drain and remove the top shells. Arrange clams in a serving dish and sprinkle on the chopped ginger and chives.
❀ Mix the soy sauce and sesame oil together and divide between several small dishes. Serve as dips with the clams.

## Beijing 北京

# STEAMED DRIED SCALLOPS

*Scallops are an expensive seafood found right along the coast of China, although the best come from Shandong Province. The scallops used in the following recipe are sun-dried, which preserves them as well as intensifying their flavour. Good quality dried scallops are large, reddish yellow, fine grained and aromatic.*

10-12 large dried scallops
½ cup (125 mL/4 fl oz) chicken stock (broth)
1-2 teaspoons chilli oil or chilli sauce
1 tablespoon cornflour (cornstarch)

SEASONING

1 cup (250 mL/8 fl oz) chicken stock (broth)
2 tablespoons rice wine or dry sherry
1 teaspoon ginger juice

Rinse the scallops and soak in cold water for about 1 hour until they swell up and become pliable.
❀ Place in a heatproof dish and add the seasoning ingredients. Set the dish on a rack in a wok or in a steamer and steam, covered, over gently simmering water for about 1 hour.
❀ Strain, retaining the seasoning liquid, and arrange on a serving plate. Set aside to keep warm. Mix about ½ cup (125 mL/4 fl oz) of the retained liquid with the chicken stock, chilli oil and cornflour. Simmer for 1 minute, stirring until thickened, adjust the seasoning and pour over the scallops before serving.

STEAMED DRIED SCALLOPS

## Beijing 北京

# STIR-FRIED DRIED SCALLOPS WITH CELERY

*There are many ways to cook dried scallops, but when combined with crisp young celery the result is outstanding.*

*In ancient China there are detailed records about the medicinal and dietary values of celery. In particular it is suggested that celery may help to reduce high blood pressure.*

*This dish must be eaten hot or its subtle flavours will be lost.*

12 dried scallops, soaked for 25 minutes
¾ cup (175 mL/6 fl oz) chicken stock (broth)
250 g (8 oz) fresh young celery stems
2 tablespoons oil for frying
1 spring onion (shallot/scallion), sliced
2 slices fresh (root) ginger
2 teaspoons rice wine or dry sherry
½ teaspoon salt

Rinse the celery, drain well and cut into 7.5 cm (3 in) lengths.
❀ Place the scallops in a wok or saucepan with the stock and bring to the boil. Cover and steam for about 40 minutes over moderately high heat until the scallops are tender and the stock full of their flavour. Set aside.
❀ Heat the oil in a wok and stir-fry the celery, spring onions and ginger for about 3 minutes until tender. Add the scallops in their liquid, the rice wine and salt, simmer together very briefly and serve immediately.

STIR-FRIED DRIED SCALLOPS WITH CELERY

HERO'S THREE-IN-ONE FISH

# Beijing 北京

## HERO'S THREE-IN-ONE FISH

*This innovative Chinese dish is spectacular enough to impress a returning hero. One large fish is cut across into three pieces which are prepared in three different ways, and then arranged on a serving platter with the head and tail to resemble two fish side-by-side. Fresh carp is the fish favoured for this dish, but pearl perch (sea bass) gives excellent results.*

1 x 1½ kg (3 lb) fresh carp or pearl perch (sea bass)
60 g (2 oz) Yunnan or other salty ham, finely shredded
5-6 slices white radish, finely shredded
1 tablespoon rice wine or dry sherry
1 spring onion (shallot/scallion)
3 slices fresh (root) ginger
1 tablespoon lard

2 tablespoons peanut oil
1 tablespoon lard
1 spring onion (shallot/scallion), chopped
2 slices fresh (root) ginger, chopped
1 clove garlic, chopped
1 tablespoon hot bean paste
2 teaspoons rice wine or dry sherry
1 tablespoon brown vinegar
2 teaspoons dark soy sauce
1 tablespoon sugar
½ cup (125 mL/4 fl oz) fish or chicken stock (broth)
oil for deep-frying
2 tablespoons rice wine or dry sherry
¾ cup (90 g/3 oz) cornflour (cornstarch)
1 egg white, well beaten

Clean and scale the fish, rinse in cold water and dry well. Cut off the head, slice in half and set aside. Cut the body of the fish across into three portions, leaving the tail on the lower part.

Make shallow cuts across the central section on both sides, place on a lightly oiled, heatproof plate and top with the ham and radish. Add the rice wine and place the spring onion and ginger on top. Melt the lard and pour over, then set the plate on a rack in a wok or steamer, cover and steam for about 20 minutes until completely tender. Keep warm.

Score diagonally across the upper part of the fish on both sides. Heat the wok and add the peanut oil and lard. Fry on both sides until cooked through and lightly coloured on the surface, then set aside. Add the spring onion, ginger, garlic and bean paste to the wok and stir-fry for 2 minutes, then add the wine, vinegar, soy sauce, sugar and stock and bring to the boil. Reduce heat, return the fish and simmer until the flavours have been absorbed. Remove and set aside, keeping warm.

In a clean wok, heat the deep-frying oil of the third part of the ingredients list. Cut the tail end of the fish in half lengthways, sprinkle with the rice wine, coat with cornflour then dip into the beaten egg and coat thickly with the cornflour again, shaking off excess. Slide into the oil and deep-fry until cooked through and golden. Lift out and drain well.

Coat the head halves with cornflour and deep-fry in the hot oil until crisp and well-coloured. Place the heads at one end of a large platter and tails at the other, and the braised and steamed parts side-by-side between the heads and tails. Serve a dish of spiced salt (1 tablespoon of warmed salt mixed with 1½ teaspoons of five-spice powder) to accompany the crisp fried section of the fish.

STIR-FRIED FISH AND PINE NUTS

## Shanghai 上海

# STIR-FRIED FISH AND PINE NUTS

250 g (8 oz) fillet of rock carp or other meaty white fish
3 tablespoons peanut or vegetable oil
½ cup (60 g/2 oz) pine nuts
1 tablespoon finely chopped red capsicum (bell pepper)
1 tablespoon finely chopped green capsicum (bell pepper)
1 tablespoon finely chopped spring onion (shallot/scallion)

SEASONING

2 teaspoons Shaoxing rice wine or dry sherry
1 teaspoon ginger juice
½ teaspoon salt
1 tablespoon cornflour (cornstarch)

Skin the fish and cut it into very small dice. Place in a dish with the pre-mixed seasoning ingredients and mix well. Leave for about 10 minutes.
❈ Heat the oil in a wok and fry the pine nuts until lightly golden, then lift out and drain well.
❈ Stir-fry the capsicums and onion in the wok over high heat until just softened, then remove from the oil with a slotted spoon.
❈ Add the fish to the wok and stir-fry for about 2 minutes until white and cooked through. Return the capsicum and onion, mix well, then pile into the centre of a serving plate, arranging the fried pine nuts in a circle around the fish.

## Guangzhou 广州

# STEAMED TENCH FISH

*Only the very best and freshest fish should be steamed, and only the merest hint of seasoning or other added ingredients is needed to high-light the freshness and flavour. At the peak of summer, when the thought of oily food dulls the taste buds, steamed tench fish is very popular, both in restaurants and at home.*

1 x 375 g (12 oz) fresh tench fish (catfish or bream)
2 dried black mushrooms, soaked for 25 minutes
6 slices young fresh (root) ginger
60 g (2 oz) lean pork fillet
2 spring onions (shallots/scallions)
2 tablespoons superior stock (*see page 124*)

SEASONING

2 tablespoons superior or other light soy sauce
½ teaspoon sesame oil
pinch of white pepper

STEAMED TENCH FISH

Clean and scale the fish and slash along the top of the back bone on either side. Place in the centre of an oval heatproof dish which will fit inside a wok or steamer.
❈ Drain the mushrooms, squeeze out excess water and shred finely. Shred the ginger, pork fillet and the white parts only of the spring onions. Arrange these ingredients along the top of the fish, set the dish on a rack in a wok or in a steamer, cover and cook the fish over gently simmering water for about 15 minutes, or until very tender.
❈ Bring the stock and the seasoning ingredients to the boil separately, pour over the fish and serve at once.

## Sichuan 四川

# CRUCIAN CARP WITH BEAN JELLY

*Jelly is a popular snack in Sichuan Province and is sold throughout the year in cities and in the country at hawkers' stands or in restaurants. The jelly can be made from powdered rice, beans or buckwheat, and is usually eaten cold.*

*This particular combination of crucian carp with cubes of mung bean jelly is unique to Sichuan cooking.*

2 x 315 g (10 oz) crucian carp or other meaty white fish
1 tablespoon rice wine or dry sherry
1 teaspoon salt
1 sheet pork fat net (caul lining)
3 spring onions (shallots/scallions), finely chopped
1 teaspoon grated fresh (root) ginger
¾ teaspoon ground Sichuan peppercorns (Fagara or Sansho)
185 g (6 oz) green mung bean jelly

SEASONING

1½ tablespoons fermented black beans, chopped
1 teaspoon chopped garlic
2 tablespoons finely chopped bean sprouts or celery
2 tablespoons light soy sauce
1 teaspoon chilli oil or chilli sauce
¾ teaspoon sesame oil

Clean the carp and score diagonally across each side. Place in a heatproof dish and sprinkle with the wine and salt. Leave for 5 minutes, then wrap each fish in a piece of the pork fat net and return to the dish. Cover with the spring onions, ginger and Sichuan pepper. Place on a rack in a wok or in a steamer, cover and steam for about 20 minutes until cooked.
❈ Dice the jelly and simmer in boiling water for 2-3 minutes, then drain. Mix with the seasoning ingredients in the wok and heat through. Remove the fish from the steamer and remove the pork fat. Slide the fish into the wok and simmer gently for 2-3 minutes with the jelly and seasonings.
❈ Lift onto a serving plate and serve.

SILVER CARP AND TURNIP IN BROTH

Sichuan 四川

# SILVER CARP AND TURNIP IN BROTH

*Fish simmered in broth is a great favourite throughout China. As far back as the Tang Dynasty (618-907 AD) chefs cooked fish supplemented with mutton, rabbit and deer meat to make delicious pot meals. This dish was devised fifty years ago by the well-known chef Liao Chin-tin, who adapted the following recipe from an ancient one.*

500 g (1 lb) silver carp steaks or other meaty white fish
4 tablespoons lard
1 fresh turnip
4 cups (1 L/32 fl oz) superior stock (*see page 124*)

SEASONING

4 spring onions (shallots/scallions)
3 slices fresh (root) ginger
2 pickled red chillies
½ cup (125 mL/4 fl oz) rice wine or dry sherry
1 teaspoon salt

DIPPING SAUCE

3 tablespoons superior or other light soy sauce
1 tablespoon red or brown vinegar
1 teaspoon grated fresh (root) ginger
1 teaspoon sesame oil

Wipe the fish steaks dry with paper towels. Heat the lard in a wok and fry the steaks on both sides until lightly browned. Drain and transfer to a casserole with a tight-fitting lid.

Peel and shred the turnip. Stir-fry it in the remaining lard for 2 minutes, then add the stock and bring to the boil. Pour into the casserole.

Shred or dice the spring onions, ginger and chillies and add all the seasoning ingredients to the casserole.

Cover and simmer for 20 minutes or until the fish is tender. Do not overcook or the fish will begin to dry out.

Mix the dipping sauce ingredients together and serve it in several small dishes with the pot of broth.

Sichuan 四川

# SPECIAL BRAISED ROCK CARP

*Sichuan is a vast territory laced with rivers. The warm climate and fine water favour the reproduction of many different varieties of fish; rock or black carp in particular grow abundantly. Rock carp is characterised by its small head, thick body, small bones and rich meat. It is regarded as one of the most delicious freshwater fish in China.*

1 x 500 g (1 lb) rock carp or other meaty white freshwater fish
185 g (6 oz) yam
3 spring onions (shallots/scallions)
3 slices fresh (root) ginger
3 cloves garlic
2 tablespoons lard

SPECIAL BRAISED ROCK CARP

SAUCE

2 cups (500 mL/16 fl oz) water
1 tablespoon rice wine or dry sherry
1 tablespoon hot bean paste
1 tablespoon sugar
1 tablespoon brown vinegar
1 tablespoon red fermented rice (wine lees)
1 tablespoon light soy sauce
pinch of salt

Clean the fish and make several diagonal slashes across each side. Peel and finely dice the yam. Chop the spring onions, ginger and garlic finely.

※ In a wok, sauté the yam in the lard for about 2 minutes until lightly coloured, then place in the bottom of a casserole. Add the fish to the wok, sauté on both sides until lightly coloured and place on top of the yam. Lightly fry the spring onions, ginger and garlic in the lard and add to the casserole with the pre-mixed sauce ingredients.

※ Bring to the boil, skim any froth and residue from the surface and reduce the heat. Simmer very gently, partially covered, until the fish is tender and the stock reduced to a thick clear layer over the fish.

※ Chinese chefs call this method "gaining wonder from fire".

103

CARP WITH SICHUAN HOT BEAN SAUCE

## Sichuan 四川

# CARP WITH SICHUAN HOT BEAN SAUCE

4-6 crucian carp or other meaty white fish,
    150-200 g (5-7 oz) each
¾ cup (175 mL/6 fl oz) oil for frying
3 cloves garlic, chopped
1½ tablespoons hot bean sauce (chilli bean sauce)
1 spring onion (shallot/scallion), chopped (garnish)

SEASONING/SAUCE
¾ cup (175 mL/6 fl oz) water or fish stock (broth)
1 tablespoon brown vinegar
1 tablespoon rice wine or dry sherry
1 pickled red chilli, chopped
2-3 slices fresh (root) ginger, chopped
1 tablespoon dark soy sauce
1 tablespoon sugar
½ teaspoon salt
1½ teaspoons cornflour (cornstarch)

Clean the fish and rinse in cold water, then drain and dry thoroughly. Heat a wok with half the oil to smoking point and fry half of the fish until lightly browned on both sides. Remove to a plate and keep warm.

❋ Add the remaining oil and fry the other fish until browned, then place with the first batch. Cover and keep warm.

❋ Pour the oil out, rinse the wok, then return about 2 tablespoons of the oil. Stir-fry the garlic briefly, then add the bean sauce and stir-fry for about 40 seconds. Add the pre-mixed sauce ingredients and bring to the boil, stirring constantly. Slide the fish into the sauce, reduce heat, cover and simmer gently for about 20 minutes. Splash in a little more water from time to time if it begins to dry up during cooking.

❋ Use a wide spatula to transfer the fish onto a serving plate, stacking them together in the same direction. Scatter the spring onion over the fish and pour on the sauce.

# WHOLE GRASS CARP BARBECUED IN A BAMBOO TUBE

*The fish cooked in the following typical country fashion is insulated by green bamboo and a net of pork fat to keep it tender and moist with no risk of burning. During cooking the marinade ingredients slowly permeate the fish, which loses its usual fishy smell and takes on some of the unusual fragrance of the fresh bamboo.*

1 x 750 g (1½ lb) whole grass carp or other meaty white fish
1 sheet pork fat net (caul lining)
a thick tube of green bamboo, or several layers of bamboo
  leaves and aluminium foil
thin wire to fasten

SEASONING

1 teaspoon salt
1 tablespoon ginger juice
1 tablespoon rice wine or dry sherry
pinch of white pepper

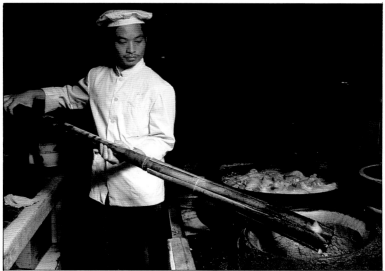

SAUCE

juice of 2 oranges
½ cup (125 mL/4 fl oz) water
1 tablespoon sugar
½ teaspoon sesame oil
1½ teaspoons cornflour (cornstarch)

Scale, gut and thoroughly wash the fish. Place the pork fat on a board and lay the fish in the centre. Rub the seasonings over the fish, inside and out, and wrap it in the pork fat net.

※ Split the bamboo in half lengthways and place the wrapped carp in the hollow. Cover with the other piece of bamboo and tie the bundle securely with wire. Have ready a quantity of glowing charcoal. Place the bamboo in the charcoal to roast slowly until the fish is cooked, 30-40 minutes. If using bamboo leaves and aluminium foil the dried leaves must be soaked first to soften. Wrap the fish in at least 8 leaves and a double layer of aluminium foil. Roast for about 30 minutes only.

※ Mix the sauce ingredients together and stir in a wok or saucepan over gentle heat until thickened. Pour into a jug or small bowl. Unwrap the fish and serve with the sauce.

WHOLE GRASS CARP BARBECUED IN A BAMBOO TUBE

## Sichuan 四川

# CRUCIAN CARP WITH LOTUS EGG

*In Sichuan Province, the word lotus has several meanings and chefs have got into the habit of calling steamed egg white "lotus egg". This very popular steamed dish uses crucian carp and lotus egg as its main ingredients. The result is very light and delicious.*

3 x 200 g (6½ oz) small crucian carp or other meaty white fish
4 egg whites
⅓ cup (75 mL/2½ fl oz) fish stock (broth)
1 tablespoon cornflour (cornstarch)
½ teaspoon salt
¼ red capsicum (bell pepper) (garnish)
lemon rind or grated hard-boiled egg yolk (garnish)
fresh coriander (garnish)

### SEASONING

1 tablespoon rice wine or dry sherry
½ teaspoon grated fresh (root) ginger
1 tablespoon finely chopped spring onion (shallot/scallion)
pinch of white pepper
dash of chilli oil or chilli sauce

### SAUCE

½ cup (125 mL/4 fl oz) fish or chicken stock (broth)
salt and pepper
1 teaspoon rice wine or dry sherry
1 teaspoon cornflour (cornstarch)

### DIP

1 tablespoon finely minced (ground), young fresh (root) ginger
1 tablespoon sesame oil

Clean the carp and place in a saucepan of boiling water to cook briefly. Lift out, drain well and scrape off the skin. Arrange them side by side in a heatproof dish and add the pre-mixed seasoning ingredients. Place on a rack in a wok or in a steamer, cover and steam for about 15 minutes until tender.
❋Beat the egg whites, fish stock, cornflour and salt together and pour into a flat, heatproof dish. Steam for about 6 minutes until set, then cut into lotus petal shapes.
❋Finely shred the capsicum and blanch in boiling water.
❋Mix the sauce ingredients, except the cornflour, together, pour into a wok and bring to the boil. Mix the cornflour with a little cold water, stir in and simmer until thickened. Add any liquid from the dish in which the fish were steamed and simmer again briefly.
❋Arrange the lotus egg around the fish and pour on the sauce. Add the garnish of capsicum, lemon rind or grated egg and fresh coriander. Serve at once with the minced ginger and sesame oil in a separate dish to use as a dip.

CRUCIAN CARP WITH LOTUS EGG

CARP WITH TRI-HOT FLAVOURS

## *Sichuan* 四川

# CARP WITH TRI-HOT FLAVOURS

1 x 440 g (14 oz) carp or other meaty white fish
oil for deep-frying
2-3 dried red chillies
1 teaspoon Sichuan peppercorns (Fagara or Sansho)

SEASONING

2 teaspoons fermented black beans
1 cup (250 mL/8 fl oz) water
1¼ teaspoons sugar
1 teaspoon rice wine or dry sherry
1 teaspoon vinegar
pinch of salt

Clean and scale the carp, rinse under running cold water, then dry well inside and out. Make several diagonal slashes across each side.

❋ Heat the oil in a wok to smoking point, lower the heat and deep-fry the fish on both sides until golden. Lift out and drain well.

❋ Pour off all but 2 tablespoons of the oil and stir-fry the whole chillies and peppercorns for about 1 minute or until crisp and dry. Remove from the oil, drain well, then chop or grind coarsely.

❋ Chop the fermented beans finely, place in the oil and stir-fry for 30-40 seconds. Add the remaining seasoning ingredients and bring to the boil. Skim off any froth, then place the fish in the pan, cover and simmer gently for about 3 minutes on each side. If the pan is tightly covered the liquid will not evaporate; if it does, add a little more water during cooking.

❋ Lift the fish onto a serving plate, pour on the sauce, sprinkle with the ground pepper and chilli and serve.

## *Shanghai* 上海

# CRUCIAN CARP STEAMED WITH EGG

1 x 375 g (12 oz) crucian carp or other meaty white fish
3 large eggs
¾ cup (175 mL/6 fl oz) chicken stock (broth)
½ teaspoon salt
1 slice cooked salted ham

Clean and scale the carp and make several deep diagonal slashes across each side.

❋ Lightly beat the eggs, add the chicken stock and salt and pour into an oval heatproof dish. Place the fish on top, then set the dish on a rack in a wok or in a steamer, cover and steam for about 12 minutes over simmering water until the fish is cooked through and the egg firm. When the dish is removed from the steamer the fish will have sunk halfway into the egg.

❋ Finely chop the ham and sprinkle over the top of the fish and serve at once.

❋ For extra flavour, add the ham halfway through cooking, when the egg has firmed up enough to prevent it from sinking through to the bottom.

CRUCIAN CARP STEAMED WITH EGG

FRIED BLACK CARP IN A GRAPE-BUNCH SHAPE

## Shanghai 上海

# FRIED BLACK CARP IN A GRAPE-BUNCH SHAPE

*This unusual traditional dish from Anhui Province is made from a big fillet of fish cut from a large black carp, scored and coated so that when crisply fried it takes on the appearance of a bunch of grapes. Grape juice in the sauce adds to the flavour.*

375-440 g (12-14 oz) thick central piece of white fish fillet
1 teaspoon grated fresh (root) ginger
1 tablespoon finely chopped spring onion (shallot/scallion)
1 teaspoon salt
1½ cups (185 g/6 oz) cornflour (cornstarch)
oil for deep-frying
grapevine leaves and stem (garnish)

SAUCE

3 tablespoons chicken stock (broth)
1 cup (250 mL/8 fl oz) dark grape juice
1½ tablespoons red vinegar
2 tablespoons light soy sauce
1 teaspoon sugar
1 teaspoon lard
½ teaspoon salt
1 tablespoon cornflour (cornstarch)

Place the piece of fish, skin side downwards on a cutting board and cut a criss-cross pattern diagonally across it, cutting down to the skin but not through it. Place in a dish and scatter on the ginger, onion and salt. Leave for 15 minutes, then coat thickly with cornflour.

In a small wok or saucepan, boil the pre-mixed sauce ingredients for about 3 minutes, stirring constantly. Check the seasoning and keep warm.

Heat the oil in a large wok to smoking point, then reduce the heat slightly. Slide in the fish, skin side upwards, and deep-fry for about 5 minutes until golden and cooked through. As it cooks, the skin will curl up, giving the fish the appearance of a bunch of grapes.

Drain, place on a dish and arrange the vine leaves and stem at the top of the "bunch". Pour on the sauce and serve.

GOLDEN CRISP FISH WITH SWEET AND SOUR SAUCE

## Sichuan 四川

# GOLDEN CRISP FISH WITH SWEET AND SOUR SAUCE

*In a small town near a river, many many years ago, there was a popular snack called "Aromatic Fried Fish". The fish, probably a carp from the river, was cleaned and marinated, then coated thickly with a paste of soy bean powder and water before frying. This dish has been developed from the original by skilful Sichuan chefs.*

1 x 1 kg (2 lb) carp or other meaty white fish
¾ cup (90 g/3 oz) soya bean powder or cornflour (cornstarch)
oil for deep-frying
3 spring onions (shallots/scallions), shredded
2-3 fresh red chillies, shredded
fresh coriander leaves

### MARINADE

2 tablespoons light soy sauce
1 tablespoon rice wine or dry sherry
½ teaspoon salt
2 teaspoons ginger juice (optional)

### SAUCE

2 tablespoons vegetable oil
2 cloves garlic, crushed
1 teaspoon grated fresh (root) ginger
1-2 fresh red chillies, chopped
2 tablespoons vinegar
1½ tablespoons sugar
¾ teaspoon sesame oil
1½ teaspoons cornflour (cornstarch)
¾ cup (175 mL/6 fl oz) fish or chicken stock (broth)
pinch of salt and white pepper

Clean and scale the carp, rinse well, then dry thoroughly inside and out. Place in a dish, rub on the pre-mixed marinade ingredients and leave for 15 minutes. Mix the soy bean powder or cornflour with enough water to make a batter of coating consistency.

Use a sharp knife or cleaver to cut deep scores across each side of the fish, cutting at an angle so that each segment of fish stands out like a large fish scale. Coat the fish lightly with additional soy bean powder or cornflour, then dip into the batter, holding the fish by the tail so that the "scales" open and all the meat is covered evenly with the batter.

In a large wok heat the oil to smoking point, put in the fish, then lower the heat slightly and deep-fry for about 10 minutes, turning once. Lift out and drain well.

In another wok heat the oil for the sauce and then fry the garlic, ginger and chillies over moderate heat for about 1½ minutes. Add the vinegar, sugar and sesame oil and increase the heat slightly, then stir the cornflour into the stock and pour the mixture in the wok. Boil briefly, adding salt and pepper.

Reheat the deep-frying oil and fry the fish again for about 2 minutes to make the surface very crisp. Drain and place on a serving plate. Pour the sauce into a jug.

Scatter the spring onions, chillies and coriander leaves over the fish and pour the sauce on immediately before serving.

## Shanghai 上海

# SMOKED POMFRET

1 x 750 g (1½ lb) pomfret or John Dory
½ cup (60 g/2 oz) black Chinese tea leaves
1½ tablespoons sugar
mayonnaise or salad dressing
cucumber fans (garnish)
pickles or tomato slices (garnish)

### SEASONING/MARINADE

1 tablespoon Shaoxing rice wine or dry sherry
1 teaspoon salt
3 teaspoons sugar
1½ tablespoons finely chopped spring onion
  (shallot/scallion)
1 tablespoon grated fresh (root) ginger

Clean the fish and cut through the body diagonally in three places. Place in a dish. Mix the seasoning/marinade ingredients together and rub thoroughly over the fish, then leave for at least one hour to absorb the flavours.

Line the bottom of a heavy duty wok, preferably an old iron one, with aluminium foil and put the tea leaves and sugar on this. Place over high heat until they begin to smoke. Set the fish on a metal rack over it, cover and smoke the fish over slightly reduced heat for about 25 minutes. The fish will take on a rich deep colour, and the heat within the wok should be sufficient to cook the fish through.

Transfer to a serving plate, garnish attractively with fans of cucumber, a little brightly coloured pickled vegetable or tomato slices and serve with the mayonnaise.

SMOKED POMFRET

MANDARIN FISH COOKED IN CHILLI BEAN SAUCE

## Shanghai 上海

# MANDARIN FISH COOKED IN CHILLI BEAN SAUCE

1 x 500 g (1 lb) mandarin fish (perch/sea bass)
125 g (4 oz) lard
2 spring onions (shallots/scallions)
6 slices young fresh (root) ginger
¾ cup (175 mL/6 fl oz) water

SEASONING

1 tablespoon chilli bean paste
1-2 pickled red chillies
1 tablespoon rice wine or dry sherry
1 tablespoon sugar
½ teaspoon red vinegar

Select a live fish if possible, kill and clean it. Heat the lard in a wok and fry the fish on both sides until golden. Lift out and set aside.

❀ Cut the spring onions into 2.5 cm (1 in) lengths and fry with the ginger in the wok for about 30 seconds. Add the seasoning ingredients except the vinegar, and simmer for 1 minute, stirring constantly. Add about ¾ cup (175 mL/6 fl oz) water and bring to the boil. Return the fish and simmer, covered, for about 3 minutes, then remove the lid and continue simmering the fish until tender and the sauce well reduced. A little cornflour (cornstarch) can be used to thicken the sauce, if necessary.

❀ Transfer to a serving plate and sprinkle on the vinegar before serving.

BRAISED CHUB'S HEAD IN AN EARTHENWARE POT

## Shanghai 上海

# BRAISED CHUB'S HEAD IN AN EARTHENWARE POT

*Chub is variegated carp, a delicious freshwater fish. All four kinds of carp – rock, silver, grass and variegated – are eaten and cooked in many different ways throughout China.*

*Chub's head is especially large, accounting for about one-third of the body size. The flesh near the gills and jaw, especially the walnut-shaped flesh inside the mouth is fatty, tender and full of flavour.*

*The clay pot used to cook the fish heads allows them to simmer slowly, thus retaining their shape and producing a richly flavoured clear sauce. This famous dish is served in the autumn and winter.*

1 x 1¼ kg (2½ lb) variegated carp (chub) head or several large
   meaty fish heads, supplemented with extra fish meat,
   if necessary
125 g (4 oz) lard
2 bean sheets, soaked to soften*

SEASONING
3 tablespoons superior or other light soy sauce
1 tablespoon Shaoxing rice wine or dry sherry
1½-2 teaspoons salt
½ teaspoon white pepper
1 teaspoon sugar
1½ tablespoons soybean oil (optional)

Rinse the fish head and wipe dry. Heat the lard in a large wok
and stir-fry the fish head until it takes on a light colour, then
transfer to an earthenware pot or casserole.

�khCut the bean sheets into squares and place in the pot,
adding the seasoning ingredients. Add enough water to just
cover the fish, then cover the pot and bring almost to the boil.
Simmer gently for about 1½ hours until the fish is completely
tender and the stock has become rich, whitish in colour and
well reduced. Serve in the pot.

*Transparent edible sheets made from a paste of ground mung beans and water. If unavailable,
substitute mung bean vermicelli, or use strips of beancurd skin, cubes of fried beancurd or soaked
dried "wood ear" fungus.*

## Beijing 北京

# PAN'S FISH

*This dish was created by the chef of a high-ranking official in the
Qing Dynasty (1644-1911 AD). This official, whose name was Pan,
loved fish but abhorred the grease that normally results from frying.
So Pan's chef steamed the fish and named the dish after him.*

1 x 410 g (13 oz) fresh carp or other meaty white fish
4 dried black mushrooms, soaked for 25 minutes
6-8 dried shrimps, soaked for 25 minutes
1 spring onion (shallot/scallion), chopped
3 slices fresh (root) ginger

SEASONING
¾ cup (175 mL/6 fl oz) chicken or fish stock (broth)
2 tablespoons rice wine or dry sherry
2 tablespoons light soy sauce
⅓ teaspoon salt

Scale and clean the fish, wash in cold water, then dip into a
pot of boiling water for a few seconds and drain well. Make
several slashes diagonally across each side and place in a
heatproof bowl.

✖Drain the mushrooms and remove the stems. Then drain
the shrimps and arrange both over the fish, adding the spring
onion and ginger. Pour on the pre-mixed seasoning ingredients, place on a rack in a wok or in a steamer, cover and steam
for about 20 minutes. The fish is ready when the thick flesh
adjoining the head is tender and flakes easily.

✖Serve at once in the same bowl.

STEAMED TRI-SHREDS ROLLED IN FISH

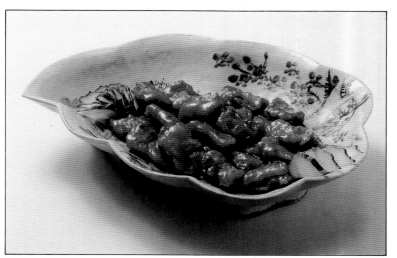

ZHUA CHAO YU FRIED FISH SLICES

## Shanghai 上海

# STEAMED TRI-SHREDS
# ROLLED IN FISH

*A variety of foods can be used as filling for these slender fish rolls. Although this dish is called tri-shreds, the number of ingredients can vary and include ham, winter bamboo shoots, black mushrooms, chicken meat, spring onions and ginger.*

*By cooking them in a steamer, the original textures of the different ingredients are preserved, while the various flavours are able to permeate each other. In one tiny roll, you can experience the tender smoothness of fish, the salty flavour of ham, the crispness of bamboo shoots, and the tasty, somewhat chewy consistency of mushroom, complemented by the pungency of onion and ginger.*

625 g (1¼ lb) thick central piece of fresh rock carp or other white fish fillet
60 g (2 oz) salted ham
60 g (2 oz) fresh or canned winter bamboo shoots
2-3 dried black mushrooms, soaked for 25 minutes
2-3 spring onions (shallots/scallions)
12 slices fresh (root) ginger

SAUCE

1 tablespoon rice wine or dry sherry
2 teaspoons light soy sauce
1 teaspoon rendered chicken fat, melted
½ teaspoon salt
1 teaspoon cornflour (cornstarch)

Holding the knife at a sharp angle, slice the fillet into very thin slices.

Drain the mushrooms, remove the stems and finely shred the caps, together with the ham, bamboo shoots, spring onions and ginger, keeping the slices about 5 cm (2 in) long.

Place a few pieces of each ingredient in the centre of each slice of fish and roll it around the filling, squeezing firmly into a smooth roll – the ingredients may be allowed to protrude slightly past the ends of the roll. Arrange on an oiled heatproof plate, place on a rack in a wok or in a steamer, cover and steam over gently simmering water for about 20 minutes until cooked and tender. Remove, retaining the cooking liquid and keep warm.

Mix the sauce ingredients together, adding the liquid from the steamed fish, and simmer, stirring, until thickened. Check the seasoning, then pour over the fish rolls and serve at once.

## Beijing 北京

# ZHUA CHAO YU
# FRIED FISH SLICES

*The story is told of the time the Empress Dowager Cixi picked out one dish of smooth, shining and tender fish slices from the many dishes on a table. When asked for the name of the dish the cook, caught unawares, called it Zhua Chao Yu, which means "grasping and frying".*

*The distinctive feature of the dish is that the fish is first deep-fried and then stir-fried. Its flavour is slightly sweet and sour, with a touch of saltiness.*

315 g (10 oz) fresh white fish fillets
1 cup (125 g/4 oz) cornflour (cornstarch)
oil, preferably peanut oil, for deep-frying

SAUCE

2 spring onions (shallots/scallions), white parts only
2 slices fresh (root) ginger
2 tablespoons lard
1 tablespoon light soy sauce
1 tablespoon brown vinegar
2 teaspoons sugar
1 teaspoon rice wine or dry sherry
pinch each of salt and pepper
½ teaspoon cornflour (cornstarch)

Cut the fish into long thin slices. Mix the cornflour with enough cold water to make a thin paste.

Heat the oil in a wok to smoking point then reduce the heat. Dip the fish slices into the cornflour paste and deep-fry 8 pieces at a time for about 1½ minutes until golden and crisp on the surface and cooked through. Lift out, drain well and keep warm while the sauce is prepared.

Very finely chop the spring onions and ginger. Heat a wok with the lard and stir-fry the spring onion and ginger for about 45 seconds, add the remaining pre-mixed sauce ingredients and heat through. When the sauce begins to thicken, slide in the fried fish and stir-fry, turning the fish carefully until coated with all the sauce. Serve at once.

STEAMED THREE-LAYER FISH

BRAISED FISH WITH MINCED MEAT

# Beijing 北京

## STEAMED THREE-LAYER FISH

1 x 625 g (1¼ lb) garoupa or other meaty white fish (coral cod or grouper)
9 dried black mushrooms, soaked for 25 minutes
185 g (6 oz) fresh or canned winter bamboo shoots
6 slices Yunnan or other salty ham
3 tablespoons fish or chicken stock (broth)
1 tablespoon rice wine or dry sherry
1 teaspoon melted lard
pinch of salt and pepper
4 slices fresh (root) ginger
3 spring onions (shallots/scallions)
250 g (8 oz) choy sum or other Chinese green vegetable
6-8 slices young fresh (root) ginger

### SAUCE

½ cup (125 mL/4 fl oz) chicken or fish stock (broth)
1 teaspoon melted lard
½ teaspoon salt
pinch of white pepper
½ teaspoon cornflour (cornstarch)

Clean and wash the fish, then scald with boiling water and drain. Cut off the head and tail and set aside. Use a sharp knife to remove the fillets from each side, then place skin-side down on a board and carefully detatch the skin from the fillet by holding firmly at the tail end and running the knife between skin and meat. Hold the knife at a sharp angle to the fillet and cut across it into slices. There should be 18 slices of fish, 9 from each fillet.

Drain the mushrooms, remove the stems and cut each cap in half. Cut the bamboo shoots and ham into pieces the approximate size of the fish slices.

Arrange the fish, mushrooms, bamboo and ham alternately in two rows along an oval heatproof plate, then position the head and tail at either end. The head can be halved so that it will remain flat on the plate.

Mix the stock, wine, melted lard, salt and pepper together and pour over the fish, then place the ginger and spring onion on top. Place on a rack in a wok or in a steamer, cover and steam over simmering water for about 20 minutes, until done. Discard the spring onions, ginger and the liquid.

Trim the choy sum and drop into a saucepan of boiling water with a tablespoon of oil. Simmer until tender, then drain well and arrange around the edge of the plate and along the centre between the two rows of ingredients.

Cut the ginger for the garnish into butterfly or other decorative shapes and use to decorate the dish.

Boil the sauce ingredients in a small pan until thickened and pour over the fish immediately before serving.

# Sichuan 四川

## BRAISED FISH WITH MINCED MEAT

*Braised Fish with Minced Meat is one of the many famous fish dishes of the Sichuan cuisine, and very popular at banquets. The fish is supplemented by special Shiu Fu pickled potherb mustard and pickled red chillies, and is cooked using a special braising technique. The dish is known for its bright red colour, fragrant aroma and slightly spicy, yet delicate taste.*

2 x 250 g (8 oz) crucian carp or other meaty white fish
2 cups (500 mL/16 fl oz) lard or oil for frying
90 g (3 oz) belly pork (fresh bacon)
30 g (1 oz) pickled potherb mustard
2 spring onions (shallots/scallions)
1½ pickled red chillies
2 slices fresh (root) ginger

### SAUCE

2 cups (500 mL/16 fl oz) fish stock (broth)
1 tablespoon rice wine or dry sherry
1 tablespoon dark soy sauce
1 teaspoon light soy sauce
1 teaspoon salt
1 teaspoon sesame oil
1 teaspoon sugar

Clean and scale the fish, make several deep scores diagonally across each side and dry well with paper towels. Heat the lard or oil in a wok and slide in the fish. Fry gently on both sides until crisp and partially cooked, then lift out carefully and drain well.

Finely chop (coarsely grind) the pork, mustard, spring onions, chillies and ginger.

Drain the wok, wipe out and return about 2 tablespoons of the oil. Sauté the pork until lightly coloured, then add the mustard, spring onions, chillies and ginger and stir-fry briefly. Pour in the pre-mixed sauce ingredients and bring to the boil.

Place the fish in the sauce, cover and simmer over gentle heat for about 45 minutes until the fish is completely tender and the sauce well flavoured.

Serve the fish with the sauce in a deep serving dish.

SANDWICHED PERCH

## Guangzhou 广州

# SANDWICHED PERCH

155 g (5 oz) perch fillets, skinned
125 g (4 oz) fresh chicken livers
90 g (3 oz) fat pork
2 teaspoons rice wine or dry sherry
1/2 teaspoon sesame oil
1/3 teaspoon salt
1/2 cup (60 g/2 oz) cornflour (cornstarch)
2 eggs
oil for deep-frying
12 stalks young choy sum or other Chinese green vegetable

Cut the perch and pork into pieces about 4 x 3 cm (1½ x 1¼ in) and slice the livers thinly. Place the fish in a dish and add the rice wine, sesame oil and salt and leave for 20 minutes.
❋ Sandwich the ingredients together, layering fish, chicken liver and fat pork, and coat each sandwich thickly with cornflour. Beat the eggs thoroughly.
❋ Heat 4–5 cups (1–1¼ L/32–40 fl oz) of oil in a wok to moderately hot. Dip the fish into the egg, coating evenly, then deep-fry (preferably in two batches) until cooked through and golden – about 6 minutes. Drain well and arrange on a serving plate.
❋ Drop the vegetables into a pan of boiling water and simmer briefly. They should remain crisp and brightly coloured. Drain and arrange around the fish.

## Beijing 北京

# LIGHT-FRIED AND SIMMERED MANDARIN FISH

*The rivers and lakes to the south of the Yangtze River are teeming with mandarin fish. The method of preparing this dish, called "ta" in Chinese, allows time for the seasoning to penetrate the meat and means that the sauce will be well reduced and concentrated.*

1 x 250 g (8 oz) piece of mandarin fish (perch/sea bass) fillet
1 tablespoon light soy sauce
1/2 cup (60 g/2 oz) flour
185 g (6 oz) lard
2 eggs, well beaten
2 tablespoons onion oil*

SAUCE

1½ cups (375 mL/12 fl oz) chicken stock (broth)
1 tablespoon light soy sauce
1½ tablespoons rice wine or dry sherry
2 teaspoons ginger juice
1/2 teaspoon salt

*Made by heating peanut or vegetable oil with sliced spring onions or red onions until the onions are well coloured. Strain and store the oil in a jar.*

LIGHT-FRIED AND SIMMERED MANDARIN FISH

Cut the fish into a fish shape and pound with the side of a cleaver to tenderise, sprinkle on the soy sauce and then coat with the flour. Heat the lard in a wok, dip the fish into the beaten egg, coating it thickly and fry on both sides until golden. Lift out and place in a casserole.
❋ Add the pre-mixed sauce ingredients and bring just to the boil. Cover and simmer very gently for about 20 minutes. Pour on the onion oil and serve in the casserole.

## Sichuan 四川

# STIR-FRIED SQUID SHREDS

*Squid can be dry and tough, unless it is gently cooked or soup is added. However, the chefs in Sichuan do not follow these common rules but cook squid using the stir-fry method. By cleverly handling the duration and degree of heat, they turn the dryness into crispness and toughness into puffiness, the result being tasty and aromatic.*

1 x 60 g (2 oz) piece dried squid
125 g (4 oz) pork belly (fresh bacon)
250 g (8 oz) lard
2 teaspoons rice wine or dry sherry
90 g (3 oz) fresh silver sprouts*
1 tablespoon light soy sauce
1 teaspoon sesame oil
salt

Use a sharp cleaver to cut the dried squid and the pork into very fine shreds and set aside.
❋ Heat the wok and add the lard. Stir-fry the squid shreds for about 2 minutes until they are crisp and red-brown. Drain off the excess lard and add the pork and the rice wine. Stir-fry together until the pork is done, then add the beansprouts and the remaining ingredients. Stir-fry together over high heat for 45 seconds, then serve.

*Fresh mung beansprouts from which the yellow seed pods and long tapering roots have been removed, leaving a slender, silver-coloured sprout.*

STIR-FRIED SQUID SHREDS

## Sichuan 四川

# FRIED WHOLE FISH WITH DUMPLINGS

1 x 500 g (1 lb) fresh carp or other meaty white fish
185 g (6 oz) semi-fat pork
1 egg white
1 cup (125 g/4 oz) cornflour (cornstarch)
oil for deep-frying
five-spice salt*

SEASONING

1 tablespoon rice wine or dry sherry
2 tablespoons finely chopped spring onions
    (shallots/scallions)
1 teaspoon grated fresh (root) ginger
1/2 teaspoon salt
pinch of white pepper

STUFFING

30 g (1 oz) pickled pot-herb mustard
2 spring onions (shallots/scallions)
2 slices fresh (root) ginger
1 teaspoon rice wine or dry sherry
2 teaspoons light soy sauce
1 teaspoon sugar
1/4 teaspoon sesame oil
lard or oil for frying

DUMPLINGS

60 g (2 oz) flour
250 g (8 oz) spinach
2 cabbage leaves
1/3 teaspoon sesame oil

Clean the carp and make several slashes diagonally across each side. Place in a dish and add the pre-mixed seasoning ingredients, rub in well and set aside for 1 hour.

Very finely mince (grind) a third of the pork and cut the remainder into fine shreds.

To prepare the stuffing, finely shred the pot-herb mustard, spring onions and ginger and mix with the remaining stuffing ingredients. Heat a little lard or frying oil in a wok and sauté the stuffing mixture and the shredded pork briefly until the pork turns white, then set aside to cool.

For the dumplings, sift the flour into a mixing bowl. Very finely chop the spinach and cook without water for about 7 minutes, then transfer to a colander and allow the liquid to drip onto the flour. Knead into the flour to make a soft dough.

Finely chop the cabbage leaves, mix with the minced pork and season with the sesame oil.

Roll the dough out into a long sausage shape and divide into 18 pieces. Roll or pull each piece into a thin round dumpling wrapper and fill with a portion of the pork and cabbage filling. Fold over and pinch the edges together to enclose the filling. Arrange the dumplings on an oiled, heatproof plate and set on a rack in a wok or in a steamer, cover and steam for about 14 minutes until tender.

Stuff the prepared stuffing into the cavity of the fish. Make a paste with the egg white and a little cornflour to seal the opening, then brush the remaining paste over the fish and coat thickly with cornflour.

Heat the oil in a wok to smoking point, put in the fish, then lower the heat. Deep-fry for about 5 minutes, turning once, until cooked through and golden brown on the surface.

Lift out and drain well. Place in the centre of a large serving plate and surround with the steamed dumplings. Pour the five spice salt into a small dish and serve separately as a dip for both the dumplings and the fish.

*To make the five-spice salt, heat 1 1/2 tablespoons of fine table salt in a wok until it begins to crackle, add 1 teaspoon of Chinese five-spice powder, remove from the heat, stir and cool.

CRISP FISH WITH SPRING ONION SAUCE

## Guangzhou 广州

# CRISP FISH WITH SPRING ONION SAUCE

1 x 1¼ kg (2½ lb) whole fresh fish
1 teaspoon salt
2 egg whites
1 cup (125 g/4 oz) cornflour (cornstarch)
oil for deep-frying

SAUCE

3 tablespoons peanut oil
¼ red capsicum (bell pepper), finely diced
¼ green capsicum (bell pepper), finely diced
3 spring onions (shallots/scallions), finely chopped
1 clove garlic, crushed
1 teaspoon grated fresh (root) ginger
2 dried black mushrooms, soaked then diced
60 g (2 oz) cha siew (Chinese roast pork), diced
2 tablespoons light soy sauce
½ teaspoon sesame oil
½ teaspoon salt
1 cup (250 mL/8 fl oz) fish or chicken stock (broth)
1 tablespoon cornflour (cornstarch)

Clean, scale and wash the fish, then drain and dry thoroughly inside and out. Make several deep diagonal slashes across each side, then cut in the other direction to create a diamond-shaped pattern on each side, and sprinkle on the salt.

Beat the egg whites until frothy and brush all over the fish. Coat thickly with the cornflour and set aside.

To prepare the sauce, heat the peanut oil in a wok and stir-fry the capsicums, onion, garlic and ginger for 2 minutes. Add the mushrooms and pork and stir-fry for another minute, then add the soy sauce, sesame oil and salt and toss together. Mix the cornflour with the stock and pour into the pan. Simmer gently, stirring until thickened and set aside.

Heat the deep-frying oil in a very large wok to smoking point, slide in the fish and deep-fry for about 7 minutes, turning once or twice, until the fish is cooked through and crisp and golden on the surface.

Reheat the sauce to boiling point and pour into a jug.

Carefully lift the fish onto a wide serving plate and take to the table with the hot sauce, which should be poured over the fish in front of the diners.

## Guangzhou 广州

# BRAISED FISH HEAD, COUNTRY-STYLE

*Dishes offered by the teahouses in the Guangdong countryside generally use local ingredients, skilfully prepared in ways unfamiliar to town dwellers. Some even have their own small vegetable plots and fish ponds from which customers can select the ingredients for their meals.*

*Carp can grow to a massive size, and the heads, although bony, have deliciously sweet pockets of meat and give a unique gelatinous texture to a dish.*

1 kg (2 lb) variegated carp (chub) head or several other meaty fish heads, supplemented with extra fish meat, if necessary
oil for deep-frying
12 cloves garlic
90 g (3 oz) lean pork
8 small cubes dried beancurd, soaked for 10 minutes
4-6 slices fresh (root) ginger
6 dried black mushrooms, soaked for 25 minutes
12 small, fresh (or canned) straw mushrooms, trimmed
12 stalks choy sum or other Chinese green vegetable

SEASONING/STOCK

3 tablespoons superior or other light soy sauce
1 teaspoon sesame oil
½ teaspoon salt
1 teaspoon sugar
¼ teaspoon ground white pepper
3 cups (750 mL/24 fl oz) superior stock (*see page 124*)

Rinse the fish head, drain and wipe dry. Heat the oil and fry the head for several minutes until it takes on a good colour. Drain and transfer to a casserole.

Peel the garlic, shred the pork, drain the beancurd and squeeze out all the water. Place in a frying basket or large perforated ladle and deep-fry in hot oil for about 2 minutes, drain and arrange over the fish. Add the ginger, mushrooms and the seasoning/stock ingredients. Bring just to the boil, then braise gently, half covered, until the fish is completely tender and the sauce well reduced.

The green vegetable can be boiled or stir-fried separately then arranged around the dish to serve.

BRAISED FISH HEAD, COUNTRY-STYLE

SHREDS OF FISH, GINGER AND PICKLED CUCUMBER

*Shanghai* 上海

# Shreds of Fish, Ginger and Pickled Cucumber

*The following recipe describes a seasonal dish prepared at the end of summer and the beginning of autumn. Each ingredient complements the other to make this a sweet, tasty, tender, yet crisp and delightfully light dish.*

375 g (¾ lb) mandarin fish fillets or other meaty fish
1 egg white
pinch of salt
8 slices young fresh (root) ginger
2 tablespoons lard
½ teaspoon sesame oil

### SEASONING

1 teaspoon Shaoxing rice wine or dry sherry
⅓ cup (75 mL/2½ fl oz) chicken or fish stock (broth)
½ teaspoon sugar
½ teaspoon salt
½ teaspoon cornflour (cornstarch)

### PICKLED CUCUMBER

2 small cucumbers
1 cup (250 mL/8 fl oz) boiling water
1 tablespoon sugar
2 tablespoons white vinegar
2 teaspoons salt

Make the pickled cucumber first as it should be allowed to marinate for several hours before use. Peel the cucumbers thinly, cut into matchstick strips, discarding the ends and seed cores and place in a bowl. Mix the remaining ingredients together, pour over the cucumber and leave to stand. Drain very thoroughly before use.

🌸 Cut the fish into shreds, place in a dish with the lightly beaten egg white and the salt and set aside.

🌸 Shred the ginger slices.

🌸 Heat a wok and add the lard. Stir-fry the fish shreds until white and firm, then remove to a strainer to drain.

🌸 Stir-fry the drained cucumber and the ginger together, adding the wine after about 30 seconds. Pour the remaining pre-mixed seasoning ingredients into the pan, and when the sauce begins to thicken, return the fish and stir-fry all together over high heat for a few moments.

🌸 Transfer to a serving plate and sprinkle on the sesame oil before serving.

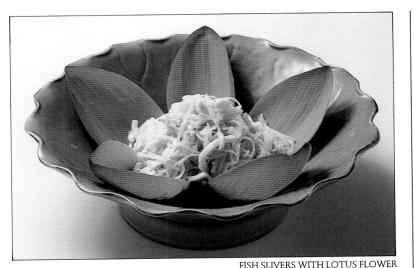

FISH SLIVERS WITH LOTUS FLOWER

*Beijing* 北京

# Fish Slivers with Lotus Flower

*The lotus flower with its light and pure fragrance and exquisitely shaped petals found its way into the hearts of the Chinese people long ago, as a symbol of beauty and perfection. The eating of lotus seeds is recorded in ancient Chinese writings, but the flower is bitter, and is only used for its colour and fragrance.*

125 g (4 oz) white fish fillets
90 g (3 oz) canned bamboo shoots, drained
1 lotus flower
1 egg white, lightly beaten
1 tablespoon cornflour (cornstarch)
1 teaspoon rice wine or dry sherry
1½ cups (375 mL/12 fl oz) oil for frying

### SEASONING

2 slices fresh (root) ginger, shredded
1 teaspoon rice wine or dry sherry
½ teaspoon salt
⅓ teaspoon sesame oil

Hold the knife at a 45° angle to cut each fish fillet into thin slices and then into shreds. Shred the bamboo shoots and rinse the petals of the lotus flower.

🌸 Arrange the lotus petals on a serving plate, preferably jade green, in a lotus leaf shape.

🌸 Place the sliced fish in a dish. Add the egg white, cornflour and rice wine and stir together lightly.

🌸 Heat the oil in a wok and deep-fry the fish in several batches over moderate heat until cooked through but not coloured on the surface. Lift out and drain well.

🌸 Pour off all but 2 tablespoons of the oil. Stir-fry the bamboo shoots for 1 minute, then add the seasoning ingredients and stir-fry together briefly. Add the fish and cook slowly, mixing lightly so as not to break up the fish.

🌸 Transfer to the serving platter, placing the fish in the centre of the "flower" and serve.

SAUTÉED FISH SLICES

# Beijing 北京

# FIVE WILLOW FISH

*Mandarin fish is a freshwater fish found in China's large rivers and lakes. They live in the Yihou Imperial Garden Lake in Beijing, where legend has it that every spring they feast on the peach blossoms that fall into the lake. As a result the meat of the mandarin fish is supposed to be especially fragrant. In reality, however, these fish are quite aggressive and their diet consists of prawns and smaller fish.*

*This recipe, with the fish garnished with five different ingredients, was inspired by the Five Willow Hermit, so called because he dwelt near a lake surrounded by five willow trees. He loved to sit under one of these trees to write and recite poetry and essays. At times he would just scoop up a big fat fish, cook it on the spot and eat it all by himself.*

1 x 440 g (14 oz) mandarin fish (perch/sea bass)
1 small carrot
2 slices pickled cabbage, soaked for 10 minutes
2 dried black mushrooms, soaked for 25 minutes
½ green capsicum (bell pepper)
5 slices young fresh (root) ginger
2 tablespoons oil for frying

SEASONING/SAUCE

½ cup (125 mL/4 fl oz) fish or chicken stock (broth)
2 teaspoons rice wine or dry sherry
1 tablespoon rendered chicken fat, melted
½ teaspoon salt
½ teaspoon sugar
small pinch of ground star anise
1 teaspoon cornflour (cornstarch)

Clean and scale the fish and make several diagonal cuts across each side. Set the fish in a heatproof dish and place on a rack in a wok, or in a steamer, cover and steam over simmering water until almost cooked through, then remove and place on a rack to drain.

※ Shred the carrot, drained cabbage and mushrooms, the capsicum and ginger.

※ Heat the oil in a wok and slide in the fish. Carefully fry over moderate heat until cooked and lightly crisp on both sides, then lift onto a serving plate and keep warm.

※ Add the shredded vegetables in separate piles to the wok and pour in the pre-mixed seasoning/sauce ingredients except the cornflour. Simmer gently, occasionally stirring carefully so as not to disorganise the groups of ingredients. Lift out separately and arrange across the top of the fish. Mix the cornflour with a little cold water and stir into the sauce, boiling until the sauce thickens and clears. Pour over the fish and serve at once.

# Beijing 北京

# SAUTÉED FISH SLICES

*This dish is said to have appeared at every birthday banquet held for the Empress Dowager Cixi. It is especially suitable for the elderly because the fish has been deboned and the meat is extremely tender.*

375 g (12 oz) white fish fillets
5-6 slices carrot, parboiled
2 tablespoons oil for frying
3 tablespoons fish or chicken stock (broth)
cucumber slices (garnish)
fresh coriander or watercress (garnish)

SEASONING

1 tablespoon rice wine or dry sherry
1 teaspoon melted lard
1 egg white, well beaten
½ teaspoon sugar
½ teaspoon salt
1 tablespoon cornflour (cornstarch)

Skin the fish and pat dry with a paper towel. Holding the knife at a sharp angle to the cutting board, cut each fillet into thin slices. Place in a dish with the pre-mixed seasoning ingredients and leave for 20 minutes.

※ Cut the carrots into decorative shapes.

※ Heat the oil in the wok and quickly stir-fry the fish for about 2 minutes over high heat. Add the carrot slices and stir-fry for another minute, then pour in the stock and simmer briefly. Check the seasoning, transfer to a serving plate and garnish with cucumber slices and a sprig of watercress or fresh coriander. Serve immediately.

FIVE WILLOW FISH

STEAMED PORGY

# Beijing 北京

# STEAMED PORGY

*This fish is commonly found in the East China Sea. Its flesh is snow white and very finely textured; it is full of nutritional value, and is said to have properties that keep it fresh longer than other fish.*

*There is a legendary figure in Japan that carries such a fish under his arm. It is said to bring blessings of peace and prosperity to the country and its people.*

1 x 500 g (1 lb) bream (sea bass/porgy)
3 slices Yunnan or other salted ham
1 fresh bamboo shoot, parboiled or canned
3 dried black mushrooms, soaked for 25 minutes
2 tablespoons melted lard
2 spring onions
3-4 slices fresh (root) ginger
2 teaspoons cornflour (cornstarch)

SEASONING

2 teaspoons rice wine or dry sherry
½ teaspoon salt
¼ teaspoon white pepper

Clean and scale the fish. Make diagonal slashes across each side then hold it by the tail and dip briefly into a pot of boiling water. Lift out and dry thoroughly.

Rub with the seasoning ingredients and place in a heatproof shallow dish. Cut the ham into decorative oval shapes and insert a piece into each of the cuts on the top side of the fish. Thinly slice the bamboo shoot, cut it decoratively, and arrange along the fish. Drain the mushrooms well, remove the stems and halve the caps. Use the point of a sharp knife to shred the caps, leaving them connected in the centre to give a chrysanthemum-like appearance. Place along the fish. Sprinkle on the lard, arrange the spring onions and ginger along the fish and pour the seasoning ingredients over it. Leave for about 10 minutes to absorb the flavours, then place on a rack in a wok or in a steamer, cover and steam for 20 minutes until tender.

Discard the spring onion and ginger, remove the fish to a serving plate and pour the liquid from the steaming dish into a wok. Bring to the boil and add the cornflour mixed with a little cold water, stirring until the sauce is clear and thick. Pour over the fish before serving.

FRIED PERCH AND PORK WITH CRAB SAUCE

## Guangzhou 广州

# FRIED PERCH AND PORK WITH CRAB SAUCE

185 g (6 oz) perch fillets, skinned
125 g (4 oz) pork fat*
1 tablespoon rice wine or dry sherry
1 cup (125 g/4 oz) cornflour (cornstarch)
3 egg whites
salt and white pepper
oil for deep-frying

CRAB SAUCE

90 g (3 oz) fresh crabmeat
60-90 g (2-3 oz) fresh crab roe
⅔ cup (150 mL/5 fl oz) fish stock (broth)
2 egg whites
½ teaspoon salt
pinch of white pepper
1½ teaspoons cornflour (cornstarch)
¾ teaspoon sesame oil

Cut the fish and the pork fat into pieces about 3 x 2 cm (1¼ x ¾ in). Place in a dish and sprinkle with the wine. Leave for 20 minutes, then sandwich pieces of pork and fish together. Coat each parcel thickly with cornflour.
✯ Lightly beat 3 egg whites, adding a pinch of salt and pepper.
✯ Heat the oil to smoking point, then reduce heat to moderate. Dip the meat parcels into the egg and fry gently in two or three batches, turning once or twice, until golden and cooked through – about 6 minutes. Lift out and drain well.
✯ Pour the oil from the wok, rinse out and return about 1 tablespoon of oil. Add the crabmeat and roe and stir-fry briefly. Pour in the stock and bring just to the boil. Lightly beat 2 egg whites and pour into the hot stock in a slow stream. Do not stir for about 40 seconds while the egg cooks. Add salt and pepper. Mix the cornflour with a little cold water and stir into the sauce.
✯ Arrange the perch and pork sandwiches on a serving platter. Cover with the crab sauce and sprinkle with sesame oil.

*The fat just beneath the skin of a pork leg roast (fresh ham) is ideal.*

FISH BALLS WITH STRAW MUSHROOMS

## Guangzhou 广州

# FISH BALLS WITH STRAW MUSHROOMS

*In many Guangdong dishes a starch dressing (sauce thickened with cornflour or pea starch) is used to enhance the appearance of the food. This also increases the density of the dish, so it lingers on the taste buds, and keeps it moist.*

250 g (8 oz) white fish fillets
1 egg white
¾ teaspoon salt
2 tablespoons flour
12 fresh or canned straw mushrooms
1 spring onion (shallot/scallion)
3 slices fresh (root) ginger
2 teaspoons rice wine or dry sherry
oil for deep-frying
2 teaspoons cornflour (cornstarch)
1 teaspoon sesame oil
fresh coriander and carrot slices (garnish)

SIMMERING SAUCE

½ cup (125 mL/4 fl oz) fish stock (broth)
½ teaspoon sugar
pinch each of salt and white pepper

STARCH DRESSING

⅓ cup (75 mL/2½ fl oz) water
1 teaspoon mushroom soy sauce
1 teaspoon cornflour (cornstarch)

Check the fish for bones, cut into small pieces and pound to a paste using the flat side of a cleaver or a food processor. Add the egg white, salt and flour and mix with your fingers to a smooth and sticky paste. Form into about 12 balls.
✯ Trim the straw mushrooms, removing the straw and dirt fragments from the bases. Place in a wok with the spring onion, ginger and wine and add 1 cup (250 mL/8 fl oz) of water. Cover and bring to the boil, remove the lid and simmer for about 10 minutes.
✯ Meanwhile, heat the oil in another wok and deep-fry the fish balls until golden, stirring with chopsticks to turn and colour evenly. Remove and drain. Drain the oil from the wok and add the simmering sauce ingredients. Simmer for 5-6 minutes, turning from time to time.
✯ Add 2 teaspoons of cornflour mixed with a little cold water to the simmering mushrooms and stir until thickened, then transfer the mushrooms and sauce to a serving plate. Place the fish balls on top of the mushrooms.
✯ Boil the starch dressing separately, stirring until thickened. Pour over the dish and sprinkle the sesame oil on top. Garnish with carrot slices and fresh coriander.

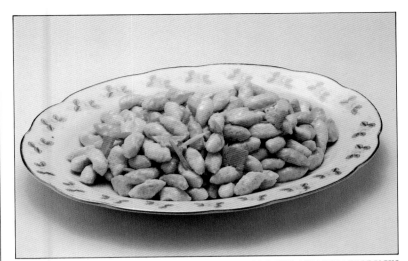

FISH CAKES AS MANDARIN DUCKS

FRIED FLAT FISH

## Beijing 北京

# FISH CAKES AS MANDARIN DUCKS

*Mandarin ducks live in lifelong couples, and the Chinese often compare them to husbands and wives. Guangdong people like to refer to things that are matching yet not completely alike as "mandarin ducks". A pair of chopsticks of different colours, for example, is called "yuan yang kuai zi" (mandarin duck chopsticks).*

*This dish is called "Fish Cakes as Mandarin Ducks" because the fish cakes have been coloured and flavoured in two different ways. One batch is simmered in a milky soup and the other in a clear soup coloured with molasses.*

250 g (8 oz) dace or whiting
½ cup (125 mL/4 fl oz) water
pinch of salt
3 egg whites
½ teaspoon salt
2 tablespoons rendered chicken fat, melted
1 spring onion (shallot/scallion), shredded
2 slices fresh (root) ginger, shredded
1½ teaspoons Shaoxing rice wine or dry sherry
1 teaspoon molasses
1 cup (250 mL/8 fl oz) chicken stock (broth)
½ cup (125 mL/4 fl oz) milk
½ cup (125 mL/4 fl oz) water

Finely chop the fish, then beat to a smooth paste with the side of a cleaver or use a food processor. Mix in ½ cup (125 mL/ 4 fl oz) of cold water, stirring in one direction only, and add a large pinch of salt. Beat the egg whites until stiff, then fold in the fish mixture and add half of the chicken fat.

❊ Heat a large pan with water and add ½ teaspoon of salt. When simmering, form the fish batter into ovals by moulding between two wet tablespoons. Slide them into the water and simmer for about 5 minutes in gently bubbling water, until they are cooked through but retain their shape. Lift out with a slotted spoon and drain.

❊ Heat the remaining chicken fat in a wok and gently stir-fry the spring onion and ginger for 40 seconds. Add the rice wine and boil briefly, then add the molasses and chicken stock and stir until dissolved. Add half the fish cakes and simmer gently, turning carefully when the underside is well coloured. Continue to cook until there is little sauce left.

❊ In another pan, bring the milk and ½ cup (125 mL/4 fl oz) of water to a slow boil and add the remaining fish cakes. Simmer uncovered until the liquid is well reduced, then thicken with a little cornflour mixed with cold water. Turn the fish cakes in the thickened sauce until well coated.

❊ Arrange the fish cakes on a platter in pairs of gold and white.

## Beijing 北京

# FRIED FLAT FISH

1 x 375 g (12 oz) flat fish (sole, flounder or turbot)
2 teaspoons rice wine or dry sherry
½ teaspoon salt
1 teaspoon sesame oil
2 tablespoons cornflour (cornstarch)
1 egg white, well beaten
oil for frying
carrot slices (garnish)
sprigs of fresh coriander (garnish)

SAUCE

2 slices fresh (root) ginger
2 spring onions (shallots/scallions), roughly chopped
2 tablespoons rice wine or dry sherry
1 teaspoon sugar

With slightly diagonal cuts, separate the head and tail of the fish and discard. Use a knife with a flexible blade to carefully trim off the skin of the remaining central section, scrape out the gut, then rinse the fish and dry well. Place in a dish, add the wine, salt and sesame oil and leave for 1 hour, turning once.

❊ Coat the fish with cornflour, then dip into the beaten egg white and coat with cornflour again.

❊ Heat the oil in a wok and fry on both sides until golden and cooked through. Transfer to a serving plate.

❊ Pour off the oil, rinse out the wok, then return to the heat and add about 2 tablespoons of the oil. Stir-fry the ginger slices and spring onions until lightly browned, then discard. Add the rice wine and sugar with a pinch of salt and bring to the boil.

❊ Spoon the sauce over the fish, then garnish with attractively cut carrot slices and sprigs of fresh coriander and serve.

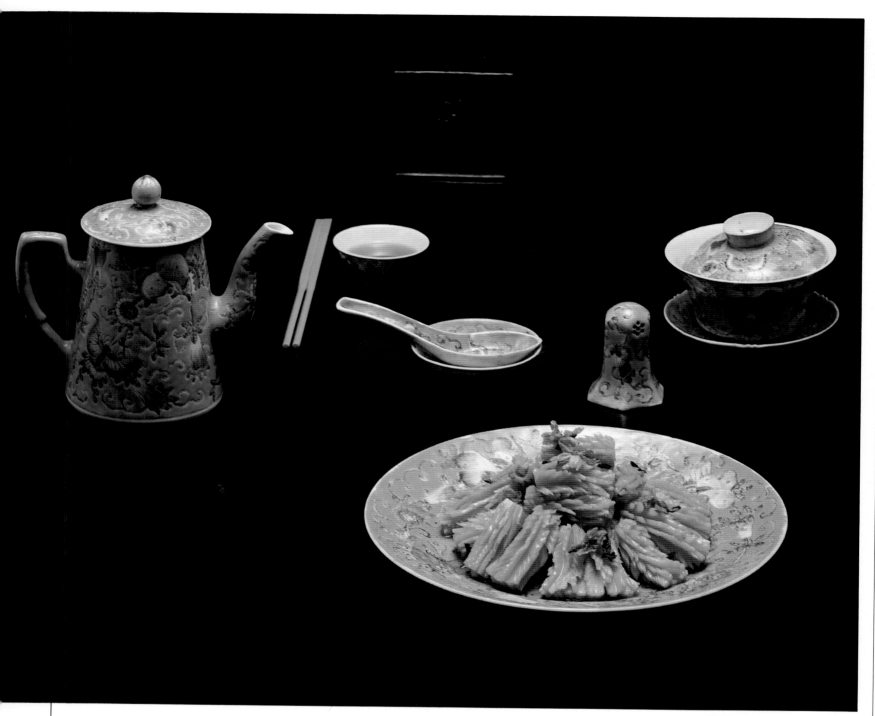

SQUID SLICES WITH JASMINE TEA

## Shanghai 上海

# SQUID SLICES WITH JASMINE TEA

*Artistically cut, curled slivers of pearly white squid, presented in a sauce flavoured with fragrant jasmine tea and strewn with jasmine flowers, is an unforgettable dish.*

500 g (1 lb) fresh squid
2 teaspoons jasmine tea leaves
2 teaspoons rice wine or dry sherry
²⁄₃ teaspoon salt
2½ teaspoons cornflour (cornstarch)
1 tablespoon vegetable oil
3 cloves garlic, finely chopped
4 slices fresh (root) ginger
1 spring onion (shallot/scallion), roughly chopped
jasmine flowers (garnish)

Pull away the head, tentacles and stomach of the squid and dislodge the transparent cuttle. Cut the squid open and pull off the fins and skin. Rinse well under cold water and drain.

Place outerside downwards on a cutting board and score the inside very lightly lengthways, then turn over. Holding the knife at a 45° angle to the board, make deep diagonal scores across the surface, then score from the other direction so that the surface has been dissected into points giving the appearance of the spines of a pine cone.

Drop the squid into a bowl of boiling water, leave for about 20 seconds, then drain. The squid should curl attractively and the points rise up.

Place the tea leaves in a pot or jug and add 1 cup (250 mL/ 8 fl oz) of boiling water, leave for 2-3 minutes, then pour the water off. Add another cup (250 mL/8 fl oz) of boiling water, cover and leave for 2 minutes.

Pour the tea into a wok, add the rice wine and salt, bring to the boil, then drop in the squid and poach for 1 minute. Mix the cornflour with a little cold water and stir into the sauce, simmering briefly.

In another wok heat the vegetable oil and add garlic, ginger and spring onion. Stir-fry for 1 minute until the garlic is lightly coloured, then pour in the squid with its tea sauce and simmer briefly. Pick out the ginger and spring onion and transfer the dish to a serving plate.

Strew with fresh jasmine flowers, and serve at once.

COUNTRY-STYLE FRIED STUFFED DACE

FRIED MELON DATES

## Guangzhou 广州

# COUNTRY-STYLE FRIED STUFFED DACE

*The people of Guangdong are particularly fond of the smooth flesh, delicate flavour and rich protein of the dace. Its fine bones do, however, make it less enjoyable, but prepared the following way, the fish is boneless, tender and more flavourful. The meat is minced and mixed with diced sausage, dried mushrooms and shrimps to make a stuffing which is filled into the skin and served in the original shape of the fish. Although it is difficult to skin fish, nearly every housewife in Shundeh County is an expert in preparing dace in this way. Whiting will give equally good results.*

2 x 375 g (12 oz) dace or whiting
2 dried Chinese sausages, or 30 g (1 oz) Yunnan or
    salted ham
2 tablespoons dried shrimps, soaked for 25 minutes
3 dried black mushrooms, soaked for 25 minutes
1-2 cloves garlic, crushed
½ cup (60 g/2 oz) cornflour (cornstarch)
2 cups (500 mL/16 fl oz) oil for frying
1 tablespoon superior or other light soy sauce
2 teaspoons rice wine or dry sherry
⅔ cup (150 mL/5 fl oz) fish or chicken stock (broth)
fresh coriander (garnish)

SEASONING

⅓ teaspoon sesame oil
½ teaspoon sugar
⅓ teaspoon salt
pinch of white pepper
2 teaspoons cornflour (cornstarch)

Clean and rinse the fish. Use a sharp knife to slit each fish closely along the backbone, severing it completely. Lift out the backbone completely and discard. Place the fish skin side down and carefully cut the meat from the skin, then do the same with the other side so that the skin remains attached to the head and tail while the meat has been completely detached. Pick or cut away the line of fine bones which runs down the centre of each fillet. Chop the fish meat roughly, then beat vigorously with a side of a cleaver until reduced to a smooth paste.

Steam the sausages on a rack in a wok or in a steamer for 5-6 minutes until softened. Drain the shrimps and mushrooms. Finely dice all three ingredients and mix with the fish, adding the seasoning ingredients and the garlic.

Dust the inside of each fish skin lightly with cornflour. Divide the mixture into two parts and spread half along the centre of each fish skin, moulding the stuffed fish into their original shape.

Coat the fish evenly with more cornflour, brushing off the excess. Heat the oil in a wok and when quite hot fry the two stuffed fish until well coloured on both sides. Carefully lift onto a serving plate.

Drain the wok, return about 1 tablespoon of the oil and add the soy sauce, wine and stock. Boil briskly, then thicken with about 1½ teaspoons of cornflour mixed with a little cold water. Pour over the fish and garnish with fresh coriander.

## Guangzhou 广州

# FRIED MELON DATES

*This is a well-known Fujian dish, but the ingredients include neither melon nor dates. Its name comes from the yellow melon fish which is plentiful along the coast of Fujian Province. This is sliced and rolled into date shapes, which are coated and fried and served on a bed of crisply fried salted vegetable leaves.*

315 g (10 oz) melon fish or other white fish fillets
2 teaspoons rice wine or dry sherry
1 teaspoon ginger juice
½ teaspoon salt
lard or oil for frying
6-8 leaves dried salted cabbage or rape, shredded
oil for deep-frying
five-spice salt*

BATTER

3 egg whites, well beaten
3 tablespoons cornflour (cornstarch)
3 tablespoons flour

Cut the fish into strips and place in a dish, adding the wine, ginger juice and salt. Mix well and leave for 1 hour.

Mix the batter ingredients, adding just enough cold water to make a thick batter.

Heat the lard or oil in a wok to smoking point, then lower the heat slightly. Dip the fish into the batter and slide into the oil to fry for about 1¼ minutes until golden, then drain and keep warm.

Heat another wok with the oil for deep-frying to smoking point, place the shredded vegetable leaves in a frying basket, deep-fry for a few seconds until bright green and crisp, remove and arrange on a serving platter. Place the fish on top of the vegetables and serve with the five-spice salt as a dip.

*To make the five-spice salt, heat 1½ tablespoons of fine table salt in a wok until it begins to crackle, add 1 teaspoon of Chinese five spice powder, remove from the heat, stir and cool.*

JADE WHITE SLICED FISH

## Sichuan 四川

# JADE WHITE SLICED FISH

220 g (7 oz) white fish fillets
1 egg white, well beaten
3 tablespoons soy bean powder or cornflour (cornstarch)
2 cups (500 mL/16 fl oz) oil for frying

SAUCE

6 thin slices fresh young (root) ginger
1 pickled red chilli
2 spring onions (shallots/scallions), white parts only
1 clove garlic
12 sprigs fresh pea leaves or 2-3 lettuce leaves
½ cup (125 mL/4 fl oz) fish stock
1 teaspoon rice wine or dry sherry
1 teaspoon sugar
pinch each of salt and white pepper
2 teaspoons cornflour (cornstarch)

Cut the fish into thin slices and place in a dish with the egg white. Mix well, then coat each slice of fish lightly on both sides with the soy bean powder or cornflour.

❈ Heat the oil in a wok to smoking point, then reduce the heat and fry the fish, about 8 pieces at a time, over moderate heat until just cooked through and still white. Lift out and drain well.

❈ To prepare the sauce, cut the ginger into decorative shapes, slice the chilli and onions diagonally and chop the garlic. Chop the lettuce leaves into squares, if used.

❈ Drain off the oil and wipe out the wok. Return about 2 tablespoons of the oil and stir-fry the ginger, chilli, onions and garlic for 1 minute over moderate heat. Add the remaining pre-mixed sauce ingredients and bring to the boil. Add the pea leaves or lettuce squares and the fish and simmer very gently, stirring to mix evenly. Transfer to a serving dish and serve at once.

## Guangzhou 广州

# SHARKS' FINS BRAISED IN BROWN SAUCE

*Shark's fin is a delicacy that featured at most Imperial banquets of the Qing Dynasty (1644-1911 AD). Its esteem in the Chinese cuisine comes from the use of the best ingredients, the culinary skills required to prepare it, and its high nutritional value. Shark's fin cooked in the method described here is golden and translucent with a smooth texture and luscious aroma. A dish of this calibre is rarely made at home, but can be enjoyed in most fine restaurants.*

280 g (9 oz) prepared dried sharks' fins
4 slices fresh (root) ginger
2 spring onions (shallots/scallions)
2 tablespoons rice wine or dry sherry
1 tablespoon cornflour (cornstarch)
125 g (4 oz) silver sprouts*
2 red chillies
2-3 slices cooked ham
black or red vinegar

SUPERIOR STOCK

½ chicken
6 chicken feet
½ pig's trotter (knuckle)
155 g (5 oz) lean pork
1 tablespoon dark soy sauce
½ teaspoon salt
pinch of white pepper
4 cups (1 L/32 fl oz) water

Soak the sharks' fins in cold water for 2 hours, bring to the boil and simmer gently for 30 minutes. Drain and cover with more cold water, soak for a further 2 hours, bring to the boil and simmer 30 minutes again. Repeat this twice more, then rinse the fins well in cold water and drain.

❈ In the meantime, place the stock ingredients in a separate saucepan, bring to the boil and skim. Continue boiling gently, covered, for 3 hours, until the liquid has been well reduced.

❈ Place the sharks' fins on a closely woven bamboo rack and arrange the ginger and spring onions on top, then sprinkle with the wine. Place the rack in a casserole and strain over the stock. Set the pot on a rack in a wok or in a steamer, cover and steam over simmering water for about 1½ hours. Top up the water in the steamer from time to time. Remove the sharks' fins from the rack and place on a serving plate.

❈ Bring the stock to the boil, thicken with the cornflour mixed with a little cold water and simmer until the sauce becomes transparent. Adjust seasoning to taste and pour the sauce over the fins.

❈ Blanch the sprouts, finely shred the chillies and ham, and arrange the three ingredients on several small dishes. Serve with the sharks' fins, together with dishes of black or red vinegar.

*Fresh mung beansprouts from which the yellow seed pods and tapered roots have been removed, leaving the silver-coloured sprouts.*

SHARKS' FINS BRAISED IN BROWN SAUCE

BRAISED SHARKS' FINS, TAN FAMILY STYLE

## Beijing 北京

# BRAISED SHARKS' FINS, TAN FAMILY STYLE

*The famous Tan family, who started their first restaurant during the Qing Dynasty (1644-1911 AD) apparently had twenty ways of cooking sharks' fins. This one has been handed down for generations and is considered one of their best.*

75 g (2½ oz) dried sharks' fins
1 x 1¼ kg (2½ lb) chicken
½ x 1¾ kg (3½ lb) duck
5 dried scallops, soaked for 1 hour
125 g (4 oz) Yunnan or other salted ham, chopped
8 cups (2 L/64 fl oz) water
1 tablespoon rice wine or dry sherry
1 teaspoon sugar
2 tablespoons superior or other light soy sauce
salt and pepper
2-3 teaspoons dried prawn (shrimp) roe (optional)
red vinegar (dip)

Place the sharks' fins in a saucepan, cover with water and bring to the boil. Simmer for 20 minutes, then drain and cover with cold water again. Bring to the boil and simmer gently for about 2 hours. Leave to cool in the water, then pour the water off. Scrape away any tough pieces of skin, then rinse the fins, cover with cold water and bring to the boil. Reduce the heat and simmer gently for another hour. Leave to cool in the water.

Drain and place the sharks' fins on a closely woven bamboo rack in a wok and cover with another bamboo rack. Chop the chicken and duck into pieces and arrange on the top rack. Add the scallops, ham and the water. Cover, bring to the boil and simmer gently for 3 hours, or until the sharks' fins are soft and tender and the stock richly flavoured.

Remove the chicken, duck, scallops and ham to use in another dish, or discard.

Bring the sharks' fins and their stock to the boil, season with the wine, sugar and soy sauce, and add salt and pepper to taste. Sprinkle with the fish roe, if used, and simmer, uncovered, for about 15 minutes until the liquid has reduced to just cover the fins.

If shrimp roe has not been used, very finely dice a little of the ham and use this to garnish the dish.

Serve with small dishes of red vinegar dip.

125

## Shanghai 上海

# EEL SHREDS WITH SESAME OIL

*Eel is delicious and highly nutritious. Traditional Chinese folk medicine holds that eel gives one energy and helps in the treatment of rheumatism.*

*Eel has different distinctive features during each of the four seasons. It is tender and delicately flavoured in spring, most delicious during the rice transplanting time from the end of spring to early summer, tough in autumn and fat in winter.*

*Eels should be killed just before cooking as the meat deteriorates quickly and then acquires a muddy and strong fishy flavour.*

1 kg (2 lb) freshwater eels
3 tablespoons lard
6 slices young fresh (root) ginger
1 tablespoon sesame oil
½ teaspoon white pepper

SEASONING/SAUCE

¾ cup (175 mL/6 fl oz) chicken or fish stock (broth)
2½ tablespoons superior or other light soy sauce
1 tablespoon rice wine or dry sherry
1½ teaspoons sugar
⅓ teaspoon powdered ginger
1 teaspoon cornflour (cornstarch)

Drop the eels into boiling water to kill, then remove. Cut off the heads and then use a sharp knife to remove the meat in long fillets from the backbone and cut into shreds. Eels do not need to be skinned if they are young and small.

※ Rub out a wok with an oiled cloth, add the lard and heat to smoking point. Drop in the eel meat and stir-fry over very high heat until it changes colour and is cooked through. Remove to a plate. Add the pre-mixed seasoning ingredients, except the cornflour, to the wok, and stir until boiling. Return the eel, cover and simmer gently for 2-3 minutes.

※ Mix the cornflour with a little cold water and pour into the sauce, stirring until thickened. Transfer the eel and sauce to a serving dish.

※ In another pan heat the sesame oil until very hot. Make a small well in the centre of the eel meat and pour in the oil, then sprinkle on the pepper. The hot oil will sizzle and make the dish very fragrant. Serve at once.

## Guangzhou 广州

# EEL STEWED IN A CLAY POT

*"When the north wind blows, the wind eel is plump" is an old Chinese saying. The wind eel is a highly nutritious seafood delicacy. Every winter the eels swim out from the Zhu Jiang River into the ocean where spawning takes place on the sea bed some 400 metres (1,300 feet) deep. The young fry later swim back to the mouth of the river where they continue to grow buried in the silt, emerging between the end of autumn and early winter when the north winds blow and the temperature falls. Thus they have become known as "feng shan", or wind eel.*

*Apart from pot roasting and stewing, wind eels are also eaten sliced and poached, steamboat-style, or made into a porridge with glutinous rice – a milk-coloured, rich, warming dish.*

1 x 750 g (1½ lb) feng shan eel or other meaty eel
1 tablespoon mushroom soy sauce
oil for deep-frying
155 g (5 oz) roasted or boiled belly pork (fresh bacon)
10 cloves garlic
6-8 dried black mushrooms, soaked for 25 minutes
6 slices fresh (root) ginger
2 pieces dried orange peel, soaked for 10 minutes
1 tablespoon cornflour (cornstarch)
1 tablespoon vegetable oil (optional)
fresh coriander (garnish)

SEASONING/STOCK

1 tablespoon rice wine or dry sherry
2 tablespoons superior or other light soy sauce
¼ teaspoon salt
¼ teaspoon white pepper
2 cups (500 mL/16 fl oz) hot fish stock (broth) or
    superior stock (*see page 124*)

Kill the eel by severing the head. Place in a strainer and pour on boiling water, then rinse thoroughly. Cut into 5 cm (2 in) pieces, rub with the mushroom soy sauce and leave for 10 minutes.

※ Slice the pork, peel the garlic and leave whole, drain and shred the mushrooms.

※ Heat the oil in a wok and fry the eel until well coloured. Using a slotted spoon, transfer the eel to a clay pot or casserole. Fry the pork and garlic in the oil until lightly coloured.

※ Arrange the pork, garlic, mushrooms, ginger and orange peel over the eel. Add the seasoning/stock ingredients, cover tightly and simmer for about 20 minutes until the eel is tender. Thicken with the cornflour mixed with a little cold water and add the vegetable oil, if used. Garnish with fresh coriander.

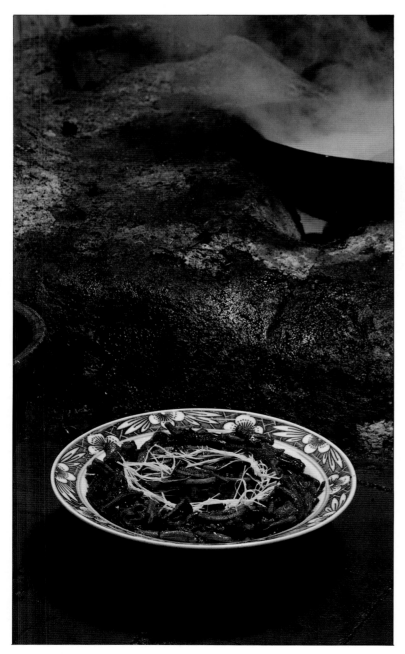

EEL SHREDS WITH SESAME OIL

EEL STEWED IN A CLAY POT

广州
Guangzhou

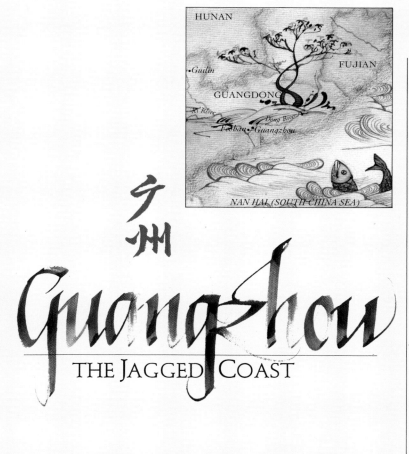

# Guangzhou
## THE JAGGED COAST

BETWEEN China's two major islands, Taiwan and Hainan, 1600 kilometres (1,000 miles) of jagged coastline curves in a gigantic arc. Taiwan, with its snowy peaks, rich rainforests and sandy beaches, straddles the straits off the province of Fujian. The island of Hainan, a tropical paradise where coconut palms wave above plantations of exotic fruit, guards the Gulf of Tonkin from the full fury of the Dai Fung, the typhoons that sweep in over the South China Sea. These two islands, and thousands of other less significant outcrops that speckle the coast, rim the southern flank of China. This indented coastline provides the rich bounty that forms the basis of China's best-known cuisine: Cantonese food, in all its diverse and splendid variety.

The coastline between the islands has everything that generous nature can bestow. Narrow river valleys broaden into fertile plains, and the sprawling estuary of the Pearl River delta provides a wonderland of twisting waterways where fish and fowl luxuriate. Countless coves and bays glow at night with the flaring twinkle of sampan lamps guiding juicy tiger prawns into the nets. On steep cliffs above azure waters fishermen tend long snap nets drooping from bamboo poles, ready to hoist ashore any school of fish unwary enough to venture past.

Out from land, on the expanse of the South China Sea, the sails of junks flap in the monsoon breeze as their nets haul taut behind. Most junks today have engines, but the romance of the sailing junk is inseparable from the legends of the China coast. Closer inshore, under the craggy rocks, tiny sampans bob in the surf as their occupants dangerously pluck shellfish from cliffs pounded by the waves. Seaweed, disdained and discarded in the West, is a profitable crop on the China coast. Jellyfish also grace the table along with sea urchins and slugs that crawl along the ocean bed.

More than half the area of the beautiful island of Hainan is an autonomous prefecture for the Li and Miao peoples. The market in their mountain capital of Tongshi offers a rewarding glimpse of their varied

A FISHING FLEET OFF HAINAN ISLAND
PAUL LAU

*(previous page)* SUNRISE OVER HAINAN ISLAND    PAUL LAU

THE YUSHAN MOUNTAINS, A MISTY BACKDROP TO THE MEI JIANG RIVER, JIANGXI PROVINCE                    LEO MEIER

WORKING IN THE FIELDS, JIANGXI PROVINCE

cuisine. Rice is the staple in this fertile paradise, but it is often accompanied by jungle delicacies such as stewed freshwater turtle or baked civet cat. Almost every Li household has a shotgun, and hunting is a passion. Even today, when much of the farmland grows rubber, sisal, peppers, cocoa, coffee and other tropical cash crops, the traditional hunting parties go out into the hills after game. The catch is still distributed in the ancient manner: the man who fired the successful shot gets a quarter and the rest of the quarry is divided between members of the hunting party, and any strangers they meet on the way home.

The southern coast, and more specifically the vast steamy delta of the Pearl River have given the Western world the flavour of Chinese food. This is not surprising, as most of the original American–Chinese came from this region: three hundred and fifty thousand Californians can trace their roots back to the county of Toishan, a former pirate haven and bandit den. The men from the delta left in a wave of despair to dig the gold mines of the sierras and hack the railroads across the Rocky Mountains. Foshan men went to the gold diggings in Australia, Hakka hill villagers left to grow pineapples in Hawaii and pan gold in New Zealand, and the Guangzhou city dwellers went to every port in the world. With them they took not only commercial cunning and a staggering ability to work, but also a gastronomic legacy that has enriched every land they reached.

The Cantonese cuisine found outside China is, however, unlike that of Guangdong Province. The dishes have been adapted to cater for local tastes: steamed chicken with bamboo shoots, for example, has a flavour in Sydney different to the dish of the same name served in San Francisco or Liverpool. It is no coincidence that all three of these great cities with their big Chinatowns are major ports, because it was by ship that the Guangdong

LEO MEIER

exodus reached the Western world, and it was by ship, when they had enough money to buy a tiny plot of the good earth of China, that they planned to come home. Very few left the delta with the intention of settling overseas. Their aim was to work to buy a wife and a plot of land back in their native village. But as the presence of thirty million overseas Chinese vividly testifies today, the dream of returning to the Middle Kingdom was for many of them a forlorn hope.

The land they left behind is very different these days from the piratical coast of the mid-nineteenth century. Nowhere in the entire country do climate and geography play a more vital role in shaping cuisine than along the jagged southern coastal rim. Food is fresh and bursting with vigour, juice and goodness. The astonishing bounty of the seas is rushed alive to market. In even the most humble of restaurants, live fish, crabs, prawns, lobsters and eels swim in large tanks before the eyes of appreciative diners. Seafood in the Cantonese kitchen has been elevated to an art. It is the supreme food of the southern school of cooking, the preparation of which calls for great skill. The love of fish is coupled with a compulsion for fresh food, so the main item on a menu is likely to be swimming in a fish tank one minute and the next served steaming on a platter with a whisper of spring onions and a hint of ginger.

To the adoration of seafood add a great desire for vegetables. Once again the gentle southern climate, hot and steamy for most of the year like some gigantic glass-

VIBRANT COSTUMES AT FOSHAN FESTIVAL, GUANGDONG PROVINCE          JACKY YIP

BOAT RACES AT FOSHAN FESTIVAL, GUANGDONG PROVINCE          JACKY YIP

HAINAN ISLAND

PAUL LAU

house given by the gods, provides the best that nature can offer. From lowland fields, which produce six crops of prime vegetables every year, farmers come to market bringing the splendid results of their labour. It is said that the Chinese agriculturalist is more a gardener than a farmer – perhaps, but the men and women who stoop endlessly over their patches of fertile earth are more lovers of the soil than simple gardeners. The earth is their passion as well as their pride. The summer rains soak deeply into the fertilised soil, the sun blazes, the tiller of the soil walks between the rows of glowing vegetables giving each plant its own private dousing from a bamboo watering can. The steam rises, the fruit hangs heavy in the summer noon, the very air reeks of fertility. The coastal rim and its inland valleys produce a range of vegetables probably unequalled on earth, and they are picked every day to be carried or trucked to markets in Fujian, Guangdong, Taiwan and Guangxi, where the housewives are unbending in their insistence on the freshest of foods, and refuse to contemplate cooking something not picked that very day.

The pride and the passion of the farmers is matched by the fanaticism to be found among the chefs in any southern kitchen. Cantonese cooks are the best in the world. Chefs in other provinces agree with this, and there is no higher praise than that. Cooking and eating the best that nature has to offer is a vital part of southern life. Much of that life is spent in the pursuit of excellent

A COLOURFUL DISH FROM GUANGXI PROVINCE             PAUL LAU

A FINE EXAMPLE OF CHINESE INTERIOR ART IN A GUANGZHOU DINING ROOM

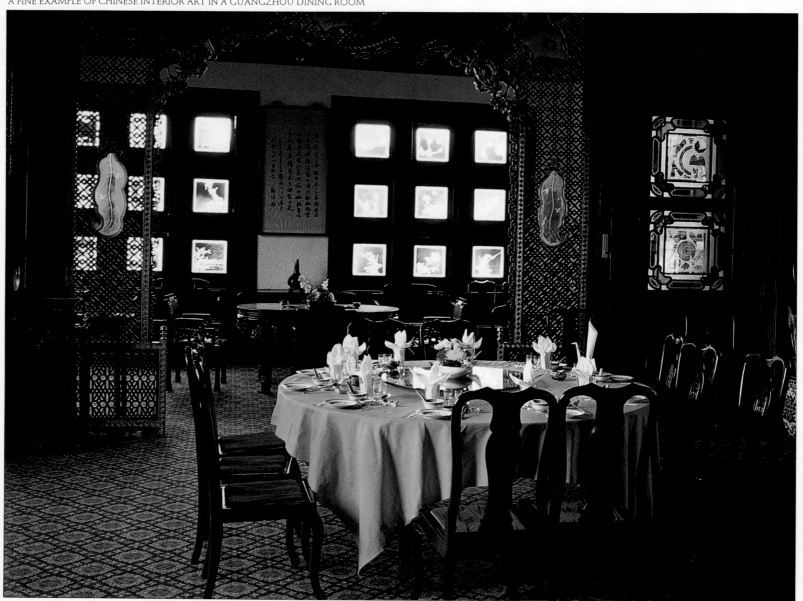

MICHAEL COOK

food. Day begins in many a city of the south with old men walking with their caged birds to special restaurants where their pets can twitter at each other as their owners eat. At the most famous teahouse on earth, the Panxi in Guangzhou, every morning long before public transport starts, regular breakfast customers walk great distances to stand in line to be first at the tables when the doors open at 6am. The Panxi is noted for its invention of thousands of new varieties of dim sum and, of course, everyone wants to be first to try the newest version of the ancient titbits.

Devotees of the southern kitchen like to announce to visitors that they will eat anything. The newcomer to their ways should not doubt it, or he might find himself feasting on owl, anteater or cobra, all firmly favoured by Cantonese gourmets. Wild cats and plump, black-tongued Chow dogs are also bred for the pot. "We eat anything whose backbone does not point to heaven" goes one old saying. True, but that was before men of the delta emigrated to South America and found the sloth that hangs upside down in trees, and discovered that this also provided the basis of a dainty treat.

"Be born in Suzhou" urges a traditional poem much quoted in the Pearl River delta. Suzhou, near Shanghai, is said to produce the most beautiful women in China. Be born in Suzhou; live in Hangzhou where the nation's finest silk comes from; die in Luzhou where the wood best suited for noble coffins grows; and eat where the best food in the world can be found – in the kitchens of Guangzhou, naturally.

The people of Guangzhou like to point out the predominant position they have held in the kitchens of China and the world over the centuries. Cantonese cuisine is, however, a varied mixture. Within the province of Guangdong alone there are major variations. The Hakka people, the gypsies of China who settled on the southern rim after fleeing from barbarian invaders in the north, have their own style of cooking. The gastronomic delights of Chiu Chow cuisine are in a class of their very own. Fujian Province rivals even Guangdong in its pursuit of treasures from the sea, and the aboriginal tribes on the east coast of Taiwan make a seafood soup that is more ambitious than the heartiest bouillabaisse to be found on the waterfront of Marseille.

The strength that underlies the region is provided by nature. From the sea, the land and the ponds that harbour fat carp and contented duck, the stress is on natural, fresh goodness. It is on this basis of fresh food that Cantonese cuisine is built. Along the entire coast nature's abundance has provided raw materials that make life easy for master chef and imaginative housewife alike. Few additional flavourings are needed: a hint of ginger, a small dash of salt, a gentle sprinkling of spring onions. The natural goodness and sweet taste of food straight from the garden or the water is the trademark of the famous Cantonese kitchen.

SUNSET OVER HAINAN ISLAND                                    PAUL LAU

(following page)
TERRACED HILL SIDES IN GUANGXI PROVINCE
PAUL LAU

NOMADS TEND THEIR SHEEP ON THE GRASSLANDS OF NORTHERN SICHUAN

LEONG KA TAI

肉類
Meat

# Meat 肉類

WHEN a Chinese chef talks of meat, it is almost certain that the animal to which he refers is the pig. In every corner of the land pork is the most common and preferred meat. The only exceptions are the Muslim areas of the northwest, and even there the increasing settlement of Han Chinese has led to pork becoming commonly available. It is no coincidence that in Chinese script the character for "home" consists of the ideogram for a "pig" under a "roof". For centuries the home was where the pig lived, often sharing a modest hut in a tiny village with its owner. Pigs are still common throughout China, although they are now raised by agronomists using more scientific methods as well as by farmers' wives in the barnyard.

Chefs use pork in at least seven out of every ten meat dishes. The reasons are historic, culinary and economic. Pigs are easy to raise and can live virtually anywhere there are people. They are cheap to feed, simple to care for and adaptable. They grow quickly and produce meat of high quality that can be sliced, shredded or cubed for any style of cooking. Pork has no strong flavour of its own, making it ideal to use as a base on which to build a combination dish with virtually any vegetable. It can be covered with honey and roasted whole, or ground to make the ideal raw ingredient for the beloved meatball. Indeed, if the pig did not exist a Chinese cook would have to invent it.

Pork in one guise or another appears prominently in every regional cuisine. A thousand years ago recipe books contained instructions for the dutiful housewife on how to prepare pork for sacrifices to ancestors and family deities. Today there is keen provincial rivalry about which area produces the best ham in China; but the most famous, with much justification, comes from Yunnan. The bacons of Hunan, laid out to dry in the winter sun, are renowned. Winter sausages, strongly akin to the spicy sausages of Hungary, are a speciality of Shanxi. Shanghai chefs use ground pork in soup and inside pastries; and heavy hearty dumplings – each large enough to feed three hungry people in the northern winter – are famous in Liaoning. Guangdong prides itself on whole suckling pigs suspended from a chain in a special kiln which bakes them crisply to produce the incomparable roast pork of Guangzhou. As the pig cooks,

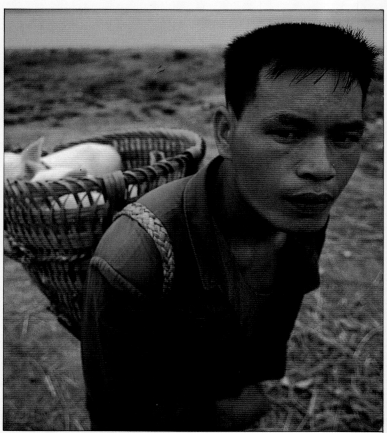

A PIG SELLER, SICHUAN PROVINCE                    PAUL LAU

the fat drains off to sizzle in a pan of water at the bottom of the huge upright oven which then fills with steam so the meat stays sweetly succulent as it roasts.

Pork may be predominant, but every other sort of meat has at one time or another, somewhere in the country, been enjoyed. Historically, beef has been rare in China. For the past two thousand years there simply has not been sufficient land to raise grazing herds. The only cattle generally seen by the average Chinese is the dignified old water buffalo, more a friend and a tool to the peasant farmer with whom the creature grows up and works the fields for most of its life. Only when old and useless, after years of toil which have developed muscles instead of meat, does the buffalo ever find its way into the pot, by which time it is disdainfully rejected by the gourmet.

A strongly held article of faith of many southerners is that they simply cannot abide the strong smell of sheep or goat. No such prejudices prevent the northerner from enjoying lamb, kid, sheep or goat. A dish that is a delight to a Beijing gourmet, like lamb fried with coriander, will be eaten swiftly and without pleasure by someone from Guangzhou who is taking it as a medicine instead of a meal. But although repelled by the thought of eating sheep, the southerner will go to considerable trouble and spend as much as necessary to enjoy a bowl of dog stew. This delicacy is not only believed to warm the blood and help the circulation during the chilly winter months, but is also a gastronome's joy.

Although they are the proud inheritors of the oldest agrarian tradition on earth, the Chinese have always been keen hunters. The hunt, strictly for the pot, is an interest that continues today all over the country except in the most densely populated areas. Even in provinces with huge populations there still remain large areas of mountain and forest where game is abundant. There is now no necessity for peasants to hunt to eat; starvation is no longer the spur, but the sport is enjoyed and rare creatures that are not grown domestically sometimes add spice to the family table. Venison, rabbit, bear, tiger, snake, boar, pangolin, mountain goat, hare and other game are prized species which feature prominently in ancient recipe books. Alas for the modern gourmet, they are now more difficult to find.

YAKS, A SOURCE OF MILK AND MEAT FOR NOMADIC TIBETAN TRIBES    LEO MEIER

GOATS AND OXEN GRAZE IN MOUNTAINOUS NORTHERN YUNNAN

GREGORY HEISLER

## Sichuan 四川

# APPETISERS IN A LACQUER BOX

*A banquet in Sichuan will often begin with an assortment of cold appetisers served in a multi-sectioned box made of lacquered wood. This classical and elegant presentation displays the efforts of the chef and the host, together with the traditional craft of lacquer work.*

*The contents of these boxes vary according to season, but each item must have a different taste and cooking method. Some may be salted, others quick-fried, others mixed. The cutting methods too must differ – slices, chunks, dice, strips, curls, rolls.*

*The colours must present attractive patterns and contrast. Flavours must complement – some mild, others strong.*

THIS SELECTION COMPRISES

Steamed, thinly sliced Yunnan ham
Salt-simmered duck with peeled broad beans
"Thousand-year" eggs
Cabbage rolls with dried chillies
Thinly sliced Chinese sausage
Sliced poached winter bamboo shoots
Dry-fried beef with Sichuan pepper and chillies
Diamonds of boiled winter melon interlaced with
    dried shrimp
Curls of spring onion centred with slivers of red chilli,
    served on a bed of edible black moss and dried shrimp

## Guangzhou 广州

# SKEWERED PORK DIPPED IN MALT SUGAR

*Slightly fatty pork should be used in this dish, otherwise it will burn and dry out during the cooking process. The malt sugar, brushed over the pork during roasting, gives a rich, red-brown glaze and adds a crisp texture and salty sweet taste.*

500 g (1 lb) pork leg with a little fat
3 tablespoons malt sugar
1/2 cup (125 mL/4 fl oz) boiling water

SEASONING

1 1/2 tablespoons light soy sauce
1 tablespoon dark or mushroom soy sauce
1 tablespoon Fen liquor, rice wine or dry sherry
2 tablespoons soy bean oil
1/4 teaspoon salt
1 tablespoon sugar
1 teaspoon sesame oil

Cut the meat into strips and place in a dish with the pre-mixed seasoning ingredients. Mix well and marinate for 2-3 hours, turning frequently.

Thread the strips of pork on a thick metal skewer and suspend them in a pre-heated hot oven (200°C/400°F) over a drip-tray to roast for 10 minutes.

Mix the malt sugar and boiling water together, stirring until the sugar has melted. Remove the pork from the oven and brush liberally with the syrup, then return to the oven to roast for a further 5 minutes. Brush again with syrup, roast again very briefly, then remove from the oven and brush with a final coating of syrup.

Cut into slices and arrange on a serving plate. Can be served warm or cold.

(*inset*) APPETISERS IN A LACQUER BOX

SKEWERED PORK DIPPED IN MALT SUGAR

LOTUS EGGS WITH BARBECUED PORK

DEEP-FRIED SHREDDED PORK

## Guangzhou 广州

# LOTUS EGGS WITH BARBECUED PORK

*The lotus "grows out of the mud but is not stained. It stands firmly against the wind, elegantly beautiful and mildly scented." Many famous people praised the lotus and even compared it to the beauty of women. In Guangdong cuisine, when egg is an important ingredient in a dish, the name of the dish often incorporates the word lotus (fuyong). This alludes to the resemblance of the egg's delicate texture and pale colour to the beauty of the lotus.*

2 eggs
4 egg whites
125 g (4 oz) barbecued pork
45 g (1½ oz) fresh or canned bamboo shoots
2 spring onions (shallots/scallions), white parts only
2-3 tablespoons lard or oil for frying
¾ teaspoon salt
pinch of pepper

Beat the eggs and egg whites together thoroughly and set aside.

Cut the barbecued pork, bamboo shoots and spring onions into fine shreds. Heat the lard or oil in a wok and sauté the shredded ingredients briefly.

Season the egg with salt and pepper, pour over the shredded ingredients and cook over moderate heat, stirring only occasionally, until golden brown underneath. Turn the whole omelet without cutting and gently cook the other side until the egg is just firm, then slide onto a serving dish.

## Beijing 北京

# DEEP-FRIED SHREDDED PORK

315 g (10 oz) pork fillet
½ cup (60 g/2 oz) cornflour (cornstarch)
2½ cups (625 mL/20 fl oz) peanut oil
¼ small red capsicum (bell pepper), shredded
¼ small green capsicum (bell pepper), shredded
2 spring onions (shallots/scallions), white parts only, shredded
1 teaspoon chilli oil or chilli sauce

### SEASONING

1 tablespoon light soy sauce
2 teaspoons ginger juice
2 teaspoons rice wine or dry sherry
2 teaspoons brown vinegar
½ teaspoon salt

Cut the pork fillet into paper-thin slices, then into shreds, finer than matchsticks. Mix the cornflour with enough cold water to make a thin paste. Add the pork and mix well until each shred is thinly coated with the paste.

Heat the peanut oil in a wok to smoking point and deep-fry the pork shreds until crisp, using wooden chopsticks to separate the shreds. The pork will turn a light golden brown and rustle slightly when drained, as soon as it is done. Remove and set aside.

Drain the oil, leaving about 1 tablespoon, add the pre-mixed seasoning ingredients and bring to the boil. Return the fried pork and stir-fry in the sauce until evenly coated, add the capsicums and onions and toss all together, then sprinkle on the chilli oil, toss well and transfer to a serving plate.

## Sichuan 四川

# PORK WITH SICHUAN PRESERVED CABBAGE

*Chinese preserved cabbage, and especially that from Fulin in Sichuan, is famous for its unique flavour and has been exported all over the world. In the preparation it is seasoned with a great variety of condiments, in particular fennel, pepper, licorice root, Chinese cassia, chilli, salt and spirits.*

185 g (6 oz) Sichuan preserved cabbage
375 g (12 oz) pork fillet (tenderloin)
1 leek or 2-3 spring onions (shallots/scallions)
3 slices fresh (root) ginger
1-2 fresh red chillies
3 tablespoons lard or vegetable oil

### SEASONING

1 tablespoon light soy sauce
2 tablespoons rice wine or dry sherry
1 tablespoon cornflour (cornstarch)
½ teaspoon sugar

Soak the salted cabbage in cold water for 1 hour. Drain and squeeze out as much water as possible, then cut into strips of about 5 x 1 cm (2 x ½ in) and set aside.

Very thinly slice the pork, cutting across the grain, then stack the slices and cut them into fine shreds. Place in a dish with the pre-mixed seasoning ingredients, mix well and leave for 20 minutes.

Cut the leek, ginger and chillies into fine shreds.

Heat the lard in a wok to smoking point. Stir-fry the pork and cabbage together until the pork changes colour. Push to one side of the pan and add the remaining ingredients, stir-frying for 1 minute. Mix with the pork and cabbage, add 1 tablespoon of water, check the seasoning and serve.

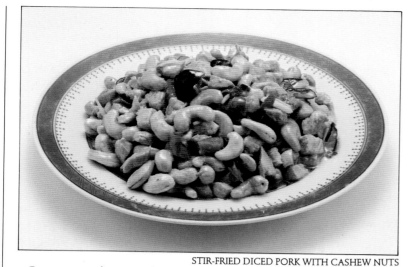

STIR-FRIED DICED PORK WITH CASHEW NUTS

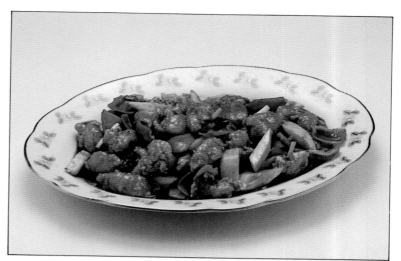

SWEET AND SOUR PORK

## Guangzhou 广州

# STIR-FRIED DICED PORK WITH CASHEW NUTS

*The cashew nut grows abundantly in sub-tropical climates. Its strange looking fruit consists of two parts: the upper part called the "pear" or "false fruit" is soft and juicy with the flavour of musk, and is eaten as a fruit; the lower part comprises the shell and crescent-shaped kernel of the cashew.*

*Deep-fried cashew nuts are extremely crisp, with a flavour surpassing peanuts which are often used in Chinese cooking.*

315 g (10 oz) lean pork
2 spring onions (shallots/scallions)
1/3 red capsicum (bell pepper)
1/3 green capsicum (bell pepper)
2 cloves garlic
2 dried black mushrooms, soaked for 25 minutes
oil for deep-frying
90-125 g (3-4 oz) raw cashew nuts

### SEASONING

1 teaspoon rice wine or dry sherry
1/2 teaspoon salt
3/4 teaspoon sugar
2 teaspoons cornflour (cornstarch)

### SAUCE

1/3 cup (75 mL/2 1/2 fl oz) chicken stock (broth) or water
1 teaspoon dark soy sauce
1/2 teaspoon salt
1/2 teaspoon sugar
pinch of white pepper
1 teaspoon cornflour (cornstarch)

Dice the pork finely, add the seasoning ingredients, mix well and leave for 20 minutes.

Cut the spring onions into short lengths, dice the capsicums, finely chop the garlic and squeeze the water from the mushrooms before cutting into small dice.

Heat the oil in a large wok and deep-fry the pork in a frying basket or large perforated ladle for about 3 minutes until cooked through. Remove and drain well. Deep-fry the cashew nuts until they begin to colour and remove quickly. Do not overcook or they will be bitter. Set aside.

Drain the wok, reserving about 1 tablespoon of the oil, and stir-fry the vegetables and garlic for 2-3 minutes. Mix the sauce ingredients together and pour into the wok, stirring to thicken. Add the pork and toss together until well coated with the sauce and mixed with the vegetables.

Transfer to a serving plate and arrange the cashews on top. Serve at once.

## Guangzhou 广州

# SWEET AND SOUR PORK

280 g (9 oz) pork belly (fresh bacon)
1/2 teaspoon salt
2 teaspoons rice wine or dry sherry
1 egg, well beaten
1 medium green capsicum (bell pepper)
60 g (2 oz) fresh or canned bamboo shoots
2-3 spring onions (shallots/scallions)
3 cloves garlic
1 cup (125 g/4 oz) cornflour (cornstarch)
oil for deep-frying
1/2 teaspoon sesame oil (optional)

### SWEET AND SOUR SAUCE

2 tablespoons sugar
1 tablespoon oil for frying
3 tablespoons brown vinegar
1/2 cup (125 mL/4 fl oz) stock (broth)
salt and pepper
1 teaspoon cornflour (cornstarch)

Use a sharp knife to closely crosshatch the pork skin, then cut the meat into cubes, each with a piece of skin attached. Place in a dish with the salt, rice wine and egg, mix well and set aside.

Cut the capsicum in half, remove the seeds, stem and inner ribs and cut into squares. Thinly slice the bamboo shoots and the spring onions and finely chop the garlic.

Place the cornflour in a plastic bag, add the pork and shake vigorously to coat thickly and evenly, transfer to a colander and shake off the excess.

Heat the oil in a wok to smoking point and deep-fry the pork for 1 minute, then lower the heat slightly and continue to fry for about 3 minutes until well cooked and crisp on the surface. Remove and drain well.

Drain off the oil and wipe out the wok. Return 2 tablespoons of the oil and stir-fry the capsicum, bamboo shoots, spring onions and garlic for about 1 1/2 minutes. Add the pork and mix well, then remove to a plate.

Pour the sugar and oil of the sauce ingredients into the wok and cook until it turns a light caramel colour, stirring minimally. Add the vinegar and remaining sauce ingredients and bring to the boil, stirring.

Return the pork and vegetables, stir in the sauce until evenly coated, sprinkle on the sesame oil and serve.

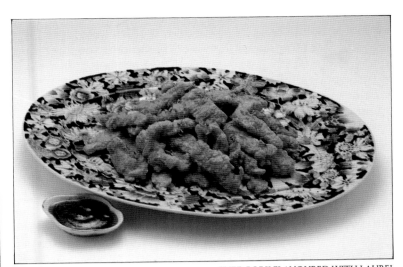

FRIED PORK FLAVOURED WITH LAUREL

PORK "COINS" WITH HONEY

## *Shanghai* 上海

# FRIED PORK FLAVOURED WITH LAUREL

*Flowering laurel is a treasured aromatic plant in China, being used for ornamental and medicinal purposes. Chefs often use the flowers in cooking to enhance the colour, taste and aroma of the food. The pork in this dish is golden, light and tender, with the added fragrance of laurel flowers. Served with a sweet and sour sauce and peppercorn salt it is especially delicious, and is a traditional speciality of the Shanghai area.*

280 g (9 oz) lean pork
2 eggs
¾ cup (90 g/3 oz) cornflour (cornstarch)
oil or lard for deep-frying
2 spring onions (shallots/scallions), white parts only
1 teaspoon sesame oil
silver laurel flowers
peppercorn salt*

SEASONING

1 tablespoon light soy sauce
1 tablespoon rice wine or dry sherry
1 tablespoon finely chopped spring onion (shallot/scallion)
¼ teaspoon salt

SAUCE

1 tablespoon light soy sauce
2 teaspoons rice wine or dry sherry
1 teaspoon sugar

Cut the pork into thin slices and pound with the side of a cleaver or a rolling pin to flatten and tenderise, then cut into strips. Place in a dish and add the pre-mixed seasoning ingredients, mix well and leave for 20 minutes.
❈ Beat the eggs and mix into a batter, adding the cornflour.
❈ Heat the oil in a wok over moderate heat. Dip the pork into the batter, then deep-fry in the oil for about 1 minute. Remove and drain well. Increase the heat and fry the pork again for about 20 seconds. Remove, drain and fry again, cooking until the surface is crisp and the pork cooked through. Remove and drain well.
❈ Finely chop the spring onions.
❈ Heat a clean wok and add a little oil. Stir-fry the spring onions with the pork, adding the sesame oil. Add the pre-mixed sauce ingredients and toss the pork over high heat until the sauce is absorbed. Sprinkle on the laurel flowers, stir in and serve with the peppercorn salt as a dip.

*To make peppercorn salt, dry-fry 1 teaspoon of Sichuan peppercorns (Fagara or Sansho) in a wok until fragrant, then grind finely. Heat 1 tablespoon of fine table salt in the wok, add the pepper, mix together and cool before using.*

## *Beijing* 北京

# PORK "COINS" WITH HONEY

*The name of this dish derives from the way the meat is skewered for cooking. When removed from the skewer each piece of meat has a hole in the centre similar to an old Chinese coin.*

*Although the meat is barbecued over an open fire, the interlayered pork fat prevents the normally dry fillet from becoming parched and tough.*

500 g (1 lb) pork fillet (tenderloin)
250 g (8 oz) duck livers or fresh ham
750 g (1½ lb) pork fat
½ cup (155 g/5 oz) clear honey
½ cup (125 mL/4 fl oz) peanut oil

PORK MARINADE

1 egg white, lightly beaten
1 tablespoon dark soy sauce
1 tablespoon rice wine or dry sherry
1½ tablespoons sugar
1 teaspoon five-spice powder
pinch of salt

PORK FAT MARINADE

2 teaspoons rice wine or dry sherry
2 teaspoons sugar
1 teaspoon salt

Cut the pork, livers and fat into thin slices, then shape into rounds of approximately 4 cm (1¾ in) diameter. Place the pork fillet and the pork fat in separate dishes and add their respective pre-mixed marinade ingredients, mix well and leave for 20 minutes.
❈ Use thick metal skewers or wooden butchers' rods soaked for one hour in water to prevent them burning during barbecueing and rub them with oil. Thread the pork, liver and fat in alternate layers along the rods.
❈ Cook over a moderately hot charcoal fire, brushing alternately with honey and oil to keep them moist. Or roast in a preheated oven at 180°C (350°F) for about 30 minutes, turning several times during cooking. Serve at once.

## Guangzhou 广州

# BARBECUED PORK

*Skewered and barbecued meat, usually lamb, is a speciality of the wandering tribes of the north-western regions of China. The southern Chinese have devised a similar recipe using pork, which they prefer to lamb. The ingredients used to flavour the meat impart a sweetish taste, a bright red-brown colour and a crispness to the surface. Cooked over charcoal, the meat gets a mouthwateringly delicious smoky taste. It can be served as a main course or as a starter with drinks.*

1 kg (2 lb) lean pork (loin or hand/picnic shoulder)
fresh pineapple (garnish)
cucumber (garnish)

### SEASONING/GLAZE

⅔ cup (125 g/4 oz) malt sugar
3 tablespoons boiling water
1 tablespoon light soy sauce
1 tablespoon oyster sauce
2 tablespoons rice wine or dry sherry
1 teaspoon sesame oil
½ teaspoon salt
½ teaspoon orange or red food colouring (optional)

Cut the pork into long strips about 4 cm (2 in) wide, and place in a dish. Mix the seasoning/glaze ingredients together, first mixing the malt sugar and boiling water until dissolved. Pour over the pork and leave for at least 5 hours, turning from time to time.

❊ Prepare a charcoal fire or pre-heat an oven to 240°C (460°F). Hang the strips of meat on metal butchers' hooks and suspend over the fire, or hang from a rack in the oven, placing a drip-tray underneath.

❊ Roast for about 15 minutes, then remove and brush thickly with the remaining marinade. Return to the oven to complete roasting until just cooked through and very crisp on the surface.

❊ Cut into thick slices and pile onto a serving plate. Surround with pineapple and cucumber. Serve warm or cold.

BARBECUED PORK

PORK IN WINE LEES

KIDNEY SLICES WITH SESAME PASTE DRESSING

## Guangzhou 广州

# PORK IN WINE LEES

*In Chinese cooking, the chef pays careful attention to the choice and use of seasoning ingredients, the red fermented rice used in this recipe being one such speciality. This is polished glutinous rice prepared through a process of steaming, fermenting and filtration, and is a local product of Fujian Province. It is bright red and has the fragrant smell of wine, and is often known as wine lees. Fujian dishes are characterised by their frequent use of this ingredient.*

315 g (10 oz) pork fillet
1 medium-sized cucumber
2 egg whites, lightly beaten
3 tablespoons cornflour (cornstarch)
3 tablespoons red fermented rice (wine lees)
250 g (8 oz) lard

SEASONING/SAUCE

¾ cup (175 mL/6 fl oz) chicken stock (broth)
2 tablespoons rice wine or dry sherry
1½ teaspoons sugar
¾ teaspoon salt
2 teaspoons cornflour (cornstarch)

Cut the pork fillet and unpeeled cucumber into small cubes, discarding any tendons and sinews from the meat and the seeds from the cucumber.

Mix the pork with the egg whites, then place in a plastic bag and add the cornflour. Shake briskly until the meat is well coated with the flour, then transfer to a plate and add the red fermented rice, mixing in well.

Heat the lard in a wok and stir-fry the pork over high heat until bright red, separating pieces that stick together. Add the cucumber and stir-fry briefly, then remove the pork and cucumber and drain off the fat.

Return the pork and cucumber and add the pre-mixed seasoning/sauce ingredients, stirring over high heat for about 45 seconds before serving.

## Beijing 北京

# KIDNEY SLICES WITH SESAME PASTE DRESSING

*The cooking method described in the following recipe is unusual. The thin slices of kidney are scalded several times in boiling water, dipped in the sesame paste dressing and then served. The scalding removes the strong taste and aroma of the kidneys while cooking it just enough to preserve its delicate texture.*

2 pork kidneys
salt
1 teaspoon rice wine or dry sherry
cucumber slices

DRESSING

½ teaspoon sesame oil
2 teaspoons dark soy sauce
2 tablespoons sesame paste (tahini)
1 tablespoon sugar
pinch of salt

Cut the kidneys in halves horizontally to expose the inner core of white fat. Remove this and the connected veins, and place the kidneys in a dish of cold water to soak for several hours. Change the water 3-4 times. Drain well, then slice the kidneys very thinly.

Bring a saucepan of water to the boil. Scald the kidneys for just a few seconds, then remove and drain. Boil a second pot of water and scald again, just long enough for them to lose their pink colour. Drain well and sprinkle with a little salt and rice wine.

Mix the dressing ingredients together, adding cold water if the paste is very thick – depending on the brand of sesame paste used.

Arrange slices of cucumber on a serving plate and pile the kidney slices on top, pour on the sesame paste and serve.

PORK SHREDS AND CAPSICUM

BALSAM PEAR WITH PORK AND PRAWN FILLING

## Sichuan 四川

# PORK SHREDS AND CAPSICUM

*Capsicum, also called "lantern" or "bell" pepper, has a sweet, yet slightly hot taste. Pickled red capsicum is served with many Sichuan meals as a side dish, as it is said to stimulate the appetite. Being a good source of Vitamin C, and growing and bearing fruit readily, it has been an essential part of the Sichuan cuisine for many centuries.*

250 g (8 oz) pork fillet (tenderloin)
1 large or 2 small red capsicums (bell peppers)
90 g (3 oz) canned or cooked fresh bamboo shoots
6 garlic chives
4 slices young fresh (root) ginger
2 tablespoons cornflour (cornstarch)
3 tablespoons lard, vegetable or rapeseed oil

SEASONING/SAUCE

²⁄₃ cup (150 mL/5 fl oz) chicken or veal stock (broth)
1 tablespoon light soy sauce
2 teaspoons rice wine or dry sherry
½ teaspoon salt
pinch of white pepper
1 teaspoon cornflour (cornstarch)

Slice the pork into paper thin slices, cutting across the grain, then stack the slices into piles of five or six, cut into matchstick shreds and set aside.

🥢 Cut the capsicums in halves, trim and cut lengthways into narrow shreds. Cut the bamboo shoots, garlic chives and ginger into similar-sized pieces.

🥢 Stir the cornflour into the pork shreds, coating them evenly.

🥢 Heat the wok over moderate heat and stir-fry the capsicum shreds without oil until browned on the edges and half tender. Add a large pinch of salt, stir, then remove.

🥢 Add the lard and stir-fry the pork over high heat until white. Add the bamboo, garlic chives and ginger and stir-fry for another minute, then add the pre-mixed seasoning/sauce ingredients and return the capsicum. Simmer, stirring, until the sauce thickens and clears, then serve.

## Guangzhou 广州

# BALSAM PEAR WITH PORK AND PRAWN FILLING

*Balsam pears are said to be able to lighten the heart and brighten eyesight, promote respiration and reduce fever. There is a folk song in Guangdong which goes: "They say the balsam pear is bitter/But I take it to be sweet/Sweet or bitter to your choice/How can there be sweetness without bitterness?" This implies that the bitter balsam pear (commonly referred to as Chinese bitter melon) can be made sweet. The bitter taste of the balsam pear is not, however, passed on to other ingredients cooked with it. Hence it is said to possess a "gentleman's behaviour".*

3-4 balsam pears (Chinese bitter melons)
pinch of bicarbonate of soda (baking soda)
185 g (6 oz) fatty pork
90 g (3 oz) fresh prawn (shrimp) meat
½ teaspoon salt
cornflour (cornstarch)
oil for frying

SAUCE

1 tablespoon fermented black beans
3 cloves garlic
1 teaspoon finely chopped fresh (root) ginger
2 teaspoons rice wine or dry sherry
2 teaspoons mushroom soy sauce
1 teaspoon sugar
pinch of white pepper
½ cup (125 mL/4 fl oz) chicken stock (broth)
1 teaspoon cornflour (cornstarch)

Cut the balsam pears into 1.5 cm (½ in) slices, scoop out the seeds and fibrous centres, then place in a saucepan with cold water to cover. Add the bicarbonate of soda and bring to the boil. Simmer until the pears are beginning to soften, then drain.

🥢 Very finely mince (grind) the pork and prawn meat to a smooth paste, using two cleavers simultaneously, or a food processor. Add the salt and mix well. Dust the inside of the pear rings with cornflour and fill with the pork and prawn paste, smoothing the tops. Coat lightly with cornflour.

🥢 Heat about 1.5 cm (½ in) of oil in a flat pan and fry the pears gently on both sides, until the filling is crisp on the surface and the pear rings are bright green and tender. Remove from the pan, drain and arrange on a serving plate.

🥢 Drain the pan, reserving about 2 tablespoons of the oil. Finely chop the black beans and garlic and fry briefly in the hot oil, add the ginger and fry briefly again. Add the wine and soy sauce, then after a few seconds add the sugar, pepper and the stock mixed with the cornflour. Bring to the boil, stirring, then pour over the prepared dish and serve at once.

## Guangzhou 广州

# Roast Suckling Pig

*Roast suckling pig is a renowned traditional Chinese delicacy. During the fifth century, it was considered by the common people to be "Yao Shu" (important art). In the Qing Dynasty (1644-1911 AD), it was one of the dishes featured in banquets held at the Qing Palace, and even today, roast suckling pig appears only at grand banquets and is always considered one of the highlights of the meal.*

*The pig has a characteristic bright red colouring, a sweetish flavour and skin that is smooth as glass, yet crisp and feather light. Special large iron forks are used to hold the prepared pig over glowing charcoal, and it is slowly rotated – usually by hand – until cooked to perfection. In a quality restaurant one of the masterchefs will often tend the roasting over a tub of charcoal on the verandah or footpath outside the restaurant.*

1 x 6-8 kg (12-16 lb) suckling pig (to serve about 24)
1 cup (185 g/6 oz) malt sugar
½ cup (125 mL/4 fl oz) red vinegar
boiling water

SEASONING

1 tablespoon crushed garlic
½ cup (155 g/5 oz) bean paste
½ cup (155 g/5 oz) sesame paste (tahini)
½ cup (125 mL/4 fl oz) sweet vinegar
3 tablespoons Fed liquor, rice wine or dry sherry
3 tablespoons peanut oil
½ cup (125 mL/4 fl oz) soy bean milk
1 tablespoon mushroom soy sauce
½ cup (125 g/4 oz) sugar

Have the butcher slit the pig down the centre underneath, cutting through the head as well so that the whole pig can be pressed out as flat as possible. Pierce with a large iron fork which will hold the pig open, or devise a cooking method which suits your equipment or circumstances. Have ready a large quantity of charcoal for roasting.

⚒ Hold the pig over the sink and pour over plenty of boiling water. This will contract the skin and help make it crisp. Mix the malt sugar and red vinegar with enough boiling water to make a thick syrup and paint this over the skin of the pig. Hang in an airy place for several hours until the skin feels dryish to the touch.

⚒ Mix the seasoning ingredients together, stirring until the sugar has dissolved and all ingredients are well blended. Coat the pig thickly on the underside with some of the seasoning mixture and rub the remainder over the skin.

⚒ Roast slowly over glowing charcoal until no pink liquid runs off when the pig is pierced through the thickest part of the thigh. This will take several hours. During cooking, pierce any bubbles which appear on the skin with a large needle or skewer to ensure the skin remains flat and smooth.

⚒ There is a traditional way to serve this delicious dish. First, slice the crisp red skin from the back of the pig, place the whole pig on a large platter and put the skin back in place. At the first serving, only the skin will be eaten. Return the pig to the kitchen where the choicest pieces of meat will be cut into serving portions and reassembled on the carcass. This is presented as the second course.

⚒ The first and second courses are usually accompanied by multi-layered white buns or thin pancakes and dips of sweetened soy sauce or sweet bean paste. Spring onion (shallot/scallion) bulbs or curls, and crisp sweet-sour pickled vegetables, such as beetroot, cucumber, turnip or radish, are also served. The meat is dipped into the sauce, then eaten with the bread or pancake and a piece each of vegetable and onion. This combination of ingredients counteracts the richness of the pork and provides an interesting contrast of tastes and textures.

⚒ Finally, the bones may be simmered and made into a rich broth, or the remaining pieces of meat stir-fried – usually with ginger and onions – to make a third course.

ROAST SUCKLING PIG

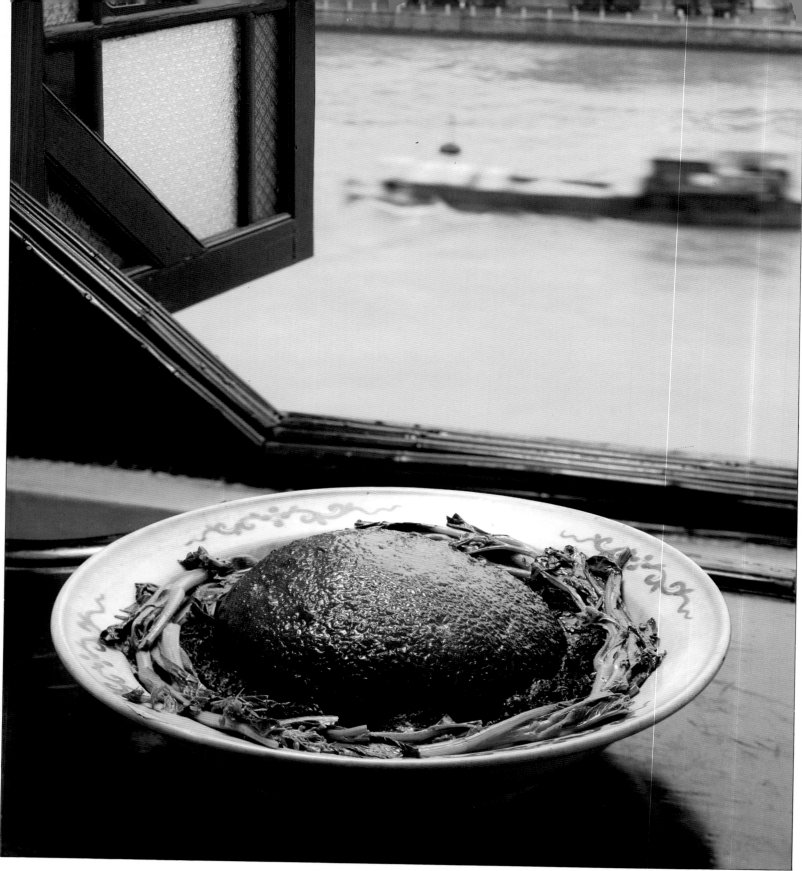

BRAISED RUMP OF PORK

## Guangzhou 广州

# BRAISED RUMP OF PORK

1 kg (2 lb) pork rump (upper leg/fresh ham)
8 cups (2 L/64 fl oz) oil for deep-frying
8 slices fresh (root) ginger
4-5 spring onions (shallots/scallions)
12 dried black mushrooms, soaked for 25 minutes
250 g (8 oz) choy sum or other Chinese green vegetable
vegetable oil

### SEASONING/SAUCE

3 tablespoons light soy sauce
1 tablespoon dark soy sauce
1 tablespoon rice wine or dry sherry
1½ teaspoons salt
1 tablespoon sugar
1 teaspoon sesame oil

Wipe the skin of the pork with kitchen paper. Heat the oil in a large wok and when quite hot, deep-fry the pork, skin side downwards, until it turns a light golden colour and bubbles have appeared on the skin. Take care at this stage, as the frying pork is inclined to spatter. Lift out and place immediately in a casserole half filled with cold water. This causes the skin to ripple and it will be very tender when braised.

❖ Add the ginger, whole spring onions, drained mushrooms and the seasoning ingredients. Cover and bring to the boil, then simmer gently for about 2 hours until the meat is very tender.

❖ Trim the choy sum or other vegetables and stir-fry in a hot wok with a little vegetable oil. Add 2-3 tablespoons of water, cover and cook until almost tender.

❖ Arrange around the edge of a serving dish. Place the pork in the centre, and slice. Arrange the mushrooms over the meat and pour over a generous serving of sauce.

## Shanghai 上海

# MEATBALLS IN MYRICA BERRY SHAPES

*Including the juice of the myrica berry in the preparation of meatballs is a speciality of Anhui Province. They are both sweet and sour, invigorating and useful for treating hangovers.*

*The Chinese have an expression, "looking at the berry quenches one's thirst", which derives from the late Han Dynasty, around the year 200 AD, when General Cao Cao was leading his exhausted soldiers on a long march. To revitalise them he told them of a forest of berry trees ahead, their spirits picked up and they marched swiftly towards their imaginary goal.*

410 g (13 oz) pork belly (fresh bacon)
3 tablespoons myrica berry juice, tamarind water
    or a tart mixture of fruit and lemon juice
1 cup (125 g/4 oz) dry breadcrumbs
4 cups (1 L/32 fl oz) oil for deep-frying

SAUCE

¾ cup (175 mL/6 fl oz) water
2 tablespoons sugar
2 tablespoons vinegar
pinch of salt
2 teaspoons light soy sauce
2 teaspoons cornflour (cornstarch)
1 tablespoon lard

Finely mince (grind) the pork and mix with the fruit juice. Form into small balls and coat with the breadcrumbs.

✿ Heat the oil in a wok to smoking point and put in one-third of the meatballs. Deep-fry until cooked through and golden brown, for about 3 minutes, then cook the remainder in two batches.

✿ Insert a small twig or toothpick into the top of each meatball so that they resemble myrica berries or small plums, and pile on a serving plate.

✿ Boil the sauce ingredients in another wok, stirring until thickened. Pour over the meatballs and serve.

MEATBALLS IN MYRICA BERRY SHAPES

PORK TWICE-COOKED

## Sichuan 四川

# PORK TWICE-COOKED

*Sichuan cooking makes much use of pork. Records show that even six thousand years ago the inhabitants of Ba and Shu (the ancient names of the east and west parts of Sichuan) kept domesticated pigs.*

*The following recipe, incorporating two separate cooking processes, is especially good with pork. It eliminates some of the fat, making it easier to digest and very tender.*

375 g (12 oz) belly pork (fresh bacon)
1 medium-sized red capsicum (bell pepper)
60 g (2 oz) canned or cooked fresh bamboo shoots
2 spring onions (shallots/scallions) or garlic chives
4 slices fresh (root) ginger
2 tablespoons lard

SEASONING

1 tablespoon sweet bean paste
2 teaspoons hot bean paste
1 tablespoon light soy sauce
1 teaspoon mushroom soy sauce
1½ teaspoons sugar
2 teaspoons rice wine or dry sherry
2 tablespoons water

Place the pork, skin upwards, on a rack in a wok or in a steamer over simmering water. Cover and steam gently for about 25 minutes until the pork is soft, but not completely cooked through.

✿ Cut the capsicum and bamboo shoots into squares, the spring onions or garlic chives into 2.5 cm (1 in) lengths, and shred the ginger.

✿ Remove the pork from the steamer and leave for about 20 minutes to cool and firm up.

✿ Use a very sharp knife to cut the pork into thin slices, then into pieces about 5 cm (2 in) long. The slices should curl up like rose petals during frying.

✿ Heat the lard in a wok and stir-fry the capsicum and bamboo shoots until softened, then add the spring onions or garlic chives and ginger and stir-fry briefly. Push to one side of the pan or remove, and stir-fry the pork slices until cooked through and crisp on the edges. The fat should turn translucent, like bacon fat. Mix in the pre-mixed seasoning ingredients and stir-fry with the capsicum and other vegetables over high heat for about 1½ minutes, then serve.

CANDIED FRIED PORK

PORK WITH FRUIT SAUCE

## Beijing 北京

# CANDIED FRIED PORK

375 g (12 oz) belly pork (fresh bacon)
6 cups (1½ L/48 fl oz) chicken stock (broth)
125 g (4 oz) Chinese rock candy or caramelised white sugar
1 teaspoon finely chopped fresh red chilli
1 tablespoon finely chopped spring onion (shallot/scallion)
oil for deep-frying

BATTER

2 egg whites, well beaten
½ cup (60 g/2 oz) flour
½ cup (60 g/2 oz) cornflour (cornstarch)

Cover the belly pork with stock and simmer gently for about 1 hour until very tender. Cool in the stock, drain and remove the fat. Cut the meat into slices approximately 5 x 2 cm (2 x 1 in).
Crush the rock candy finely and set aside.
Mix the egg whites, flour and cornflour to make a batter of coating consistency (add a little cold water if needed). Dip the pork into the batter and deep-fry several pieces at a time until golden and crisp on the surface. Drain and keep warm.
Heat the rock sugar in a heavy wok or saucepan until it caramelises. Add the chilli and spring onion, turn off the heat and turn each piece of meat in the caramel until coated.
Arrange on a lightly oiled plate and serve at once.

## Guangzhou 广州

# PORK WITH FRUIT SAUCE

280 g (9 oz) boneless lean pork
1 egg, well beaten
1 cup (125 g/4 oz) cornflour (cornstarch)
oil for deep-frying
12 prawn crackers (krupuk)
1 cup (250 mL/8 fl oz) pineapple or apricot juice
½ teaspoon sesame oil

SEASONING

2 teaspoons rice wine or dry sherry
½ teaspoon salt
1 teaspoon grated fresh (root) ginger
1 tablespoon finely chopped spring onion (shallot/scallion)

Cut the pork into slices and place on a board. Pound with the side of a cleaver or a rolling pin to tenderise. Place in a dish, add the pre-mixed seasoning ingredients, mix well and leave for 20 minutes.
Add the egg to the above ingredients, mix well and then coat each slice thickly with cornflour.

Heat the oil in a large wok to smoking point. Deep-fry the pork slices for about 3 minutes, until crisp and well coloured on the surface, stirring constantly to prevent them from sticking together. Lift out and drain well.
Fry the prawn crackers in the oil until puffed up and lightly coloured, lift out and drain. Arrange in the centre of a serving plate.
Pour off the oil and return the meat, adding the fruit juice. Simmer until the juice has been absorbed, then transfer to a plate. Sprinkle with the sesame oil and serve at once.

## Beijing 北京

# PLAIN BOILED PORK SLICES

*This dish was introduced with the Manchurians who conquered and ruled the country as the Qing Dynasty (1644-1911 AD). It was a custom during that era for the king to bestow his favour on the subjects who came to wish him happiness during New Year by treating them to this simple, but delicious dish. Similarly Manchurian nobility offered this speciality at weddings and other festive occasions. Each person would cut meat for himself from a large piece of pork and guests were invited to eat as much as they could. The more one ate of this dish, the more delighted the host would be.*

1 kg (2 lb) meatier portion of pork hand (picnic shoulder)
1 teaspoon salt

BROWN BEAN SAUCE DIP

1 tablespoon brown bean sauce
1 teaspoon sugar
1 teaspoon sesame oil

GARLIC SAUCE DIP

3 cloves garlic, crushed
1 teaspoon salt
1 tablespoon vegetable oil

CHILLI SAUCE DIP

1 fresh red chilli, finely chopped
2 tablespoons light soy sauce

Place the pork in a wok with the skin downwards, add the salt and cover with water. Bring to the boil, cover and simmer for at least 2 hours until the pork is very tender. A chopstick will easily penetrate the skin when the pork is cooked through. Remove from the heat but leave in the stock to cool.
Cut off the skin and part of the fat before cutting the pork into paper-thin slices. Arrange in overlapping rows on a serving plate.
Mix the sauce ingredients together and serve as cold dips in small dishes.

DICED PORK, STIR-FRIED WITH SOY BEAN PASTE AND CAPSICUM

## Shanghai 上海

# DICED PORK, STIR-FRIED WITH SOY BEAN PASTE AND CAPSICUM

375 g (12 oz) belly pork (fresh bacon)
2 tablespoons dried shrimps, soaked for 25 minutes
½ green capsicum (bell pepper)
½ red capsicum (bell pepper)
1-2 dried red chillies
2 tablespoons soy bean paste
3 tablespoons vegetable oil

SEASONING/SAUCE

1 tablespoon rice wine or dry sherry
1½ tablespoons light soy sauce
¼ teaspoon salt
1 teaspoon sugar
⅓ cup (75 mL/2½ fl oz) chicken stock (broth)
1 teaspoon cornflour (cornstarch)

Cut the pork into very small dice, discarding any skin and fragments of bone. Drain the shrimps. Cut the capsicums into small squares, removing the stems, seeds and inner ribs. Finely chop the chillies.

Heat the vegetable oil in a wok to smoking point. Stir-fry the capsicums for about 1½ minutes, then remove and set aside. Stir-fry the pork until it changes colour. Add the chilli and soy bean paste and continue to cook over high heat for 3-4 minutes until the meat is cooked through, stirring continually.

Add the capsicums and the seasoning ingredients except the chicken stock and cornflour, and stir-fry briefly. Mix the stock and cornflour together and stir into the dish. Simmer until thickened, then serve.

DRAGON AND PHOENIX HAM

## Sichuan 四川

# DRAGON AND PHOENIX HAM

*There are many legends about the dragon and the phoenix in China. In ancient times, people thought of the dragon as the embodiment of a king and the phoenix as that of a queen. Sometimes the dragon and phoenix are combined into one symbol of glory, honour, riches and good luck. At wedding or birthday celebration banquets people always like to have dishes using dragon and phoenix names.*

375 g (12 oz) boneless duck meat
250 g (8 oz) pork
90 g (3 oz) water chestnuts
10 chicken wing bones
2 pieces pork fat net (caul fat)
5 slices salted ham
5 slices white bread
oil for deep-frying

SEASONING

2 tablespoons water
2 teaspoons rice wine or dry sherry
2 tablespoons light soy sauce
¾ teaspoon salt
¼ teaspoon white pepper
1 egg yolk
3 tablespoons cornflour (cornstarch)

Very finely mince (grind) the duck meat and pork together with the water chestnuts until reduced to a smooth, sticky paste. Add the pre-mixed seasoning ingredients and stir briskly with a wooden spoon until completely amalgamated, then form into 10 oblong shapes resembling drumsticks. Cut each pork fat net into 5, giving 10 similar-sized pieces. Insert one chicken bone into the narrow end of each drumstick, wrap them in pieces of the pork fat net and set aside.

Cut the ham and bread slices in halves and trim them into rectangular shapes of equal size. Place the ham on a rack in a wok or in a steamer, cover and steam until tender. In the meantime lightly toast the bread.

Heat the oil in a wok to smoking point and slide in the drumsticks, several at a time. Deep-fry for about 3 minutes until cooked through, then drain well.

Place a piece of ham on top of each slice of toast, arrange the drumsticks and ham sandwiches alternately around a large platter and serve.

YUNNAN HAM SHAPED AS PLUM FLOWERS

## Sichuan 四川

# YUNNAN HAM SHAPED AS PLUM FLOWERS

*The Chinese love plum flowers as much as the Japanese revere the cherry blossom. For three thousand years they have cultivated plum trees and praised the characteristics of the plum. It can bloom in snow, is very resistant to bitter cold and hardship, and it is the first to greet the spring. The poet Chen Liang of the Song Dynasty (960-1279AD) said: "One plum flower blooms first, hundreds of flowers follow; they spread the news of spring, even while it is behind the snow".*

5 slices Yunnan ham or other well-salted ham
185 g (6 oz) white fish fillets
1 spring onion (shallot/scallion), minced (ground)
⅓ teaspoon grated fresh (root) ginger
⅓ teaspoon salt
pinch of white pepper
1 egg white
125 g (4 oz) pork fat
lard
lemon peel (rind), optional

Use a sharp knife or vegetable cutter to cut or stamp out plum flower designs from the ham. Make a hole in the centre of each, then cut small pieces of the lemon rind, if used, to fill these holes, to create the centre of the blossoms.

❋ Cut the fish into small pieces and bat with the flat side of a cleaver, or use a food processor, to make a smooth paste. Add the spring onion, ginger, salt, pepper and egg white and mix with your fingers until smooth.

❋ Spread the fish over a large sheet of very thinly sliced pork fat, then cut into diamond shapes, large enough for the ham blossoms to fit in the centre (*see photograph above*). Place the ham in position.

❋ Heat a wide flat pan and wipe out with a little melted lard. Gently fry the fish cakes until the pork fat is crisp and melting. Cover halfway through cooking so that the top is cooked by steam.

❋ Lift onto a serving plate, arrange attractively and garnish with a carved vegetable rose.

BRAISED PORK WITH DRIED VEGETABLE

## Guangzhou 广州

# BRAISED PORK WITH DRIED VEGETABLE

*The meat used for this dish is pork belly (fresh bacon) which consists of alternating layers of fat and meat with a thin skin. The dried vegetable is a salted and sun-dried leaf mustard, the best of which is the "Huizhou" dried vegetable which is exported around the world. This has a thick heart and well flavoured leaves and is frequently used in vegetarian cooking.*

750 g (1¹⁄₂ lb) pork belly (fresh bacon)
1 heart of Huizhou dried vegetable (mui-choy)
2 tablespoons peanut oil
2 tablespoons mushroom soy sauce
2 tablespoons sugar
¹⁄₂ teaspoon sesame oil

Scald the pork in boiling water, then leave to drain. Soak the vegetable in cold water for 30 minutes, rinse well and squeeze dry; repeat several times.
❀ Heat a wok or large saucepan and add the peanut oil. Fry the pork over high heat until brown on both sides. Add the mushroom soy sauce and sugar, then reduce the heat. Turn the pork several times until it is coated with the sauce. Add the whole piece of vegetable, cover the meat with boiling water and bring back to the boil.
❀ Reduce heat to very low and simmer for at least 2 hours until the pork is very tender and has a smooth, almost gelatinous texture. Add the sesame oil.
❀ Lift out the vegetable, cut into pieces and arrange on a serving plate.
❀ Carefully lift out the pork and cut into slices. Arrange in its original shape on top of the vegetable.
❀ Reduce the sauce further, if it is not yet thick and syrupy, or add a little extra water if it has become too concentrated. Spoon over the pork and serve.

## Shanghai 上海

# BOILED AND FRIED PORK LEG IN BROWN SAUCE

*Boil and fry is a cooking method particularly suitable for the cooking of large joints of meat such as pork leg. It reduces the fat content while tenderising the meat and enhancing the flavour.*

*In ancient times, the village people in the Shanghai area often cooked large fish or massive joints of meat for wedding banquets, funeral gatherings, and other celebrations.*

BOILED AND FRIED PORK LEG IN BROWN SAUCE

750 g (1¹⁄₂ lb) pork leg/butt (boneless)
1¹⁄₂ teaspoons salt
1 tablespoon dark soy sauce
3 cups (750 mL/24 fl oz) lard or vegetable oil
12 stalks Chinese kale (gai larn) or spinach
2 tablespoons superior or other light soy sauce
1¹⁄₂ tablespoons rice wine or dry sherry
1 teaspoon sugar
salt and pepper

Place the pork in a saucepan, cover with water and add the salt. Bring to the boil, then reduce heat and simmer for about 30 minutes. Drain, then wipe the skin and meat as dry as possible with kitchen paper, piercing any bubbles in the skin, as these can expand during frying and splatter.
❀ Rub the pork with the dark soy sauce, leave for 1 hour.
❀ Heat the lard or vegetable oil in a wok, put in the pork, skin side downwards, and deep-fry over moderate heat for about 3 minutes. Turn and cook the other side for 1-3 minutes, then lift out, drain and place in a clean casserole.
❀ Cover with cold water and set aside for 10 minutes, then add the remaining ingredients and simmer gently until the meat is very tender with a texture similar to beancurd.

## Shanghai 上海

# FRIED AND BRAISED SPARE RIBS

*Spare ribs are an inexpensive ingredient, being quite bony with little meat. However, when cooked in the following way the result is lustrous, with finger-licking succulence.*

750 g (1¹⁄₂ lb) pork spare ribs
³⁄₄ cup (90 g/3 oz) waterchestnut powder or cornflour (cornstarch)
prawn crackers (krupuk)
oil for deep-frying

SEASONING

2 tablespoons Jizhi or other ketchup
2 tablespoons tomato juice
2 tablespoons sweet vinegar
2 tablespoons sugar
³⁄₄ cup (175 mL/6 fl oz) superior stock (*see page 124*)

Cut the ribs into short lengths and toss in the waterchestnut powder or cornflour to coat thickly. Shake off the excess.
❀ Heat the oil in a wok to moderately hot and deep-fry the prawn crackers until well expanded and crisp. Do not allow to colour. Remove, drain well, then place around the edge of a serving dish and set aside.
❀ Place the ribs in the oil and deep-fry for about 6 minutes until well coloured, crisp on the surface and almost cooked through. Remove with a slotted spoon and set aside.

FRIED AND BRAISED SPARE RIBS

SHREDDED PORK WITH SPECIAL SAUCE

✳ Drain off the oil and add the pre-mixed seasoning ingredients to the wok. Bring to the boil and boil for 2-3 minutes, then add the ribs, cover and braise for about 10 minutes until the ribs are very tender and the sauce has reduced to a thick glaze on the meat.

✳ Spoon into the centre of the dish and serve.

## Beijing 北京

# MEATBALLS WITH SESAME SEEDS

500 g (1 lb) belly pork (fresh bacon)
½ cup (125 mL/4 fl oz) water
2 tablespoons cornflour (cornstarch)
3 cups (750 mL/24 fl oz) peanut oil
¾ cup (90 g/3 oz) white sesame seeds
1 cup (220 g/7 oz) sugar

Mince (grind) the pork finely, adding first the water, then the cornflour. The mixture should be very smooth.

✳ Heat the peanut oil in a wok to smoking point, then reduce the heat slightly.

✳ Form the meat into small balls about the size of a walnut and drop into the oil. Fry in several batches for about 3 minutes until cooked through and well coloured on the surface. Lift out and drain well.

✳ Spread the sesame seeds on a plate.

✳ Pour the sugar into a clean wok adding 2 tablespoons of the hot oil. Cook gently without stirring until it turns to a pale caramel colour, then turn off the heat and quickly roll each meatball through the caramel to coat evenly. Roll in the sesame seeds and place on a lightly oiled serving plate.

## Sichuan 四川

# SHREDDED PORK WITH SPECIAL SAUCE

220 g (7 oz) lean pork, preferably fillet (tenderloin)
½ teaspoon salt
pinch of white pepper
1½ tablespoons cornflour (cornstarch)
1-2 pickled red chillies
2 slices fresh (root) ginger
2 cloves garlic
2 spring onions (shallots/scallions)
2 tablespoons lard or oil for frying

SAUCE

3 tablespoons stock (broth)
1 tablespoon light soy sauce
1 teaspoon brown vinegar
2 teaspoons sugar
¾ teaspoon sesame oil
½ teaspoon cornflour (cornstarch)

Very thinly slice the pork across the grain, then cut into fine shreds and place in a dish. Add the salt, pepper and cornflour, mix well and set aside.

✳ Finely chop the chillies, ginger, garlic and spring onions. Mix the sauce ingredients.

✳ Heat the wok and stir-fry the pork shreds in the lard or oil until white. Push to one side of the pan and add the chopped chillies, ginger, garlic and spring onions and stir-fry quickly, then mix in with the pork.

✳ Add the sauce ingredients and heat quickly over high heat, stirring into the pork, and serve.

MEATBALLS WITH SESAME SEEDS

STIR-FRIED PORK TENDERLOIN

FRIED MEAT-FILLED EGG ROLLS

## Beijing 北京

# STIR-FRIED PORK TENDERLOIN

375 g (12 oz) pork fillet (tenderloin)
3 tablespoons peanut oil
1 tablespoon finely chopped spring onion (shallot/scallion)
½ teaspoon finely chopped fresh (root) ginger
1 tablespoon brown vinegar
2 teaspoons sugar

SEASONING

1 tablespoon rice wine or dry sherry
1 tablespoon dark soy sauce
1 tablespoon cornflour (cornstarch)
½ teaspoon salt
pinch of pepper

Cut the pork into thin slices and place in a dish with the pre-mixed seasoning ingredients, mix well and leave for 20 minutes.

✄ Heat the wok and add the peanut oil. Stir-fry the pork for about 2 minutes over high heat until lightly coloured and cooked through. Remove and set aside.

✄ Add the spring onions and ginger and stir-fry briefly, then add the vinegar and sugar and toss together for a few seconds. Return the meat and stir-fry together until the meat is well coated with the ingredients. Serve immediately.

## Beijing 北京

# FRIED MEAT-FILLED EGG ROLLS

315 g (10 oz) fat pork, finely minced (ground)
4 eggs
2 tablespoons peanut oil
½ cup (60 g/2 oz) flour
oil for deep-frying

SEASONING

1 tablespoon finely chopped spring onion (shallot/scallion)
½ teaspoon grated fresh (root) ginger
1 teaspoon cornflour (cornstarch)
1 teaspoon sesame oil
½ teaspoon salt
pinch of white pepper

Mix the pork with the seasoning ingredients, squeezing the mixture through your fingers until it is smooth and sticky and set aside.

✄ Add enough water to the flour to make a sticky paste.

✄ Beat the eggs with 2 teaspoons of the peanut oil. Heat a wok or omelet pan over moderate heat and wipe out with a cloth dipped in the peanut oil. Pour in half of the egg batter and tilt

the pan so that the egg spreads out as much as possible, and is very thin. Cook evenly, moving the pan constantly until lightly-coloured underneath, then cook the other side briefly. Cook the other omelet and leave them both on a work top to cool.

✄ Spread the flour paste over the omelets, then spread on a layer of the pork filling, leaving a border all around. Roll up, tucking the sides in securely. Heat the deep-frying oil to smoking point, then reduce heat slightly. Cut the rolls into 4 cm (2½ in) lengths and deep-fry in several batches until golden. Lift out and drain well, then serve at once.

## Beijing 北京

# STIR-FRIED KIDNEYS

4 pork or lamb kidneys
2 tablespoons lard
1 teaspoon finely chopped fresh (root) ginger
1 tablespoon sugar

SAUCE

1 tablespoon water or chicken stock (broth)
1 tablespoon rice wine or dry sherry
1 tablespoon dark soy sauce
1 tablespoon finely chopped spring onion (shallot/scallion)
½ teaspoon salt
1 teaspoon cornflour (cornstarch)

Soak the kidneys in cold water for 1 hour, then drain. Cut in halves, remove the fatty core then turn the cut sides downwards and score deeply with diagonal cuts.

✄ Soak in cold water for 20 minutes, then drain very thoroughly and cut each kidney into several pieces.

✄ Heat a wok and add the lard. Stir-fry the ginger briefly, then add the kidneys and stir-fry over high heat until just cooked through. They should remain pink inside but no blood should run out when pierced. Do not overcook or they will become tough. Stir the sugar in and place on a serving plate.

✄ Add the pre-mixed sauce ingredients to the wok and bring to the boil. Simmer, stirring, until slightly thickened. Return the kidneys and toss in the sauce until thoroughly coated and the sauce reduced to a glaze, then serve immediately.

## Shanghai 上海

# STEWED LARGE MEATBALLS

*The Chinese call these meatballs "lion heads". Stewed large meatballs have long been a traditional speciality in the Yangzhou area and are prepared principally with minced (ground) pork, although they may consist of a combination of meats and sometimes contain a delicious filling, such as crabmeat. The delicate colours of the dish – the light pink of the meatballs and the bright green of the tender cabbage – plus the rich aroma and flavour create a meal to delight the senses.*

750 g (1½ lb) lean pork (preferably fillet/tenderloin)
2½ tablespoons finely chopped spring onion
   (shallot/scallion)
1 teaspoon grated fresh (root) ginger
1½ teaspoons salt
1 tablespoon Shaoxing rice wine or dry sherry
500-750 g (1-1½ lb) Chinese cabbage
lard or vegetable oil for frying
chicken stock (broth) or superior stock (*see page 124*)

Cut the pork into small pieces, then mince (grind) it finely, using two cleavers simultaneously or a food processor.

❀ Mix in the spring onion, ginger, salt and wine and work the meat with your fingers until smooth and sticky. Form into 3-4 large meatballs.

❀ Wash the cabbage and cut lengthways into quarters. Stir-fry it briefly in a wok, in lard or vegetable oil, adding a generous pinch of salt.

❀ Spread half of the cabbage across the bottom of a casserole and place the meatballs on top, then cover with the remaining cabbage.

❀ Add enough boiling stock to just cover the meatballs. Cover the casserole tightly and simmer over low heat for about 1½ hours until the meatballs are melt-in-the-mouth tender.

❀ Serve in the casserole, pushing the vegetables to one side to expose the meatballs.

161

MANDARIN DICED KIDNEY

FRIED BEEF AND WATER SPINACH WITH SHRIMP PASTE

## *Sichuan* 四川

# MANDARIN DICED KIDNEY

250 g (8 oz) pork kidneys
1½ tablespoons cornflour (cornstarch)
2 cloves garlic
3 slices fresh (root) ginger
2 spring onions (shallots/scallions)
2 dried red chillies
3 tablespoons lard or oil for frying
1 teaspoon ground Sichuan peppercorns (Fagara or Sansho)
1 teaspoon rice wine or dry sherry
large pinch of red chilli powder or chilli oil (optional)

### SEASONING/SAUCE

½ cup (125 mL/4 fl oz) chicken stock (broth)
2 tablespoons light soy sauce
2 teaspoons red vinegar
2 teaspoons sugar
pinch of salt
2 teaspoons cornflour (cornstarch)

Cut the kidneys in halves horizontally, remove the skin and cut away the fatty inner section. Use a sharp knife to deeply score each piece in crosshatch fashion. Place in a dish and sprinkle on the cornflour, mixed to a thin paste with water. Stir until the kidney pieces are evenly coated, then set aside.
※ Finely chop the garlic, ginger, spring onions and chillies.
※ Heat the lard or oil in a wok to smoking point. Stir-fry the chopped chillies and Sichuan peppercorns for 20-30 seconds, then add the kidneys and the garlic, ginger and onions and stir-fry together over high heat until the kidneys are partially cooked. Add the wine and chilli powder, if used, reduce heat and continue cooking until the kidneys are tender. Then add the pre-mixed seasoning/sauce ingredients and simmer, stirring, until the sauce thickens and serve.

## *Guangzhou* 广州

# FRIED BEEF AND WATER SPINACH WITH SHRIMP PASTE

*Water spinach is one of the main green vegetables available in Guangdong during the hot summer. It is cultivated on floating rafts made of reeds with small holes, through which the water spinach grows. The jade-like vegetable must be cooked with care. If under-done, it will be astringent; if overdone, yellow, dull and with little flavour.*

185 g (6 oz) beef fillet (tenderloin)
250 g (8 oz) water spinach, or young English spinach
1 spring onion (shallot/scallion)
2 cloves garlic
½ cup (125 mL/4 fl oz) vegetable oil
salt
½ teaspoon fresh (root) ginger
2 teaspoons shrimp paste
1 teaspoon rice wine or dry sherry
3 tablespoons chicken stock (broth)
½ teaspoon cornflour (cornstarch)
⅓ teaspoon sesame oil

### SEASONING

1 teaspoon dark soy sauce
1 teaspoon fish sauce or anchovy essence
1 tablespoon vegetable oil
1 tablespoon water
1 teaspoon cornflour (cornstarch)
½ teaspoon bicarbonate of soda (baking soda)

Very thinly slice the beef, cutting across the grain, then cut into narrow, short strips. Place in a dish and add the pre-mixed seasoning ingredients. Mix well and leave for 20 minutes.
※ Thoroughly wash the spinach and drain well. Chop the spring onion into 2½ cm (1 in) lengths. Finely chop the garlic.
※ Heat the vegetable oil in a wok and stir-fry the spinach over high heat for about 2 minutes until the leaves wilt and the stems soften but retain crispness. Add a sprinkling of salt, then use chopsticks to lift onto a serving plate.
※ Reheat the wok, add the beef and stir-fry over very high heat until it changes colour. Remove from the pan. Stir-fry the ginger, garlic and spring onion until tender, then return the beef. Add the shrimp paste and wine and toss all ingredients together until well mixed. Stir the cornflour into the stock and pour over the beef, stirring until the sauce thickens.
※ Arrange the beef on or near the vegetables, sprinkle over the sesame oil and serve.

## Sichuan 四川

# BOILED BEEF WITH CHILLI

*This is a traditional dish famed for its characteristically heavy, hot and spicy, yet tender and delicious flavour. It originated in the salt mining area of Sichuan, where people usually cooked beef by boiling it in a soup heavily seasoned with chilli, bean paste and pepper. This old recipe was very popular for its heavy flavour which banishes cold and whets the appetite. Over the years many improvements have been made to the dish and it is now a local speciality.*

315 g (10 oz) beef steak (rump/sirloin/loin)
6-8 lettuce leaves
1 tablespoon hot oil
½ teaspoon fried Sichuan peppercorns (Fagara or Sansho), ground
1 teaspoon finely chopped garlic (optional)

SAUCE

2 tablespoons lard or oil for frying
6 dried chillies
1 teaspoon Sichuan peppercorns (Fagara or Sansho), ground
1 tablespoon fermented black beans, finely chopped
3 cloves garlic, finely chopped
3-4 slices fresh (root) ginger, finely chopped
6-8 garlic chives or 3 spring onions (shallots/scallions), chopped
1 tablespoon hot bean paste
½ cup (125 mL/4 fl oz) water

Cut the meat across the grain into paper thin slices and set aside. Rinse the lettuce and tear into small pieces.

To make the sauce, heat the lard or oil in a wok and fry the dried chillies and Sichuan peppercorns for about 30 seconds, then remove and chop the chillies finely. Add the black beans to the wok and fry for about 30 seconds, then add the garlic, ginger, garlic chives or spring onions and the bean paste and fry together until aromatic. Return the chillies and pepper, add the water and bring to the boil, then set aside.

Heat a large saucepan of water to boiling point. Add the beef and cook just long enough for the meat to change colour, then drain well.

Add the meat to the wok with the sauce, reheat and stir-fry together until all the sauce has adhered to the meat slices, then stir in the lettuce.

Transfer to a serving plate and splash on the hot oil. Sprinkle on the ground Sichuan pepper and the chopped garlic, if used, and serve at once.

STEWED BEEF WITH TENDER GARLIC CHIVES

## *Sichuan* 四川

# STEWED BEEF WITH TENDER GARLIC CHIVES

500 g (1 lb) stewing/braising beef
2 tablespoons lard or vegetable oil
1 tablespoon soy bean paste or mashed fermented black beans
3 cups (750 mL/24 fl oz) beef stock (broth)
10 slices fresh (root) ginger
2 spring onions (shallots/scallions), halved
1 tablespoon soy bean powder or cornflour (cornstarch)

SEASONING

1 tablespoon rice wine or dry sherry
½ teaspoon Sichuan peppercorns (Fagara or Sansho)
1 teaspoon salt
2 teaspoons sugar

GARNISH

2 fresh red chillies
20 garlic chives or spring onions (shallots/scallions)
1 tablespoon oil for frying

Cut the beef into slices about 1 cm (½ in) thick, then into sticks about 8 x 2 cm (3 x 1 in).

Heat a wok over moderate heat and add the lard. Stir-fry the bean paste or mashed black beans for about 40 seconds until fragrant, then add the beef and stir-fry over high heat until lightly coloured and well sealed on all surfaces.

Pour in the stock, heat through briefly over high heat, then reduce the heat and simmer for about 1 hour, covered, until the beef is tender and the liquid reduced to about 1 cup (250 mL/8 fl oz).

Halfway through cooking, add the ginger and spring onions and the pre-mixed seasoning ingredients.

Meanwhile prepare the garnish. Cut the chillies into long thin shreds, discarding the seeds. Use only about 5 cm (2 in) of the white end of the chives or spring onions. Use a toothpick or bamboo skewer to make a hole in one end of each piece of onion and insert a sliver of chilli to resemble the wick of a candle or firecracker. Heat another wok or pan and add the oil. Stir-fry the onions quickly and carefully. Sprinkle with 1 tablespoon of water to help them to soften, simmer until evaporated, then set the garnish aside.

Mix the soy bean powder with a little cold water and stir into the sauce with the beef. Simmer, stirring, until it thickens and the oil floats on the surface.

Spoon into the centre of a serving plate and arrange the onions around the edge of the plate.

## *Shanghai* 上海

# STEAMED THREE SHREDDED MEATS

*This much revered dish, incorporating pork, ham and chicken meat with cooked bamboo shoots is a traditional food in Shanghai homes. Locals often serve it during festival times and family get-togethers. The three kinds of shredded meats packed closely together imply a reunion.*

250 g (8 oz) ham
250 g (8 oz) lean pork
250 g (8 oz) chicken breast
2 dried black mushrooms, soaked for 25 minutes
185 g (6 oz) canned or cooked fresh bamboo shoots, thinly sliced
1 cup (250 mL/8 fl oz) clear chicken stock (broth)

Place the ham, pork and chicken in a saucepan, cover with water, bring to the boil, then simmer gently for one hour. Remove, drain and cut the meat into fine shreds.

Select one or two heatproof bowls large enough to contain all of the ingredients. Place a black mushroom, cap downwards, in the bottom of the bowl. Arrange the shredded meats and the bamboo shoots in the bowl and set on a rack in a wok or in a steamer with simmering water. Cover and steam for about 10 minutes until the meat is compact.

Turn the bowl upside down into a serving dish and remove the bowl so that the meat retains its shape. Boil the stock up, pour over the meat and serve.

This is delicious either as a main course or is enough for 12 guests as an appetiser.

STEAMED THREE SHREDDED MEATS

DEEP-FRIED BEEF ROLLS FILLED WITH QUAIL EGGS

## Guangzhou 广州

# DEEP-FRIED BEEF ROLLS FILLED WITH QUAIL EGGS

250 g (8 oz) lean beef steak
1 small carrot
2 teaspoons cornflour (cornstarch)
½ teaspoon bicarbonate of soda (baking soda)
10 quail eggs, fresh or canned
¼ teaspoon powdered cloves (optional)
oil for frying

SEASONING

2 teaspoons superior or other light soy sauce
1 teaspoon rice wine or dry sherry
½ teaspoon sesame oil
½ teaspoon salt
1 teaspoon sugar
pinch of ground star anise
pinch of white pepper

Using two cleavers, one in each hand, mince (grind) the meat very finely, or process to a smooth pulp in a food processor. Grate the carrot finely and add to the beef with the cornflour, bicarbonate of soda and the seasoning ingredients. Mix with your fingers until a smooth paste. On a piece of greaseproof paper or thick plastic wrap spread the meat in a rectangle about 30 cm (12 in) long and 12 cm (5 in) wide.

❀ Boil the fresh quail eggs for 5 minutes, place under cold running water to cool and remove the shells. Dry the eggs and arrange end to end along the centre of the meat. Use the paper or plastic to lift the meat up around the eggs, so that they are completely encased within a long sausage of meat. Pinch the ends together. Coat the roll thickly with cornflour, brushing off the excess.

❀ Heat about 2.5 cm (1 in) of oil in a wide flat frying pan or large wok and fry the beef roll over moderate heat until well and evenly coloured all over. Roll it gently in the pan, using two wide spatulas to ensure it does not break during cooking. Lift out, drain and sprinkle over the powdered cloves, if used. Slice to serve.

## Beijing 北京

# TWICE-COOKED BEEF

1 kg (2 lb) beef top rump (bottom round)
3 tablespoons peanut oil
3 pieces star anise
2 pieces dried mandarine/tangerine peel
3 spring onions (shallots/scallions)
6 slices fresh (root) ginger
4 cloves garlic
2 teaspoons Sichuan peppercorns (Fagara or Sansho)
3 tablespoons rice wine or dry sherry
½ cup (125 mL/4 fl oz) light soy sauce
3 tablespoons dark soy sauce
2 tablespoons brown bean sauce
1 tablespoon sugar
salt and pepper
2 teaspoons cornflour (cornstarch)
1 teaspoon sesame oil

Cut the beef into thick slices, then into square pieces. In a wok, heat the oil to smoking point and fry the beef in several batches until well coloured. Lift out and set aside.

❀ Drain off most of the oil. Stir-fry the star anise, peel, whole onions, ginger, garlic and peppercorns for 2 minutes until fragrant. Add the wine and soy sauces and simmer for 4 minutes. Discard the star anise, spring onion, ginger and garlic, then add the beef slices, bean paste and sugar and cover with water.

❀ Bring to the boil, then reduce heat to very low and simmer, covered, for about 3 hours until the beef is very tender.

❀ Season the sauce with salt and pepper and thicken with cornflour mixed with cold water. Sprinkle on the sesame oil and serve at once.

TWICE-COOKED BEEF

DEEP-FRIED BEEF CROQUETTES

KASAYA BEEF

Beijing 北京

# DEEP-FRIED BEEF CROQUETTES

*This dish is also called "Tien Dan Regains Chi", a name which can be traced back to 279 BC. Tien Dan, the great general of the Kingdom of Chi, was suffering from the onslaught of the warring Kingdom of Yen, which had captured some seventy Chi cities. In desperation he devised a remarkable plan.*

*His men gathered together a thousand cows, tied swords and knives to their horns and hay soaked with oil to their tails. In the dead of night they set fire to the hay and sent the cows charging into the enemy camp, followed by five thousand soldiers.*

*Victory was theirs, the cities were recovered and great honours were bestowed on Tien Dan.*

*The red beef fillet in this dish represents the fire-cows of Tien Dan, hence its name.*

375 g (12 oz) beef fillet
4 water chestnuts, finely shredded
155 g (5 oz) ham, finely shredded
1 stem Chinese kale (gai larn) or spinach, shredded
1 tablespoon rice wine or dry sherry
1 teaspoon salt
375 g (12 oz) chicken meat
½ egg
1 tablespoon cornflour
pinch of salt
deep-fried, dried vegetable leaves or fresh sprigs of coriander (garnish)

COATING
½ cup (60 g/2 oz) flour
1 egg, beaten
1 cup (125 g/4 oz) dry breadcrumbs
oil for deep-frying

Cut the beef into long thin slices, then beat gently with the side of a cleaver to flatten.
❊ Season the shredded ingredients with the rice wine and salt.
❊ Mince (grind) the chicken meat finely and mix with the egg and cornflour, adding a pinch of salt.
❊ Place a few strands of shredded ingredients in the centre of each strip of beef and roll up into cylinders. Cover each roll with a thin coating of chicken paste, then dust with flour, dip into beaten egg and coat with breadcrumbs.
❊ Heat the oil in a large wok and deep-fry the croquettes in batches until cooked through and golden brown. Lift out and drain well.
❊ Arrange the croquettes on a bed of deep-fried vegetable leaves or surround them with sprigs of fresh coriander and serve at once.

Beijing 北京

# KASAYA BEEF

*China raises a great number of cattle of many varieties, including Mongolian cattle and the pien niu – the offspring of a bull and a female yak. The pien niu can withstand hardship better than cattle, it produces more milk than a yak and is easy to tame.*

*Beef used in Beijing cooking usually comes from Inner Mongolia, being rich and tender with a delicious aroma. It is said to strengthen bones and muscles and to reduce water retention.*

*In this recipe the fillet is pounded to a paste and spread between two layers of omelet before being crisp-fried.*

250 g (8 oz) beef fillet
2 egg whites, lightly beaten
2 tablespoons cornflour (cornstarch)
2 teaspoons rice wine or dry sherry
2 tablespoons finely chopped spring onion (shallot/scallion)
1 teaspoon finely grated fresh (root) ginger
2 cloves garlic, finely chopped
¾ teaspoon salt
2 eggs
2½ cups (625 mL/20 fl oz) peanut oil
½ teaspoon sesame oil
3 tablespoons cornflour (cornstarch)

Very finely mince (grind) the beef, removing any sinews. Add the beaten egg white, cornflour and rice wine and mix well, then add the spring onion, ginger, garlic and salt and beat with a wooden spoon until the mixture is very smooth and slightly sticky.
❊ Beat the eggs well. Heat a wok and rub with a piece of kitchen paper, dipped in sesame and peanut oil. Pour in half of the egg mixture and tilt the pan until it spreads into a thin, wide sheet of about 33 cm (13 in) in diameter. When firm and lightly coloured on the underside, turn and lightly cook the other side. Repeat with the remaining egg.
❊ Lay out one omelet and spread the beef paste over it. Cover with the other omelet, pressing it firmly into place. Cut into diamond shapes and dip the cut edges into the cornflour. Heat the peanut oil and add the sesame oil. Fry the "sandwiches" in batches over moderate heat until crisp and golden. Ensure that the meat filling is cooked through before removing from the oil. Drain well and stack on a serving plate. Serve at once.

BEEF SLICES STIR-FRIED IN OYSTER SAUCE

## Guangzhou 广州

# BEEF SLICES STIR-FRIED IN OYSTER SAUCE

250 g (8 oz) fillet of beef (tenderloin)
1 egg white, well beaten
3 tablespoons oil for frying
1 spring onion (shallot/scallion), chopped
2 slices fresh (root) ginger, shredded
2 teaspoons cornflour (cornstarch)
2 tablespoons water

SEASONING

2 tablespoons oyster sauce
1 tablespoon rice wine or dry sherry
1 tablespoon light soy sauce
1 teaspoon mushroom soy sauce
1 teaspoon sugar
pinch of salt and white pepper
2 tablespoons beef stock (broth)

Cut the beef across the grain into very thin slices, then cut into small squares. Place in a dish with the egg white and mix well. Add the pre-mixed seasoning ingredients and leave to marinate for 20 minutes.

Drain the beef, reserving the marinade. Heat the wok with the oil and stir-fry the beef over high heat until it changes colour. Remove immediately.

Add the spring onions and ginger to the wok and stir-fry for 45 seconds, then return the beef, the marinade ingredients and the cornflour mixed with water. Stir over very high heat until thickened, then serve at once.

## Beijing 北京

# STIR-FRIED FILLET OF LAMB

185 g (6 oz) lamb fillet (tenderloin)
1 egg white
1½ tablespoons cornflour (cornstarch)
½ teaspoon salt
pinch of pepper
60 g (2 oz) canned bamboo shoots, drained
5 cm (2 in) piece cucumber
1 small red capsicum (bell pepper)
2 spring onions (shallots/scallions)
3 slices fresh (root) ginger
2½ cups (625 mL/20 fl oz) peanut oil
2 teaspoons rice wine or dry sherry

Use a sharp knife to cut across the fillet into thin slices. Stack the slices together and cut into narrow shreds. Place in a dish.

STIR-FRIED FILLET OF LAMB

Lightly beat the egg white, adding the cornflour, salt and pepper and pour over the lamb. Mix in well and leave for 20 minutes.

Shred the bamboo shoots, the skin and flesh of the cucumber, the capsicum, onions and ginger.

Heat the oil in a wok and deep-fry the lamb strips for 1½ minutes over moderate heat, using chopsticks to separate the shreds. Lift out and drain well.

Pour off all but 2 tablespoons of the oil and stir-fry the bamboo shoots, cucumber and capsicum for 2 minutes, then add the onions and ginger and stir-fry together briefly.

Return the lamb and toss the ingredients together over very high heat. Add the rice wine and toss again, then serve.

## Beijing 北京

# DEEP-FRIED LAMB SLICES

280 g (9 oz) lamb fillet (tenderloin)
¾ cup (90 g/3 oz) cornflour (cornstarch)
oil for deep-frying

SAUCE

½ cup (125 mL/4 fl oz) water
2 tablespoons light soy sauce
1 teaspoon ginger juice
1½ teaspoons rice wine or dry sherry
1½ teaspoons vinegar
2 teaspoons sugar
1 teaspoon cornflour (cornstarch)

Cut across the fillet into thin slices, then thin strips.

Mix the cornflour with water to a very thin batter.

Heat a wok with the oil to smoking point. Coat with the batter and deep-fry the meat in several batches, stirring with chopsticks to separate the strips. The meat will take about one minute to be cooked through and well coloured on the surface. Remove and drain well.

In another wok bring the pre-mixed sauce ingredients to the boil, add the meat slices and simmer, stirring carefully, until the sauce glazes the meat. Spoon onto a serving plate and serve at once.

DEEP-FRIED LAMB SLICES

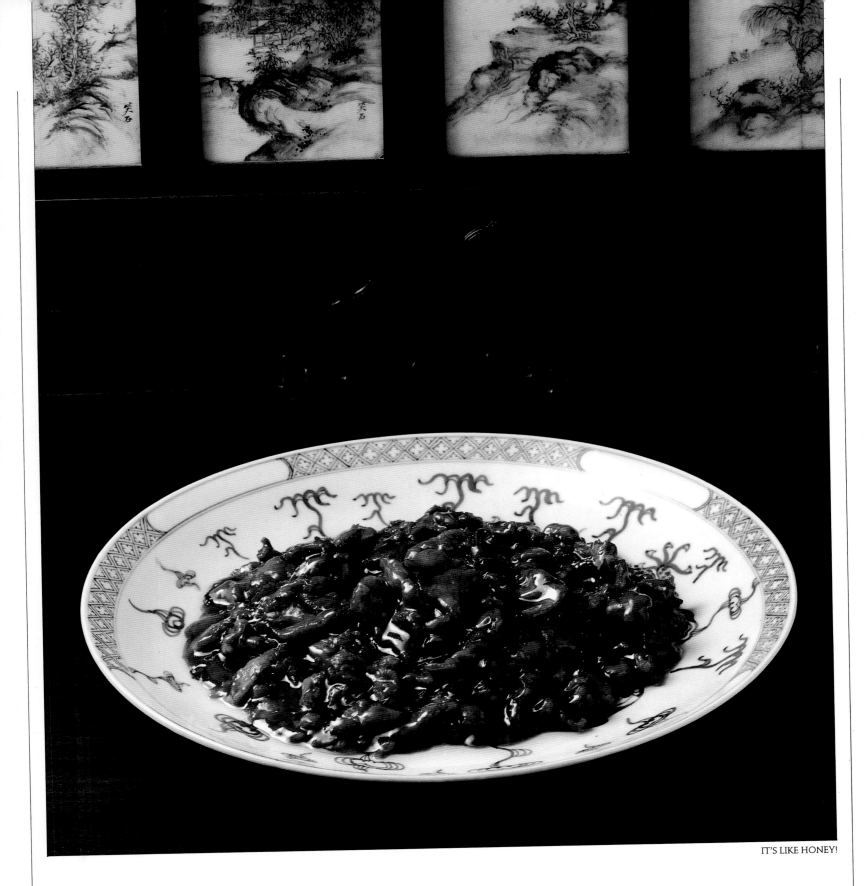

# Beijing 北京

## IT'S LIKE HONEY!

*A story is told about a special lamb dish cooked for the Empress Dowager Cixi. Being very pleased with it, she asked the chef for the name of the dish. He did not dare to venture an answer and instead asked her to name it. She said casually, "It's like honey!" and that has been the name of this dish ever since.*

*The lamb pieces in this recipe are brownish red in colour, and soft and tender. It really tastes like honey with a slightly sour aftertaste.*

220 g (7 oz) lamb fillet
1 tablespoon Hoisin sauce
2 tablespoons cornflour (cornstarch)
3 tablespoons peanut or other oil for frying
⅓ teaspoon sesame oil

SEASONING

1 tablespoon light soy sauce
1 teaspoon brown vinegar
1 teaspoon rice wine or dry sherry
1 teaspoon ginger juice
¼ teaspoon molasses or ½ teaspoon golden syrup/treacle
2 teaspoons sugar
½ teaspoon cornflour (cornstarch)

Very thinly slice the lamb across the grain into slices. Place in a dish and add the Hoisin sauce, mixing well, then sprinkle with the cornflour and mix until coated evenly.

❀ Mix the seasoning ingredients together and set aside.

❀ Heat the oil in a wok and stir-fry the lamb over moderate heat until reddish-brown and just cooked, stirring constantly with chopsticks to separate the slices. Remove and drain well.

❀ Pour off most of the oil and add the seasoning ingredients. Bring to the boil and add the sesame oil. Return the lamb and stir quickly over high heat until the seasoning ingredients coat the lamb. Serve at once.

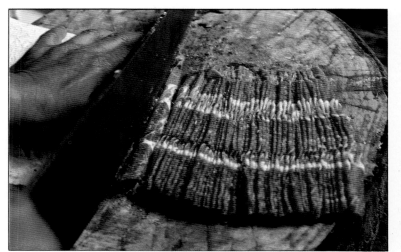

MONGOLIAN FIRE POT

## Beijing 北京

# MONGOLIAN FIRE POT

*The traditional Mongolian Fire Pot, or Hotpot as it is also known, is positioned in the centre of a large round table over a charcoal fire. The pot is filled with simmering broth and everybody cooks their own meal by using wooden chopsticks or small wire baskets to suspend pieces of meat and vegetables in the hot stock. Plates with paper-thin slices of lamb, bean thread vermicelli and different sorts of vegetables are arranged around the fire pot. The meat, or other cooking ingredients, is dipped into one or more of the seasonings, served separately in small bowls on the table. At the end of the meal all the remaining vegetables and side dishes are added to the broth and the banquet is finished off with bowls of the resulting rich soup.*

10 cups (2½ L/80 fl oz) chicken stock (broth)
2 tablespoons dried shrimp
6 dried black mushrooms, soaked for 25 minutes
1 kg (2 lb) lean lamb loin
500 g (1 lb) Chinese cabbage
90 g (3 oz) dry bean thread vermicelli
90 g (3 oz) canned pickled garlic
large bunch fresh coriander

SEASONINGS/DIPS

3 tablespoons sesame paste (tahini)
½ cup (125 mL/4 fl oz) rice wine or dry sherry
⅓ cup (125 g/4 oz) preserved beancurd
2 tablespoons chilli oil
½ cup (125 mL/4 fl oz) dark soy sauce
2 tablespoons shrimp paste
½ cup (125 mL/4 fl oz) light soy sauce

Fill the fire pot or other vessel suitable for table-top cooking with the stock and add the dried shrimp. Drain the mushrooms, remove the stems, dice the caps and add to the stock. ※ Slice the lamb very thinly (made easy by partially freezing it beforehand) and arrange on plates. Rinse the cabbage, cut into squares and place in a dish. Pour boiling water over the vermicelli to soften, drain and arrange on a plate. Place the garlic and coriander on plates. Arrange all the plates around the fire pot on the dining table. Serve at least 2 small bowls of each seasoning/dip and place these on the table with spoons. ※ Give each guest one bowl to eat from, one or two small bowls for mixing the sauce, and a pair of wooden chopsticks.

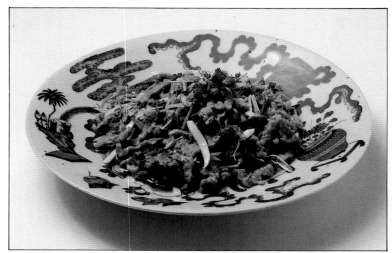

LAMB TENDERLOIN WITH FRESH CORIANDER

## Beijing 北京

# LAMB TENDERLOIN WITH FRESH CORIANDER

375 g (12 oz) lamb fillet (tenderloin)
1 tablespoon rendered chicken fat
125 g (4 oz) broccoli or other green vegetable
2 dried black mushrooms, soaked for 25 minutes
4 stalks fresh coriander
1 spring onion (shallot/scallion)
2 teaspoons rice wine or dry sherry
1 tablespoon dark soy sauce
½ teaspoon salt

SEASONING

2 teaspoons sugar
1 teaspoon sesame oil
2 teaspoons cornflour (cornstarch)

Cut the lamb into thin slices, then into strips and rinse with cold water. Drain and dry thoroughly. Place in a dish and add the pre-mixed seasoning, mix well and leave for 15 minutes.
※ Heat the chicken fat in a wok and stir-fry the shredded lamb until just cooked, then remove and set aside.
※ Trim and slice the broccoli. Drain the mushrooms, remove the stems and shred the caps. Rinse the spring onion, dry well and cut into 5 cm (2 in) lengths. Trim and chop the coriander.
※ Add the vegetables to the wok and stir-fry together until the broccoli is tender, then add the wine, soy sauce and salt, return the meat and toss together over high heat for 1 minute. Add the coriander and serve immediately.

## Beijing 北京

# ROAST LAMB ON SKEWERS

*Muslims along the north-western borders of China have a high regard for this delicious dish of cubed, seasoned lamb, tossed in sesame seed and roasted on skewers over charcoal.*

*The dish was introduced into Beijing some 20 years ago and now a number of restaurants include it in their menu.*

1 kg (2 lb) lamb fillet (tenderloin)*
3 eggs
¾ cup (90 g/3 oz) flour
1 tablespoon salt
1½ teaspoons pepper
1½ teaspoons ground Sichuan peppercorns (Fagara or Sansho)
¾ cup (125 g/4 oz) minced (ground) spring onions
    (shallots/scallions)
2 large tomatoes, finely chopped, seeds discarded
3 tablespoons white sesame seeds

ROAST LAMB ON SKEWERS

Cut all the white sinews and membrane covering off the meat, then cut into small, uniform cubes.
※ Beat the eggs lightly and mix with the remaining ingredients except the sesame seeds. Pour the marinade over the meat cubes and stir in evenly. Cover with plastic wrap and leave for at least 3 hours.
※ Toss the meat cubes in sesame seed and thread onto metal skewers which have been rubbed with an oiled cloth to make the removal of the cooked meat easier. Take 6-7 pieces of meat for each skewer.
※ For best results roast over a charcoal burner with gently glowing coals. Turn skewers over once to ensure even cooking. When the meat turns reddish brown, after 3-4 minutes, it is done. Tender lamb should be crisp and coloured on the surface, but still pink inside, as it dries out with prolonged cooking.
※ Serve on the skewers.

*\*Less expensive cuts, such as boneless leg meat, can be used, but the result will be a tougher textured meat with a stronger flavour.*

## Beijing 北京

# HAND-GRASPED LAMB

*Hand-grasped lamb is a traditional dish of the nomadic desert dwellers of north-western China. At the end of a journey they prepare a fire, slaughter a lamb, cook it simply and enjoy the hearty meal. The name of this dish comes from their practice of grasping the rib bones while eating the meat.*

2 kg (4 lb) lamb ribs (approximately 20 ribs)
1 spring onion (shallot/scallion), finely chopped
3 fresh red chillies, finely chopped
1 tablespoon grated fresh (root) ginger
2 tablespoons finely chopped fresh coriander

SEASONING

2 tablespoons rice wine or dry sherry
1 fresh red chilli, sliced
2 spring onions (shallots/scallions), roughly chopped
4 slices fresh (root) ginger
1 teaspoon salt
2 star anise
2 cloves garlic, crushed
1 x 5 cm (2 in) stick cinnamon

Cut the meat into sections of two ribs each, then trim away the meat and fat at the end of the bones.
※ Place the ribs in a large saucepan and cover with water. Add the seasoning ingredients and bring to the boil. Cover and simmer gently for about 1½ hours until the meat is very tender. Leave to cool in the stock, then drain well.
※ Arrange on a serving plate. Serve with small dishes of raw spring onion, chilli, ginger and coriander.

BARBECUED MUTTON

## Beijing 北京

# BARBECUED MUTTON

*When night falls on the northern seafront of China, all is peaceful and quiet except for the brightly lit small restaurants along the shore, filled with the laughter of happy diners. The aroma of barbecued mutton fills the air.*

*The meat chosen for this traditional dish comes from the hind leg of a certain type of sheep. The crescent-shaped knife used to slice the meat, and even the grid on which the mutton is cooked, are especially made for this purpose. In the past even a special pose was adopted as one cooked and feasted on the barbecued meat. With one foot on the ground and the other on top of a stool, the cooking, chatting and feasting might have brought to mind stories handed down by nomadic ancestors.*

*The following recipe shows an improved version of the traditional dish, consisting of richly marinated shreds of mutton, quickly barbecued with shredded leeks. It is stuffed into sesame-covered pocket bread and eaten sandwich-style, often with pickled garlic.*

500 g (1 lb) lean mutton or lamb
3 tablespoons light soy sauce
1½ tablespoons rice wine or dry sherry
2 teaspoons ginger juice
1½ tablespoons sugar
2 teaspoons sesame oil
pinch of salt
2 fresh leeks
fresh coriander
pickled garlic

Cut the meat across the grain into very thin slices, then stack several slices together and cut into shreds. Place in a dish and add the soy sauce, wine, ginger juice, sugar, sesame oil and salt and mix well. Leave for at least 30 minutes.
❀ Rinse the leeks thoroughly, cut into 5 cm (2 in) lengths and shred lengthways.
❀ Heat a ribbed barbecue plate over a charcoal fire. Rub with oil and spread the leeks over it. Place the meat in a single layer on top of the leeks, then use a pair of long-handled chopsticks to turn the leeks and meat over and over until the leeks are soft and the meat cooked through and tender.
❀ Stuff the pocket bread with the meat and fresh coriander leaves, and serve the pickled garlic separately.

## SESAME POCKET BREAD

3 tablespoons vegetable oil
3½ cups (440 g/14 oz) flour
¾ cup (175 mL/6 fl oz) boiling water
3 tablespoons cold water
2 teaspoons salt
2-3 tablespoons white sesame seeds
oil for frying

Heat the oil in a wok, add ½ cup (60 g/2 oz) flour and cook over low heat until the mixture is smooth and golden, stirring constantly. Set aside to cool.
❀ Pour the remaining flour into a bowl, reserving 1 tablespoon. Pour in the boiling water and stir quickly, using the handle of a wooden spoon, to a smooth dough, adding the cold water to make it soft and pliable. Knead for about 7 minutes on a lightly oiled board. Roll out into a long sausage shape and divide into 10-12 pieces. Cover with a damp cloth.
❀ Roll each piece out separately into a square-shaped cake about 12 cm (5 in) wide. Spread on a coating of the flour-and-oil dough and sprinkle with salt and some of the reserved flour. Fold in two sides to overlap in the centre, seal the edges by pinching the two ends, then fold the other two sides in to just overlap in the centre. Roll in the direction of the folds into a rectangular shape. Dip the smooth side into sesame seeds, pressing on lightly.
❀ Bake on an oiled and floured baking tray in a pre-heated oven at 220°C (425°F) or fry on both sides until puffed and golden. Cut in halves to fill.

SICHUAN RABBIT CAKE

STUFFED OXTAIL

## Sichuan 四川

# SICHUAN RABBIT CAKE

*Confucius taught the Chinese to be meticulous about fine food and in particular minced meat. Food should be savoured rather than devoured: it is the quality not the quantity of the food that counts. As for minced meat, the finer the mince the better, as it should be easily digested and easily absorbed.*

*In this dish, the rabbit meat is minced, seasoned, steamed into cakes and then deep-fried until crisp. A rich Sichuan sauce containing minced ginger, spring onion and garlic is poured over before serving. The meat is tender and salty, sweet and sour, and pepper hot.*

1 x 625-750 g (1¼-1½ lb) rabbit
2 egg whites, well beaten
½ cup (125 mL/4 fl oz) water
1½ tablespoons cornflour (cornstarch)
¾ teaspoon salt
cornflour (cornstarch)
oil for deep-frying

SAUCE

2 pickled red chillies
3 cloves garlic
3 spring onions (shallots/scallions)
3 slices fresh (root) ginger
½ cup (125 mL/4 fl oz) chicken or rabbit stock (broth)
1 tablespoon sugar
1½ tablespoons brown vinegar
1 tablespoon light soy sauce
1½ teaspoons cornflour (cornstarch)
pinch of salt and Sichuan pepper (Fagara or Sansho)

Remove the rabbit meat from the bones and mince (grind) very finely. Add the egg whites, water, cornflour and salt and mix thoroughly until the paste is smooth, picking out all the fine sinews. Spread the mixture in a lightly oiled, heatproof dish and place on a rack in a wok or in a steamer, cover and steam for about 14 minutes until the cake is firm. Remove and leave to cool. Cut into thick slices, about 5 cm (2 in) long and coat thickly with cornflour.

For the sauce, finely mince (grind) the chillies, garlic, spring onions and ginger. Mix the remaining sauce ingredients together and set aside.

Heat the oil in a wok to smoking point and deep-fry the slices of rabbit cake, several at a time, until golden brown, then drain well.

In a clean wok, sauté the chillies, garlic, spring onions and ginger in a little oil until fragrant. Add the rabbit cake, mix in evenly, then pour in the other pre-mixed sauce ingredients and bring to the boil, stirring carefully, and serve.

## Beijing 北京

# STUFFED OXTAIL

*Oxtail meat is different from the meat of all other parts of the ox. It is bright red, finely textured and contains a sticky substance which is specially pleasing to some palates. In this recipe the star-shaped central bone is removed and the cavity filled with a mixture of minced (ground) fish and chicken.*

1 x 1 kg (2 lb) oxtail
5 cups (1¼ L/40 fl oz) beef stock (broth)
2 spring onions (shallots/scallions)
2 slices fresh (root) ginger
1 teaspoon salt
1 tablespoon rice wine or dry sherry

STUFFING

125 g (4 oz) white fish
125 g (4 oz) chicken meat
1 egg white
2 teaspoons rice wine or dry sherry
½ teaspoon salt

SAUCE

2 spring onions (shallots/scallions), chopped
2 slices fresh (root) ginger, chopped
2 tablespoons lard or oil for frying
¾ cup (175 mL/6 fl oz) chicken or beef stock (broth)
2 teaspoons rice wine or dry sherry
1 tablespoon cornflour (cornstarch)

Have the butcher cut the oxtail through between the joints. Place the meat in a large saucepan and add the stock, onions, ginger, salt and rice wine. Cover and bring to the boil. Skim off the froth, then reduce the heat and simmer gently for about 2 hours.

Allow to cool slightly, then remove the meat from the stock and drain well. Use a knife with a narrow sharp blade to remove the central bone from each piece of meat.

Finely mince (grind) the fish and chicken together adding the egg white, rice wine and salt. Knead to a smooth paste, then fill into the holes in the pieces of oxtail. Arrange them on a lightly oiled, heatproof plate and set on a rack in a wok or in a steamer, cover and steam for about 15 minutes until the filling is cooked through.

For the sauce, stir-fry the spring onions and ginger in the lard or oil until softened, then add the remaining sauce ingredients and bring to the boil, stirring constantly.

Stir the liquid from the dish in which the oxtail was steamed into the sauce, pour sauce over the meat and serve.

# Shanghai 上海

## COLD DISHES

*On the lower reaches of the Yangtze River, there is a shop that specialises in selling cold dishes and game. The story goes that when this shop was over a hundred years old, business was slack because of poor management.*

*One day a beggar came into the shop and asked to stay overnight. Seeing that he was tired and hungry, the owner gave him a meal. During the night the beggar spread out his mat to sleep, and before leaving the next morning the beggar left his mat in grateful repayment. The shop owner thought it useless and burnt it in his cooking fire. But the pork cooked over the fire that day was delicious, and business soon picked up. The beggar was said to have been an incarnation of the deity Lu Dongbing, and as the story spread, the owner changed the shop's name to Lu Gaojian to honour the god, selling pork stewed in soy sauce in the spring, goose pickled in grain in the summer, duck in autumn, and mutton, roast fish, roast eggs, duck stewed in soy sauce, prawns, pigs' trotters, game and more in the winter.*

### COLD DISHES ON A SINGLE PLATE

Cold, cooked food is often served as the first course at a dinner and cold dishes in Shanghai have undergone several stages of development. Over a hundred years ago, each item of food was served on a separate plate. At a banquet, there would be dried and fresh fruit, cold and hot plates, beverages and so on. Even at the simplest dinner there were at least four cold dishes, and usually there were six or eight.

The food was finely cut and served neatly on plates. For instance, ham was cut into thin slices of equal size and thickness. Pai ham was cut into squares and Qiao ham was cut into thin pieces and placed on a plate in the shape of an arched bridge.

### ASSORTED COLD DISHES OF TWO OR THREE INGREDIENTS

Forty or fifty years ago, cold dishes developed into assorted cold dishes. Usually one assorted dish was made up of two or three ingredients, and four to six such dishes were served at dinner. There were also assorted cold dishes of five or six ingredients, but these were only served at informal dinners.

Assorted cold dishes vary according to the different ingredients, shapes, colours and cuisines. Particular care is taken in selecting and arranging the ingredients so as to match the colours well.

### LARGE ASSORTED COLD PLATTERS

About thirty years ago large assorted cold dishes became popular. A large round or oval plate would contain 10 or 12 ingredients. All the ingredients were carefully prepared, boned and well presented. Preparation involved skill in slicing, matching colours and arrangement.

The photograph below shows a typical assorted cold platter of beautifully arranged cold cooked meat including ham, beef, chicken, luncheon meat, vegetarian "chicken" and bamboo shoots, with poached prawns and shredded marinated cabbage in the centre.

# Beijing 北京

# FRIED RED AND WHITE MEATS

*This is a traditional Shanxi speciality found on the menus of many of the restaurants in northern China. There are two kinds of meat in this dish, white chicken meat and red pork fillet. They complement each other and are both tender. Black wood ear fungus and green vegetable strips give additional colour.*

## RED MEAT

250 g (8 oz) pork fillet
½ egg, well beaten
3 tablespoons cornflour (cornstarch)
½ cup (125 mL/4 fl oz) peanut oil
1 tablespoon brown vinegar
1 spring onion (shallot/scallion), sliced
2 cloves garlic, sliced
3 pieces dried wood ear fungus, soaked for 20 minutes
1 stalk Chinese kale (gai larn) or spinach, sliced diagonally

## SAUCE

2 teaspoons rice wine or dry sherry
2 teaspoons dark soy sauce
½ cup (125 mL/4 fl oz) chicken stock (broth)
large pinch of five spice powder

## WHITE MEAT

250 g (8 oz) chicken breast meat
1 egg white, well beaten
3 tablespoons cornflour (cornstarch)
2 tablespoons lard
½ cup (125 mL/4 fl oz) chicken stock (broth)
¾ teaspoon salt
1 tablespoon rice wine or dry sherry
1 spring onion (shallot/scallion), sliced
3-4 slices fresh (root) ginger, shredded
3-4 slices cucumber, seeds removed
1 tablespoon rendered chicken fat, melted

Slice the pork fillet thinly, then cut into smaller pieces. Place in a dish and add the egg and cornflour, coating the pork evenly.
❀ Heat the peanut oil in a wok and fry the pork until cooked through, stirring constantly to separate the slices. Remove and set aside.
❀ Add the vinegar, spring onion, garlic, drained fungus and vegetable slices and stir-fry for 2 minutes, then return the pork and stir-fry briefly before adding the pre-mixed sauce ingredients. Cook, stirring, until the sauce coats the ingredients, then spoon onto one side of a serving dish and keep warm.
❀ Slice the chicken and place in a dish with the egg white and cornflour, mixing until each piece is well coated.
❀ Heat a wok and add the lard. Stir-fry the chicken over high heat, adding the chicken stock, salt and rice wine. Then add the spring onions, ginger and cucumber and simmer gently until the chicken is tender, and the sauce reduced to a glaze.
❀ Arrange beside the pork meat on the serving plate and serve.

THE WILD RUSH OF THE DADU RIVER, WESTERN SICHUAN

LEO MEIER

四川
Sichuan

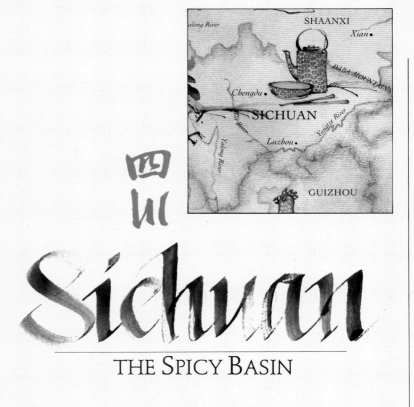

# Sichuan
## THE SPICY BASIN

IN THE geographical heartland of China is the huge natural bowl of Sichuan. Surrounded by range after range of mountains, slashed by the gathering flood of the Yangtze, the plains of the Red Basin are one of the most fertile areas in all China. Into these lowlands the Yangtze comes bursting with the ice-melt from the high ranges of remote Qinghai. When it leaves the red earth of Sichuan to carve its way through the Daba mountains to the east China plains, the Yangtze is mightier still – swollen by the waters of four substantial tributaries. These four rivers, the Min, Jialing, Yalong and To, give the province its name: Sichuan means Four Streams. They also give the area much of the agricultural muscle that has helped shape its gastronomic heritage and which today feeds a hundred million people with one of the best balanced and most spectacular cuisines on earth.

Three centuries before Christianity began, and sixteen centuries before Sichuan became a province of China, the flow of the mighty Min river was harnessed to water the thirsty land. A huge barrage built by human might diverted the river away from its natural channel into the surrounding plains. The flow was halved again and again, until countless irrigation streams trickled through the fields covering the plains on which the present provincial capital of Chengdu now stands. From these fields peasants harvested rich crops. They still do, and their produce gives the province its proud and spicy culinary legacy, which in recent years has swept the dinner tables of the world.

Sichuan cuisine today is a happy medley of many traditions and influences. The tangy tastes of India are blended into Sichuan cooking. Travellers brought Buddhism into the province more than two thousand years ago. The traders and missionaries carried Indian spices, herbs and cooking techniques with them as well as Buddhist teachings, and the strong vegetarian legacy is still very much alive in such family dishes as peppery hot beancurd and Sichuan pickled vegetables, items which sometimes take pride of place at a meatless table. The

A WARM WELCOME FROM TIBETAN VILLAGERS IN WESTERN SICHUAN
LEO MEIER

181

AT SHIMIAN VILLAGE MARKET, SICHUAN PROVINCE

HARALD SUND

SPRING ONIONS, AN ESSENTIAL INGREDIENT OF CHINESE COOKING

provincial cooking also has links with the cuisines of Indochina to the south. The Thai people trace their beginnings back through the mists of time to the shrouded mountains that surround the Sichuan basin, and many aspects of the cooking of Thailand bear a close similarity to Sichuan cooking. Thai-speaking tribes still live in the mountains, as do Miao, Li and other hill peoples whose racial relatives are scattered over the highlands of Vietnam, Laos and Kampuchea.

Vegetarian dishes flourish in Sichuan in staggering variety. For two thousand years Buddhist customs dictated a meatless diet for a large minority of the population, and imaginative chefs created an exhaustive repertoire of dishes from the abundant produce of the land. As the huge population grew, grazing space for animals dwindled as every available piece of land went under the plough. The animal that pulled the plough, the faithful, plodding water buffalo, the eternal tractor of China, was more often than not the only source of meat.

Many vegetarian dishes are garnished with the memorable and delicious, but wrongly named, Fish Flavoured Sauce. This splendid example of culinary ingenuity tastes like fish, but its unforgettable flavour comes from a careful mixing of vinegar, garlic, ginger, spring onions and hot bean paste. There is an old saying in Sichuan that a cook could pour the searingly spicy Fish Flavoured Sauce over rocks washed up on the banks of the Min River and hungry diners would devour them with enthusiasm.

LEO MEIER

Another old saying concerns the seven flavours used in the cooking of provincial specialities. This is the first lesson given to a novice cook and it stays with him throughout his career: *sweet* (tien) comes from honey or sugar; *sour* (suan) from vinegar; *salty* (tien) from salt or soy; *fragrant* (xiang) from garlic and ginger; *bitter* (ku) from spring onions or leeks; *nutty* (ma) from sesame seeds or oil; and, most importantly for Sichuan, *hot* (la) from the red chilli.

Beans and beancurd, together with flavoursome ingredients like spring onions, garlic, peppercorns and ginger, combine with sesame oil, vinegar and the ubiquitous chilli to form memorable dishes. To these are added carefully tended crops from the deep rich soil, the products of the wild mountains and steep valleys that make up ninety per cent of the 540 000 square kilometres (210,000 square miles) of the province. In these mountains, covered in semi-tropical forests rising to cool growths of pine, are gathered some of the most highly praised mushrooms and fungi in China. Here, too, in magnificent towering stands, grow the imposing bamboos for which Sichuan is famous. The bamboo provides a delicacy not only for human gourmets but for the nation's most famous animal, the giant panda. The bamboo forests are home and refuge for these bulky black and white animals, and the people of Sichuan are as proud of the pandas as they are of their distinctive cuisine. The animals are totally protected, and on cold winter nights often venture down from their mountain strongholds to seek shelter, which is given willingly, in highland farmyards. Peasants in the mountains go to the aid of the pandas during periods of drought or flood when their delicate staple diet is threatened. Like the human inhabitants of Sichuan, the pandas are connoisseurs of the food of the province, and their preferred diet

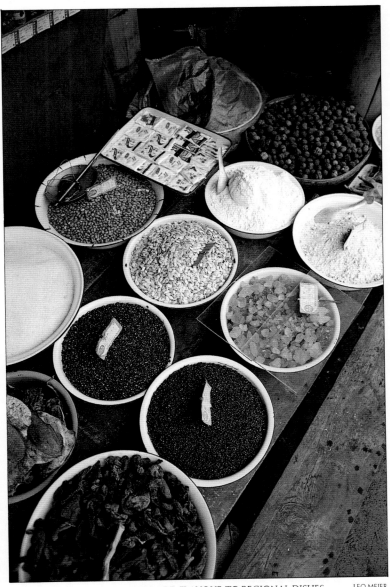

TASTY AND COLOURFUL SPICES ADD FLAVOUR TO REGIONAL DISHES    LEO MEIER

NOMADIC TIBETAN SHEPHERDS IN THE GRASSLANDS OF NORTHERN SICHUAN

LEO MEIER

is fresh bamboo shoots which grow in plenty only in their remote and misty mountains. When the supply is threatened, local farmers carry loads of bamboo on their backs up steep tracks to feed the animals that are the symbol of Sichuan.

Although Chengdu is 2900 kilometres (1,800 miles) up the Yangtze from the East China Sea, fish figures prominently in the diet. Until railways were forged through the mountains earlier this century, the great waterway provided the only reliable form of communication with the outside world. Today the waters of the Yangtze yield a good catch, but a good deal of the fish, freshwater crabs, eels and other water-dwellers consumed in the province are raised for the wok in fishponds, canals and irrigation ditches. A bonus of plump frogs, juicy turtles and tender snakes is also harvested by farmers going to their fields and children tending their flocks of wandering ducks. But despite its location, seawater fish also appear on Sichuan menus, and for many hundreds of years junks loaded with dried or salted fish and seaweed have been towed by armies of toiling coolies through the narrow Yangtze gorges.

If the cuisine of Sichuan Province is built on a solid foundation of red-hot, mouth-pursing chillies, then that tradition is even more apparent over the border in neighbouring Hunan. This landlocked province has a hot, humid summer and a winter that brings bracing chills. To open the pores and keep cool in the summer and to heat the blood in the cold months are two reasons that Hunan people give for flavouring almost every dish with chillies. As in Sichuan, there is an awesome variety of chillies and capsicums. They range from the familiar, harmless large green capsicum to the tiny red pepper known as the delayed action bomb. Why the name? Any innocent visitor can tell you that. Just ask the question five minutes after they have eaten one and, if they can

splutter out an answer while trying to quaff buckets of cold water, they will explain that the peppers take a little while to take effect. When the fire is lit, however, it is hard to put out – perhaps one reason why the people of Sichuan and Hunan are also known for their ample consumption of prime beers which wash down the hearty, spiced meals.

Not all Sichuan food is hot, either in temperature or in flavour. Especially in summer, a meal will start with a selection of cold dishes or a platter holding a selection of cold meats. And the famed peppercorn of the province, used in moderation, tends to be tasty rather than hot. But let the visitor beware the small scarlet peppers that are used as the raw ingredient of pungent red oil and to add the fire to fermented hot bean paste. When they grow, and they are harvested on every patch of earth in Sichuan, the chillies lift themselves upright on the branches. That is why they are called "reach for the sun" chillies – belief has it that they are striving to get closer to the warmth of the sun to take in more of its fire.

CARD PLAYERS IN A TRADITIONAL TEAHOUSE

HARALD SUND

THE TIBETAN VILLAGE OF ANLANG, SICHUAN PROVINCE

HARALD SUND

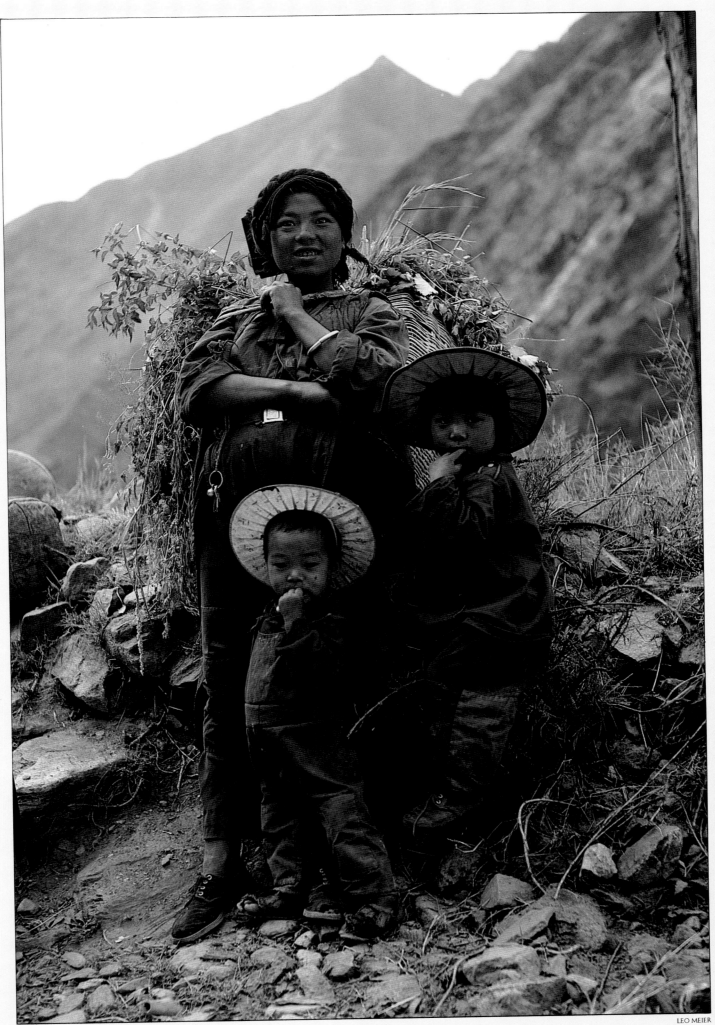

LEO MEIER

TIBETAN MOUNTAIN VILLAGERS

*(following page)* TIBETAN HOUSES CLIMB
THE QIONGLAISHAN MOUNTAINS, WESTERN SICHUAN

LEO MEIER

糧食豆品
Grains
&Curd

糧食豆品

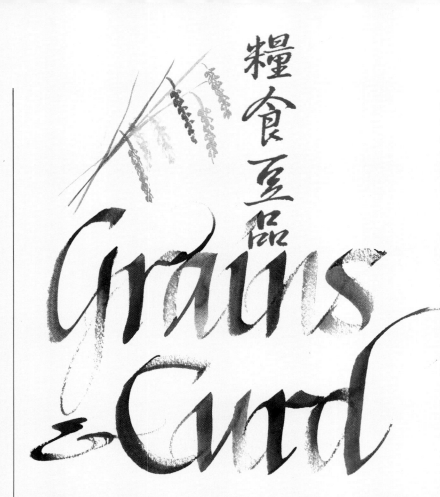

# Grains & Curd

糧食豆品

COOKING NOODLES IN A STREETSIDE RESTAURANT     WELDON TRANNIES

of water and two parts of flour are the simple ingredients of the pancake of northern China. Add a thousand choices of different stuffings or accompaniments and you have the start of many northern meals. Plain steamed buns or thin fried pancakes can be eaten with the filling stews of Hebei and Shandong or to mop up the remains of a bubbling Mongolian Fire Pot.

Whether from rice flour or wheat, a staggering variety of pasta is made in China. Fat or thin, flat or round, pasta comes in sheets, strings, strands and nodules. Noodles can be cooked by themselves or as a steaming bed on which to serve a regional delicacy. They can be fried, stewed, boiled or baked, and eaten for breakfast, lunch, dinner, as an in-between meal or a midnight snack.

While rice and bread give Chinese cuisine much of its carbohydrates, a lot of the protein comes from the miraculous soy bean. Cultivated since the beginning of China's recorded history, over five thousand years ago, there are more than two thousand five hundred varieties of the soy bean. They grow easily in the harsh climate of the north, even in frigid Manchuria; they produce an immense yield, are easy to grow, simple to harvest and are processed into a vast range of healthy and edible products. Dieticians say the beans in one form or

NORTH of the Yangtze, wheat; south of the river, rice; all over China, beancurd. Like most schoolboy maxims, this one is too simplified to be completely true, but it is basically correct. While one of the seven thousand varieties of long-grained rice is the staple staff of life for people of the south and centre of China, north-erners build their sturdy diet on a foundation of steamed buns or noodles. People don't say "Hullo" in Canton-onese, the polite phrase is "Have you eaten rice yet?" In Shanghai, holding a secure job in the government is said to be like having an iron rice bowl – the bowl can't be broken and the public servant can't be sacked. While rice-eating has been ingrained for centuries in the south where benevolent nature provides ample rain and sun-shine to harvest up to three bumper crops a year, the cold, dry plains of the north support mainly wheat, barley and millet. In Manchuria the farmers have to move quickly to harvest their crops before the freezing winter snaps down after the all too brief summer.

Throughout the southern provinces life revolves around the paddy field. Landscapes are painted in differ-ent shades of green, from the brilliant emerald of the newly transplanted rice to the deep luxuriant greens of the mature plants. Thousands of years of experience has laid down immutable laws for peasant farmers to follow as they bring in the white gold of the rice crop. The rice plant provides a greater yield in the flooded fields than any other crop, and it brings to the table a much-loved staple that plays a vital role in the daily diet of most Chinese. Eaten three times a day, it is an integral part of every meal – much more so than bread and potatoes in a Western kitchen. Rice to many Chinese is not just part of a meal, but the body on which the delicacies of meat, fish and vegetables are the gorgeous clothes: "A meal with-out rice is like a beautiful girl with one eye" says an old proverb.

The situation is quite different in the northern prov-inces, where the people feel deprived if they cannot enjoy the buns and noodles they were weaned on. The basic dough used reflects the no-nonsense approach to food of a busy farmwife who has crops, a home and chil-dren to attend to as well as a family to cook for. One part another provide almost everything needed by the human body. Certainly, in the form of beancurd, the soy bean provides a high-protein meat substitute healthier than the original animal product it so flatteringly copies.

Beancurd has for a long time provided protein for those who could not afford meat, and today, in a more health-conscious world, beancurd is often used in place of meat by the more prosperous societies. Over the centuries chefs have invented tens of thousands of recipes using beancurd. The Buddhist influence which seeped gently through many eras of China and spread the gospel of a meatless diet did much to take the humble bean and elevate it to be a gourmet's delight. Stir-fried with vegetables, stewed with seafood, braised along with meat, boiled to add body and potency to soups, beancurd is a versatile addition to the diet.

Another well-known by-product of the bean is soy sauce; indispensable in Chinese cooking, it adds a unique flavour to any dish. With sugar added the soy bean becomes a health drink or a dessert sweet. The bland bean picks up the flavour of whatever it shares a pot with. In the hard years that have come so often to China, countless lives of poor peasants have been saved by this modest culinary chameleon.

MAKING DIM SUM, A FAMILY AFFAIR                    WHEELER PICTURES

## Sichuan 四川

# PEPPERY HOT BEANCURD

*This deliciously hot and aromatic dish was created by pockmarked grandmother Ch'eng who operated a small beancurd stall on a street corner in Chengdu, centuries ago. Using a few cakes of beancurd, a little ground meat and local seasonings, she produced one of the tastiest and most nutritious of the Chinese dishes, yet one of the least expensive. Today the dish is still called after her "Ma Po Dofu" (pockmarked mother's beancurd).*

4 x 140 g (4½ oz) squares soft beancurd
185 g (6 oz) lean beef, preferably fillet (tenderloin)
3 spring onions (shallots/scallions)
2-3 tablespoons vegetable or rapeseed oil
3 cloves garlic, crushed

SEASONING/SAUCE

1 teaspoon grated, fresh (root) ginger
1 tablespoon fermented black beans, chopped
2 pickled red chillies, chopped
2 tablespoons light soy sauce
1-2 teaspoons hot bean paste
½ teaspoon salt
1½ teaspoons sugar
½ teaspoon Sichuan peppercorns (Fagara or Sansho), ground
1 cup (250 mL/8 fl oz) chicken stock (broth)
1 tablespoon cornflour (cornstarch)

Cut the beancurd into small cubes and set aside. Very finely mince (grind) the beef, and finely chop the spring onion.

🔆 Heat the oil in a wok, and stir-fry the beef, spring onions and garlic until half cooked.

🔆 Add the ginger, black beans, chillies, soy sauce and hot bean paste and stir-fry together for about 1½ minutes, then add the remaining seasoning/sauce ingredients, except the cornflour, and bring to the boil. Slide in the beancurd and simmer for about 5 minutes over gentle heat, carefully stir in the cornflour mixed with a little cold water, simmering gently until thickened.

🔆 For extra flavour, sprinkle on some flaked red chilli and a little crushed Sichuan pepper just before serving.

## Sichuan 四川

# BEANCURD IN CONSOMMÉ

6 x 140 g (4½ oz) squares soft beancurd
3 egg whites
1 tablespoon softened lard
1½ tablespoons cornflour (cornstarch)
7 cups (1¾ L/56 fl oz) clear chicken or vegetable stock (broth)
salt to taste
white pepper
500 g (1 lb) fresh lettuce, Chinese cabbage or other leafy
    Chinese green vegetable

Place the beancurd in a dish and mash smoothly. Beat the egg whites well and stir into the beancurd. Add the lard and the cornflour, mixed with a little cold water, and beat the whole mixture together until thoroughly amalgamated. Pour into a lightly oiled square tin and place on a rack in a wok or in a steamer. Cover and steam for about 14 minutes until firm, then remove and leave to cool.

🔆 Cut the beancurd mixture into rectangular-shaped pieces.

🔆 Boil the stock up and season with salt and pepper.

🔆 Rinse the vegetables thoroughly and separate the leaves, place them in the bottom of a serving bowl and arrange the beancurd on top. Upturn the sliced beancurd onto the vegetables, cover with the boiling stock and serve at once.

PEPPERY HOT BEANCURD

BEANCURD IN CONSOMMÉ

STUFFED CALTROP-SHAPED BEANCURD

## Sichuan 四川

# STUFFED CALTROP-SHAPED BEANCURD

4 x 140 g (4½ oz) squares beancurd
1 cup (250 mL/8 fl oz) rapeseed or peanut oil
2 x 45 g (1½ oz) slices ham
8 water chestnuts
125 g (4 oz) fatty pork
2 tablespoons finely chopped bamboo shoots
1 egg white, lightly beaten
½ cup (60 g/2 oz) cornflour (cornstarch)
4 slices fresh (root) ginger
2 spring onions (shallots/scallions), sliced
4 cloves garlic, chopped

### SAUCE

¾ cup (175 mL/6 fl oz) chicken stock (broth)
1 tablespoon light soy sauce
2 teaspoons rice wine or dry sherry
½ teaspoon salt
½ teaspoon sugar
2 teaspoons cornflour (cornstarch)

Hold each square of beancurd in the palm of your hand and carefully cut into four triangular-shaped pieces. Heat the oil in a wok and fry the beancurd until the surface is crisp and slightly bubbly. Lift out and drain well. Make a slit in one side of each piece of beancurd.

✺ Finely mince (grind) the ham, water chestnuts, pork and bamboo shoots, mix together and stuff into the beancurd triangles. Dip the cut edges in the egg white, then into cornflour, and fry gently in the oil for about 2½ minutes until the beancurd has become very crisp and the stuffing has cooked through. Remove, drain well and arrange on a serving plate.

✺ Sauté the ginger, spring onion, and garlic in the oil for about 45 seconds, then add the pre-mixed sauce ingredients and simmer, stirring, until the sauce thickens. Pour over the beancurd and serve at once.

## Sichuan 四川

# BRAISED CRUCIAN CARP WITH BEANCURD

1 x 625 g (1¼ lb) fresh carp or other meaty white fish
4 x 140 g (4½ oz) squares beancurd
1 cup (250 mL/8 fl oz) peanut oil
1½ tablespoons red fermented rice (wine lees)
1½ tablespoons sweet bean paste

### SEASONING/SAUCE

1½ tablespoons fermented black beans
1 teaspoon finely grated fresh (root) ginger
3 tablespoons finely chopped spring onions (shallots/scallions)
1 teaspoon finely chopped garlic
2 tablespoons dark soy sauce
½ teaspoon ground Sichuan peppercorns (Fagara or Sansho)
1 tablespoon rice wine or dry sherry
½ cup (125 mL/4 fl oz) chicken stock (broth)

Clean the fish, dip into boiling water, drain and dry well. Make several deep scores diagonally across each side. Cut the beancurd into cubes and slide into a pot of simmering water. Boil gently for 2 minutes, then drain well.

✺ Heat the oil in a wok and fry the fish on both sides until well coloured. Pour off most of the oil, then add the pre-mixed seasoning/sauce ingredients, except the stock, and fry for 1 minute. Add the stock and beancurd, cover the dish and simmer gently until the flavours are well absorbed. Add the fermented rice and sweet bean paste, simmer briefly and transfer to a serving dish. Serve at once.

BRAISED CRUCIAN CARP WITH BEANCURD

# Beijing 北京

# BEANCURD IN AN EARTHENWARE POT

3-4 dried black mushrooms, soaked for 25 minutes
1 dried scallop, soaked for 25 minutes
1 tablespoon dried shrimp, soaked for 20 minutes
60 g (2 oz) chicken breasts, finely minced (ground)
60 g (2 oz) lean pork, finely minced (ground)
30 g (1 oz) prawn (shrimp) meat, minced (ground)
4 x 140 g (4½ oz) squares beancurd
4 spring onions (shallots/scallions)
3 slices fresh (root) ginger
1 teaspoon salt
3 cups (750 mL/24 fl oz) superior stock (*see page 124*) or
　chicken stock (broth)
sesame oil

Place the mushrooms, scallops and shrimps in the heatproof dishes they have been soaked in on a rack in a wok or steamer. Cover and steam for about 15 minutes over high heat until softened, then drain well.

❈ Cut the stalks from the mushrooms and finely dice half of the tops. Mix the minced chicken, pork and prawn meat together and season lightly with salt.

❈ Cut each square of beancurd into four and make a slit through the centre of each quarter. Fill one end of each slit with the minced filling and the other with the diced mushrooms, and place in an earthenware pot.

❈ Slice the spring onions diagonally and add to the pot with the ginger, remaining mushrooms, shredded scallop and the shrimp meat, then add the salt, a dash of pepper, sesame oil and the stock.

❈ Bring to the boil and simmer gently for about 30 minutes. Serve in the pot.

SAN XIAN STUFFED BEANCURD

"SILVER FISH" WRAPPED IN SNOW

Beijing 北京

# SAN XIAN STUFFED BEANCURD

*Beancurd was first made some two thousand years ago by an emperor of the Han Dynasty (206 BC-220 AD). An accomplished scholar, well versed in medicine and astrology, he assembled a group of researchers to look for new medicines, and in the course of their research they produced beancurd. They found it both cheap and very nutritious. Since that time beancurd has remained one of the most highly regarded Chinese foods, and many different ways of preparing and cooking it have been devised.*

2 x 140 g (4½ oz) squares of firm-textured beancurd
90 g (3 oz) chicken breasts, finely minced (ground)
60 g (2 oz) fresh prawn (shrimp) meat
2 tablespoons finely chopped, soaked and prepared sea cucumber (optional)
1½ tablespoons finely chopped spring onion (shallot/scallion)
¼ teaspoon grated, fresh (root) ginger
1 egg white, well beaten
1 tablespoon rice wine or dry sherry
½ teaspoon sesame oil
½ teaspoon salt
oil for frying

BATTER

1 cup (125 g/4 oz) flour
1 egg

SAUCE

1 cup (250 mL/8 fl oz) chicken stock (broth)
1½ teaspoons rice wine or dry sherry
½ teaspoon salt
1 teaspoon cornflour (cornstarch)

ONION OIL

1 small red onion, very thinly sliced
3 tablespoons peanut oil

Cut the beancurd squares in halves and slice each piece thinly to give about 28 square slices in all.

Make a reasonably smooth filling by mixing the chicken breasts, prawn meat, sea cucumber if used, spring onion, ginger, egg white, rice wine, sesame oil and the salt. Squeeze the mixture through your fingers until thoroughly amalgamated and sticky. Divide into 14 portions and roll each into a ball, then press flat to about the size of the beancurd slices.

Place one piece of filling between two squares of beancurd to make sandwiches and coat lightly with flour. Use the remaining flour and some cold water to make a fairly thick batter for coating.

Heat enough oil in a wok to gently fry the beancurd, turning once, until lightly browned on both sides. Lift out and place on a serving plate.

Drain the wok, retaining about 2 tablespoons of the oil. Mix the sauce ingredients together and pour into the wok. Simmer, stirring, until the sauce thickens, then pour over the beancurd.

In a clean wok or saucepan heat the peanut oil until smoking. Add the sliced red onion and cook until lightly browned. Use a slotted spoon to remove the onion, drain well and reserve as a garnish for another dish. Pour a portion of the onion oil over the finished dish and serve at once.

Beijing 北京

# "SILVER FISH" WRAPPED IN SNOW

*This unusual and economical vegetarian dish goes well with wine. It is simply cooked macaroni dipped into an egg-white batter and fried. The long whitish pieces look like whitebait or silver fish dipped into snow. Silver fish come from the northern coast of China.*

45 g (1½ oz) dry macaroni
1 teaspoon salt
2 egg whites
½ cup (60 g/2 oz) cornflour (cornstarch)
2 tablespoons flour
oil for deep-frying
1 tablespoon five-spice salt*

Place the macaroni in a saucepan and add half the salt. Cover with plenty of boiling water, stir up well and cook until the macaroni is tender, then drain well and leave to cool.

Whip the egg whites until firm and fluffy, fold in the cornflour, the remaining salt and the flour and add just enough cold water to make a thick batter.

Heat the oil in a wok to smoking point, then lower the heat slightly. Dip the macaroni into the batter and deep-fry until crisp and puffy, but without turning golden. Remove and drain well.

Arrange the fried "silver fish" on a serving plate and serve with the five-spice salt in a small dish.

*To make the five-spice salt, heat 1½ tablespoons of fine table salt in a wok until it begins to crackle, add 1 teaspoon of Chinese five-spice powder, remove from the heat, stir and cool.*

## Guangzhou 广州

# SILVER NEEDLE NOODLES WITH ASSORTED MEAT SHREDS

*Guangdong has a long history of making noodles from dried rice; in one of the oldest methods, cooked rice is dried in the sun, ground to a powder, mixed with boiling water and rubbed into short noodles, sharp at both ends like needles. A better result is, however, achieved by making the noodles from wheat starch.*

90 g (3 oz) lean pork
90 g (3 oz) boneless chicken meat
90 g (3 oz) cleaned squid
90 g (3 oz) fresh prawn (shrimp) meat
3-4 dried black mushrooms, soaked for 25 minutes
1 egg
30 g (1 oz) fresh bean sprouts
1 small fresh leek, white part only
1 small slice salted ham
fresh coriander
lard or oil for frying

SEASONING

1 tablespoon light soy sauce
2 teaspoons rice wine or dry sherry
1 teaspoon salt
1½ teaspoons sugar
1 teaspoon sesame oil

SILVER NEEDLE NOODLES

1 cup (125 g/4 oz) wheat starch (gluten-free wheat flour)
½-⅔ cup (125-150 mL/4-5 fl oz) boiling water
1 teaspoon lard
2 tablespoons cornflour

Prepare the noodles first. Sift the flour and cornflour into a mixing bowl, make a well in the centre, pour the boiling water in and add the lard. Mix in quickly, working with a wooden spoon, then cover and leave for 5-6 minutes for the flour to soften. Working with oiled hands on a lightly oiled worktop, break off small pieces of the dough and roll into a ball, then rub across the worktop with the palm of your hand to form thin noodles, pointed at each end. Use up all the dough and set the noodles aside.

Finely shred the pork, chicken and squid, cut the prawns into small pieces, drain the mushrooms, remove the stems and cut the caps into shreds. Beat the egg lightly and set aside. Rinse the bean sprouts and drain well. Shred the leek and ham, rinse the coriander and drain.

Heat a wok, wipe out with an oiled cloth and pour in the egg, tilting and turning the wok so that the egg flows into a wide omelet. Cook until set, then turn and cook the other side. Lift out and spread on a cloth to cool.

Add 2-3 tablespoons of lard or oil to the wok and stir-fry the noodles over high heat for 1 minute, then reduce the heat and continue to stir-fry for another 2 minutes. Remove to a serving plate and set aside.

Add the shredded meats, except the ham, to the wok and stir-fry together until cooked, then add the mushrooms, bean sprouts and leek and stir-fry briefly.

Add the seasoning/sauce ingredients and toss together thoroughly over high heat. Spoon the cooked ingredients over the noodles.

Cut the egg into fine shreds and use together with the ham and coriander to garnish the dish. Or alternatively, stir these in with the noodles and other ingredients.

SILVER NEEDLE NOODLES WITH ASSORTED MEAT SHREDS

SHA HE NOODLES WITH LEEKS AND SHREDDED PORK

STEAMED DRAGON'S EYE ROLLS

## Guangzhou 广州

# SHA HE NOODLES WITH LEEKS AND SHREDDED PORK

*The Sha He Restaurant in Guangzhou is well known both at home and abroad for the special flavour of its sha he noodles. More than thirty dishes are offered featuring these tender noodles made from rice flour and water from the Nine Dragon Spring, which gives them their unique flavour.*

315 g (10 oz) fresh rice ribbon noodles (sha he noodles)
salt
lard or vegetable oil
125 g (4 oz) lean pork, shredded
90 g (3 oz) silver sprouts*
2 young leeks, shredded

SAUCE

⅔ cup (150 mL/5 fl oz) superior stock (*see page 124*) or chicken stock (broth)
1½ tablespoons Shuang Huang or other light soy sauce
1 teaspoon rice wine or dry sherry
⅓ teaspoon salt
½ teaspoon sugar
pinch of white pepper
½ teaspoon sesame oil
1½ teaspoons cornflour (cornstarch)

Stir-fry the noodles with the lard until soft and very slightly crisp on the edges. Lift onto a serving plate, sprinkle with salt and set aside.

Wipe out the wok, add a little more lard and stir-fry the pork until it changes colour. Remove, then stir-fry the silver sprouts and leeks until the leeks are tender and wilted. Add the pre-mixed sauce ingredients, return the pork and simmer, stirring, until the sauce thickens. Pour over the noodles and serve at once.

*Fresh mung beansprouts from which the yellow seed pods and long tapering roots have been removed, leaving a slender silver-coloured sprout.*

## Sichuan 四川

# STEAMED DRAGON'S EYE ROLLS

375 g (12 oz) pork belly (fresh bacon)*
1 tablespoon white sugar
½ cup (185 g/6 oz) sweetened red bean paste, available canned
18 glacé cherries
1 cup (155 g/5 oz) glutinous long-grain rice
1 teaspoon salt
2 tablespoons brown sugar

Place the pork on a rack, skin side upwards, and pour several cups of boiling water over it. Drain, then wipe dry. Melt the white sugar in a wok and rub over the pork skin, then use a very sharp knife to cut the pork into long, thin strips like bacon. Roll each strip of pork around a small portion of the sweetened red bean paste and top each with half a cherry. Place cherry downwards in a heatproof bowl and set aside.

Steam or boil the glutinous rice with plenty of salt until just cooked, mix with the brown sugar and pile on top of the pork rolls. Place on a rack in a wok or in a steamer, cover and steam for about 40 minutes. Invert onto a serving plate. The dragon's eyes form a beautiful pattern.

*Choose the best quality pork meat near the ribs, which should be in one piece.*

## Beijing 北京

# RICE AND DUCK MEAT IN LOTUS LEAVES

315 g (10 oz) duck breast meat
3 fresh or dried lotus or 12 bamboo leaves
oil for brushing leaves
¾ cup (125 g/4 oz) glutinous rice
¾ cup (125 g/4 oz) long-grain white rice
1 whole star anise
1 teaspoon Sichuan peppercorns (Fagara or Sansho)
2 teaspoons sesame oil

SEASONING

1 tablespoon light soy sauce
2½ teaspoons rice wine or dry sherry
¾ teaspoon salt
2 tablespoons finely chopped spring onion (shallot/scallion)
1 teaspoon grated fresh (root) ginger

Blanch the fresh leaves or soak the dried ones until softened, then squeeze out the water and brush the underside with oil.

Cut the duck into small strips, place in a dish with the seasoning ingredients, mix well and set aside.

Finely grind the glutinous and the long-grain rice together with the star anise and Sichuan peppercorns. Mix with the duck meat and sesame oil, adding just a little water to moisten.

Divide the lotus leaves into quarters, place a portion of the rice mixture onto each and fold the leaves, ribbed side inwards, around the rice to make little loose parcels.

Arrange side by side on a heatproof plate, set on a rack in a wok or in a steamer, cover and steam over gently simmering water for about 1 hour. Serve immediately.

RICE AND DUCK MEAT IN LOTUS LEAVES

COCONUT BUNS

## Guangzhou 广州

# COCONUT BUNS

2½ cups (315 g/10 oz) flour
1¾ teaspoons baking powder
3 tablespoons sugar
2 egg yolks
½ cup (125 mL/4 fl oz) lukewarm milk
3 tablespoons lard or butter
1 egg, beaten

### FILLING

45 g (1½ oz) fat bacon
1 tablespoon sugar
1½ tablespoons pine nuts
½ cup (125 mL/4 fl oz) peanut oil
¾ cup (45 g/1½ oz) shredded coconut
2 tablespoons sugar
1 small egg, well beaten

Sift the flour and baking powder into a mixing bowl, make a well in the centre and put in the sugar, egg yolks and milk, then cut the lard or butter into small cubes, add to the mixture and work in well. Transfer to a lightly floured board and knead lightly until the dough is smooth and soft. Cover and set aside.

To prepare the filling, finely chop the bacon and fry gently with the 1 tablespoon sugar until the fat is almost transparent, then set aside. Deep-fry the pine nuts in the peanut oil until lightly coloured, mix with the bacon, shredded coconut, sugar and the well beaten egg and set aside.

Divide the dough into about 12 portions and flatten each into a round shape. Place a portion of the filling in the centre of each, pull the dough up around the filling and pinch the edges together to completely enclose the filling.

Place the buns, joined edges downwards, on a lightly oiled baking sheet, brush the tops with beaten egg and set aside until it feels dry, then brush a second time.

Bake in a pre-heated hot oven, 220°C (425°F), for 20 minutes, or until crisp and golden on the surface.

## Beijing 北京

# SESAME CAKES WITH MINCED PORK

*Sesame cakes can be eaten with sweet or savoury fillings. They were a speciality of the chefs of the Qing Dynasty (1644–1911 AD), and a story is told about the Empress Dowager Cixi having a dream in which she was eating some sesame cakes. To her astonishment the next morning she was served sesame cakes for breakfast. She rewarded the chef of the imperial kitchen with peacock feathers and twenty pieces of silver. Thus the dish became famous.*

### SESAME CAKES – MAKES 18

½ cup (125 mL/4 fl oz) vegetable oil
7 cups (875 g/1¾ lb) flour
1½ cups (375 mL/12 fl oz) boiling water
½ cup (125 mL/4 fl oz) cold water
3 teaspoons salt
extra water or sugar-water for brushing cakes
½ cup (60 g/2 oz) white sesame seeds
oil for deep-frying (optional)

### FILLING

375 g (12 oz) lean pork
oil for frying
1 tablespoon dark soy sauce
pinch of salt and pepper
2 teaspoons sugar
1 tablespoon rice wine or dry sherry
chopped fresh coriander or diced pickled vegetables

Gently heat the vegetable oil in a wok and add 1½ cups (185 g/6 oz) of the flour. Mix into a thick paste and continue to cook very gently, stirring continually until it is a light, golden, smooth, soft ball. Remove and leave to cool.

Sift the remaining flour into a bowl and make a well in the centre. Pour in the boiling water and quickly work into the flour, then add the cold water and 1 teaspoon of the salt and work in thoroughly. Transfer to a board and knead until smooth and elastic.

Divide into 36 portions, rolling each into a ball, then roll or press them out flat. Spread a portion of the flour-and-oil dough over half of them and sprinkle generously with the remaining salt. Press the remaining single pieces of dough on top and pinch the edges together to seal tightly.

Brush one side of each cake with water or a mixture of sugar and water and coat thickly with sesame seeds.

Bake in a pre-heated hot oven, 200°C (400°F), until puffed, golden, firm and dry on the surface, or deep-fry in hot oil until cooked through. Set aside, keeping warm.

Very finely chop or mince (grind) the pork and sauté in 2-3 tablespoons of the oil until lightly coloured. Add the soy sauce, salt and pepper, sugar and rice wine and continue to stir-fry until there is no liquid left in the bottom of the wok.

Serve the pork with the warm buns, adding chopped fresh coriander or finely diced pickled vegetables.

CRISP DOUGH COATED WITH SUGAR AND POWDERED CANDIED ROSE

*Sichuan* 四川

# CRISP DOUGH COATED WITH SUGAR AND POWDERED CANDIED ROSE

3 eggs
¾ cup (90g/3oz) flour
3 tablespoons water
¾ cup (185g/6oz) sugar
cornflour (cornstarch)
oil for deep-frying
1 tablespoon finely chopped candied rose petals*

Beat the eggs in a mixing bowl and add the flour and water. Stir until the batter is smooth, then pour into a lightly greased, heated wok and cook gently, stirring continually, until the batter forms into a soft ball. Lift out and press out on an oiled plate to about 1.25 cm (½ in) thickness. Leave to cool.

Pour the sugar into a saucepan, add about 3 tablespoons cold water and set aside.

Cut the cooled batter into strips. Cover a plate thickly with cornflour and press the strips into this, coating them evenly with the cornflour.

Heat the oil in a wok to smoking point, then reduce the heat slightly. Deep-fry the strips, several at a time until puffed and golden, turning once. Lift out and drain well.

Bring the syrup to a slow boil and simmer for 2-3 minutes. When all of the wafers have been fried and well drained, dip them one by one into the syrup and pile on a serving plate. Sprinkle on the candied rose and serve at once.

*If candied rose petals are unobtainable add 1 teaspoon of rose water essence to the sugar syrup.*

*Guangzhou* 广州

# STEAMED MILK BUNS

MAKES ABOUT 24

DOUGH STARTER

1 teaspoon dried yeast
3 tablespoons warm water
¾ cup (90g/3oz) flour

2 cups (250g/8oz) flour
½ cup (125mL/4floz) water
¾ cup (175mL/6floz) lukewarm milk
3 tablespoons sugar
2 tablespoons softened lard
pinch of bicarbonate of soda (baking soda)
2 cups (250g/8oz) flour
1½ cups (185g/6oz) wheat starch
1½ tablespoons baking powder

To make the dough starter, sprinkle the dried yeast into the warm water and stir until completely dissolved, then sift on the flour and work into a soft dough, kneading lightly. Set aside in a warm place for about 10 hours.

Mix the water with 2 cups (250g/8oz) flour, add the dough starter and work together to a soft dough, cover again and leave a further 8-10 hours until it has at least tripled its bulk.

Pour the milk into a bowl and add the sugar and softened lard. Mix the bicarbonate of soda with a little water and add to the above, then stir in the remaining flour, the wheat starch and baking powder and mix into the risen dough. Knead together until smooth and elastic.

Divide the mixture into about 24 balls and press a small piece of paper onto the back of each. Set in a bamboo steamer basket, cover and steam for about 10 minutes until firm textured, springy and well risen. Serve at once.

An assortment of fillings can be used inside steamed milk buns. Try barbecued pork lightly sauteed with spring onions and flavoured with oyster sauce, or sweetened lotus seed or red bean paste, or mashed dates.

*Guangzhou* 广州

# FLAKY TARTS STUFFED WITH SHREDDED COCONUT

MAKES 24

PASTRY A

2½ cups (315g/10oz) flour
½-⅔ cup (125-150mL/4-5floz) water
90g (3oz) lard, melted

PASTRY B

1½ cups (185g/6oz) flour
125g (4oz) lard, melted

FILLING

¾ cup (185g/6oz) sugar
½ cup (125mL/4floz) water
1½ tablespoons butter
1½ cups (140g/4½oz) desiccated coconut
2 eggs, beaten
1 tablespoon lukewarm milk
½ teaspoon baking powder
½ teaspoon vanilla

Sift the flour for pastry A into a mixing bowl and make a well in the centre. Add the water and melted lard and work into a soft dough, then transfer to a board and knead until smooth and pliable.

Sift the flour for pastry B onto a board, make a well in the centre and work in the lard with your fingertips until the dough is smooth, adding just a few teaspoons of water to make the mixture hold together.

Cover the pastries and set aside.

Heat the sugar and water together in a saucepan for about 4 minutes, then add the butter and pour into a mixing bowl. Add the coconut, mix well and leave to cool. Add the remaining ingredients, working in well.

Roll out the two lots of pastry and cut with a fluted circular cutter into 24 rounds each. With practice they can be rolled out and cut together.

Place one round of pastry in the bottom of a patty pan and top with the other, pressing them lightly together. Place a portion of the filling in the centre of each.

Bake in a pre-heated hot oven, 200°C (400°F), for about 20 minutes until the filling is puffed and golden and feels dry to the touch, and the pastry is crisp and dry. Serve with tea.

## Shanghai 上海

# STEAMED SMALL MEAT BUNS

*These tasty little meat buns are the speciality of Nan Xiang, a suburb of Shanghai. Their special feature is their perfectly symmetrical shape, resembling a water chestnut, or sometimes a pagoda.*

*When crab is in season it may be used as the stuffing instead of the pork and cabbage described in the following recipe. The crab buns are shaped so that the opening at the top is in the shape of a crucian carp's mouth, and after steaming the orange-coloured crab oil can be seen through the opening.*

*Although this type of savoury snack is very popular, it is rarely made at home.*

WRAPPERS

2 cups (250g/8oz) flour
1 egg, beaten
¾ cup (175mL/6floz) water
1 teaspoon baking powder
¾ teaspoon salt

FILLING

185g (6oz) lean pork
2-3 fresh cabbage leaves
1½ tablespoons peanut oil
1 spring onion (shallot/scallion), finely chopped
1 clove garlic, finely chopped
1 slice fresh (root) ginger, finely chopped

SEASONING

1 tablespoon light soy sauce
2 teaspoons rice wine or dry sherry
2 teaspoons sugar
pinch of white pepper
½ teaspoon sesame oil
2 tablespoons chicken stock (broth)
2 teaspoons cornflour (cornstarch)

Make the wrappers first by sifting in the flour into a mixing bowl and dropping the egg into the centre. Mix in lightly, then add the water, baking powder and salt and mix together thoroughly. Knead until smooth, then set aside and cover with a damp cloth for 5-6 minutes to activate the baking powder which will cause the dumpling wrappers to swell and become soft when steamed.

※ Finely mince (grind) the pork and finely chop the cabbage leaves. Heat the peanut oil in a wok and sauté the pork, cabbage leaves, spring onion, garlic and ginger until the pork turns white, then add the pre-mixed seasoning ingredients and stir-fry together until there is no liquid in the bottom of the wok.

※ Roll the dough out into a long sausage shape and cut into about 24 pieces. Roll out each piece into a thin round shape and place a spoonful of the filling in the centre of each.

※ Gather up the edges, pleating them together, then bring to a point, pinch together and twist to give the right shape. Flatten the bases so that they will stand upright, then stand in a lightly oiled steaming basket or on a rack in a wok, cover and steam for about 14 minutes over high heat until done. The dumplings can be placed on cabbage leaves in the steamer to give them extra flavour and prevent them from sinking through the slats in the steaming basket.

※ Serve with the traditional dips of shredded young ginger and brown rice vinegar.

BEAN FLOUR CAKES OR DONKEY ROLLING CAKES

## Beijing 北京

# BEAN FLOUR CAKES OR DONKEY ROLLING CAKES

*Bean flour cakes make a delicious snack or dessert. In Beijing they used to be sold by hawkers, pushing their carts along the road and loudly announcing their products. The elderly people of Beijing remember these cakes as Donkey Rolling Cakes, because the hawkers often sprinkled a layer of dry bean flour over the cakes before giving them to the customers – reminding them of a donkey rolling on the sand and raising a cloud of dust.*

½ cup (125g/4oz) sugar
1 cup (315g/10oz) red bean paste
3 cups (375g/12oz) glutinous rice flour
1 cup (250mL/8floz) boiling water
½ cup (60g/2oz) white sesame seeds
1 cup (185g/6oz) yellow lentils

Mix the sugar and red bean paste together in a saucepan or wok, stirring over gentle heat until dissolved, then remove and leave to cool completely.

※ Sift the glutinous rice flour into a mixing bowl, make a well in the centre and pour in the water. Work the mixture into a smooth dough, adding a little extra water if needed, then cover and leave for a few minutes until the flour softens.

※ Dry-fry the sesame seeds until golden and beginning to pop, then remove and grind to a powder. Dry-fry the lentils until golden brown and very crisp. Grind to a fine powder and mix with the sesame seed powder.

※ Spread the dough over a work top in a large rectangular shape, about 1cm (1/3in) thick. Cover with the bean paste, leaving a border at the top. Roll up from the bottom to form a thick roll, then place on a rack in a wok or in a steamer, cover and steam for about 8 minutes, until cooked through.

※ Roll in the sesame and lentil powder, coating thickly, then cut into thick slices and serve.

STEAMED PRAWNS WITH STUFFING

## Guangzhou 广州

# STEAMED PRAWNS WITH STUFFING

*In Guangdong snacks the colour, flavour, aroma and shape are important elements. Colour is particularly highly regarded. There is a saying that "the colour is encountered before the flavour is sampled". In some snacks, artificial colouring is used to achieve the desired effect, but more often this is done by the use and blending of coloured ingredients.*

6 large river prawns (freshwater shrimps)
125 g (4 oz) chicken breast
1 thin slice Yunnan or Virginia or other well-salted ham
6 small sprigs fresh coriander
½ recipe wheat starch wrappers (*see page 209*), using plain wheat flour
light soy sauce or vinegar

### SEASONING

1 teaspoon rice wine or dry sherry
½ teaspoon sugar
pinch each of salt and white pepper

Peel the prawns, leaving the last section and the tail intact. Cut the chicken into six strips, about the size of the peeled parts of the prawns, or mince (grind) finely. Place the chicken in a dish and add the seasoning ingredients. Cut the ham into six strips.
🦐 Cut the prawns along the underside without cutting through them completely. Remove the intestinal vein, and flatten each prawn out. Place a chicken strip or a portion of minced (ground) chicken, a ham strip and a coriander sprig on each prawn and fold up.
🦐 Make the wrappers and roll out 6 large enough to enclose the filled prawns. Wrap up each prawn, leaving the tails exposed. Pinch the wrappers together underneath. Arrange on a lightly oiled heatproof plate and place on a rack in a wok, or in a steamer, over simmering water. Cover tightly and steam for about 12 minutes until the prawns are bright pink, the chicken meat white and the wrappers transparent.
🦐 Serve with soy sauce, or a vinegar dip.

## Sichuan 四川

# GLUTINOUS RICE DUMPLINGS

*The pyramid-shaped delicacies described in this recipe have a long history. They were originally made as an offering to the spirit of the great Chinese poet-statesman Qu Yuan who died in the third century BC. Although a loyal patriot, he was dismissed from the emperor's service because he complained about the corruption in the imperial court. Disappointed about his failure to save the country, he later committed suicide by jumping into the Mi Luo River in Hunan Province.*

*To commemorate his death and appease his spirit, every year on the fifth day of the fifth month, when the "Duan Wu" festival is celebrated, the locals fill sections of hollow bamboo with rice and throw them into the river.*

*Legend has it that the rice was originally thrown by people who went out in a boat to search for his body. They hoped the rice would lure the fish away and prevent them from devouring the body.*

*In later years bamboo leaves, reeds or rushes were used to wrap the glutinous rice into dumplings, and fillings of sweetened red bean paste, mashed dates or savoury meat were added. These specialities are now eaten during the "Duan Wu" festival.*

### DUMPLINGS

1 cup (125 g/4 oz) glutinous rice flour
3 tablespoons boiling water
2-3 tablespoons cold water
12 dried bamboo leaves, soaked to soften
oil for brushing leaves

### SWEET FILLINGS

6 tablespoons canned sweetened red bean paste
or
6 tablespoons sweetened date paste*

### SAVOURY FILLING

125 g (4 oz) minced (ground) lean pork
2 cloves garlic, crushed
2 tablespoons lard
2 tablespoons light soy sauce
½ teaspoon pepper
1 teaspoon sugar
pinch of salt

Place the rice flour in a mixing bowl and make a well in the centre. Add the boiling water and 2 tablespoons of the cold water and mix quickly into a pliable dough, adding the remaining cold water if needed. Knead until smooth, then roll out into a sausage shape and cut into 12 pieces.
🍚 Drain the bamboo leaves, dry thoroughly and brush with the oil.
🍚 To cook the savoury filling, stir-fry the pork and garlic in the lard until white, then add the remaining ingredients and continue frying until the liquid has been absorbed. Cool before using.
🍚 Flatten the dough pieces and place half a tablespoon of the chosen filling in the centre. Pull the dough up around the filling, pinching the edges together to seal it smoothly.
🍚 Place near the lower end of the bamboo leaf and wrap the leaf around it, so that it makes a pyramid shape. Set the dumplings on a rack in a wok or in a steamer, cover and steam over high heat for about 15 minutes, or until cooked through. Serve hot or cold. They can be dipped into sugar before eating.

*Dates simmered in water until tender, then sweetened with sugar, softened with a little lard and simmered further until all of the liquid has evaporated leaving a thick paste.*

## Guangzhou 广州

# STEAMED SHAO MAI TOPPED WITH CRAB ROE

*The steamed shao mai or dumpling of Guangdong is an adaptation of the northern xiao long shao mai. In Beijing there is a well-known shao mai shop, the Dou Yi Chu which opened for business over 200 years ago during the reign of Emperor Qian Long. It is said that when returning to the capital from a journey, the Emperor passed a small restaurant without a signboard. He entered, ordered the xiao long shao mai and found it unusually delicious. Full of praise, he named the shop the Dou Yi Chu, and through this royal patronage both the shop and the snack of shao mai became nationally famous.*

185 g (6 oz) fatty pork
125 g (4 oz) fresh prawn (shrimp) meat
3 dried black mushrooms, soaked for 25 minutes
24 wonton wrappers*
2-3 tablespoons fresh crab roe or tiny carrot cubes
   or green peas
chilli sauce
hot mustard
light soy sauce

SEASONING

1 egg white
2 teaspoons Shuang Huang or other light soy sauce
1/3 teaspoon sesame oil
1/2 teaspoon salt
1 teaspoon sugar
pinch of white pepper
2 teaspoons cornflour (cornstarch)

Finely chop the pork, prawn meat and drained mushrooms and mix with the seasoning ingredients.

※ Use a circular cutter to cut wonton wrappers into circles of about 7 cm (3 in) diameter. To fill, place a single wrapper over the thumb and curled forefinger of the left hand and press a spoonful of filling onto the wrapper, forcing the dumpling between thumb and finger into the cupped hand. Squeeze gently, then tap on the work surface to flatten the bottom. The finished dumpling should be cup-shaped and filled right up to the edge of the pastry, the top left open to expose the filling. Place a few grains of crab roe on top of each dumpling.

※ Set in a lightly greased steamer, cover and steam over simmering water for about 12 minutes until cooked through. Serve with chilli sauce, hot mustard and soy sauce.

*Available commercially, fresh or frozen.*

## Guangzhou 广州

# SISTER ER'S DUMPLINGS

### FILLING

125 g (4 oz) lean pork
75 g (2½ oz) fresh prawn (shrimp) meat
3 dried black mushrooms, soaked for 25 minutes
1 fresh or canned winter bamboo shoot, weighing approx
   75 g (2½ oz)
24 fresh coriander leaves or pieces of spring onion
   (shallot/scallion) tops
oil for frying

### SEASONING

2 teaspoons superior or other light soy sauce
1 teaspoon rice wine or dry sherry
½ teaspoon sesame oil
½ teaspoon salt
¾ teaspoon sugar
pinch of white pepper

### WHEAT STARCH WRAPPERS

1 cup (125 g/4 oz) wheat starch (gluten-free wheat flour)*
2 teaspoons cornflour (cornstarch)
½-⅔ cup (125-150 mL/4-5 fl oz) boiling water
½ teaspoon softened lard

Prepare the filling first and leave to cool while the wrappers are being made. Very finely dice the pork, prawn meat, drained mushrooms and bamboo shoot. In about 1 tablespoon of oil, stir-fry the pork until it whitens. Add the remaining ingredients, except the coriander, and stir-fry for 30-40 seconds. Add the seasoning ingredients and stir-fry a further 30-40 seconds. Transfer to a dish to cool.

🍥 Pour the flour into a mixing bowl, add the cornflour and make a well in the centre. Add the water, and, using the handle of a wooden spoon, very quickly work the hot liquid into the flour. When all is incorporated, cover with a cloth and leave for 5-6 minutes for the flour to soften. Rub the lard into the dough, kneading lightly for 1-2 minutes.

🍥 If wheat starch has been used the wrappers can be prepared in the traditional way. Roll the dough into a long sausage shape and cut into 24 pieces. Keep it covered while rolling each piece. Place a piece on a clean board, and use a blunt-bladed cleaver (these are especially made for the purpose) to spread the dough into a circle about 9 cm (3½ in) diameter. Turn over and place a spoonful of filling in the centre, top with a single coriander leaf, fold in half and pinch the edges together. Keep the board and the cleaver very lightly greased with lard.

🍥 Plain flour dough can simply be rolled into very thin circles with a rolling pin.

🍥 Place the dumplings side by side in a lightly greased steamer, cover and steam over briskly boiling water for about 15 minutes until the wrappers are clear.

🍥 Serve with soy sauce.

*If wheat starch is unobtainable, plain (all-purpose) white flour can be used, although the dumplings will be less transparent and the wrappers slightly more chewy.*

STEAMED SHAO MAI TOPPED WITH CRAB ROE

SISTER ER'S DUMPLINGS

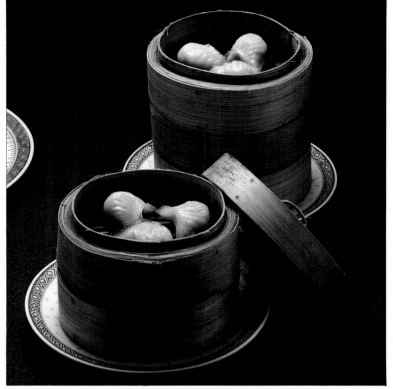

THIN PASTRY DIM SUM STUFFED WITH FRESH PRAWNS – HAW GOW

## Guangzhou 广州

# THIN PASTRY DIM SUM STUFFED WITH FRESH PRAWNS – HAW GOW

*The story behind this dish concerns the Empress Dowager Cixi who been created in a small teahouse in the Wu Chu village of Guangzhou city. Wu Chu used to be a scenic trading centre and the teahouse owner would often buy his prawns from the fishing boats of the area. But his original dumpling had a thick skin, and subsequent chefs replaced the original rice flour with wheat starch to produce the thin-skinned perfect snack known as Haw Gow.*

1 recipe wheat starch wrappers (see Sister Er's Dumplings)
155 g (5 oz) fresh prawn (shrimp) meat
45 g (1½ oz) pork fat
45 g (1½ oz) bamboo shoots, cooked or canned
1 spring onion (shallot/scallion), white part only
hot mustard
light soy sauce

### SEASONING

¼ teaspoon sesame oil
¾ teaspoon salt
½ teaspoon sugar
1 teaspoon cornflour (cornstarch)

Coarsely chop the prawn meat and finely chop the pork fat, bamboo shoots and spring onion. Mix with the seasoning ingredients, using your fingers to make it into a smooth and slightly sticky mass. Set aside while the wrappers are prepared.

🍥 As each wrapper is done, turn it over and place a spoonful of the filling in the centre. Fold the wrapper in half to enclose the filling and pinch the edges together firmly, at the same time pleating the edge of the dumplings so the smooth fold becomes the wider, curved side of the crescent shape (see photograph above).

🍥 Arrange on a lightly oiled rack in a wok or in a steamer, cover and steam over simmering water for about 7 minutes until the dumplings are as clear as crystal with the prawns showing pink inside.

🍥 Serve with hot mustard and soy sauce.

STEAMED RICE WRAPPED IN LOTUS LEAVES

## Guangzhou 广州

# STEAMED RICE WRAPPED IN LOTUS LEAVES

*"Ten miles around Ban Tang are many lotus ponds/Sisters are busy picking lotus/They do not pick lotus flowers but only pick the leaves/ Rice in lotus leaves is more fragrant than the flowers."*

*This is one of the songs from the Zhu Zi Ci collection composed during the final years of the Qing Dynasty (1644-1911 AD). Today, steamed rice wrapped in lotus leaves remains a popular dish.*

6 dried lotus or 18 bamboo leaves
2 cups (315 g/10 oz) raw, long-grain white rice
125 g (4 oz) fresh prawn (shrimp) meat
125 g (4 oz) Chinese barbecued pork
90 g (3 oz) roast duck meat
125 g (4 oz) lean pork
4 dried black mushrooms, soaked for 25 minutes
2 eggs
2 tablespoons lard

SEASONING

1 tablespoon oyster sauce
1 tablespoon light soy sauce
2 teaspoons rice wine or dry sherry
1/2 teaspoon sesame oil
1 1/2 teaspoons salt
1 teaspoon sugar
1/4 teaspoon white pepper

Soak the lotus leaves to soften them, and drain well. Partially cook the rice until it is tender but still slightly chewy, drain and set aside.

Dice finely the prawn meat, barbecued pork, duck, pork and drained mushrooms. Beat the eggs lightly in a small dish.

Heat the wok, add the lard and heat to smoking point, then pour in the eggs. Cook quickly, stirring until set, then lift out with a slotted spoon and set aside. Add the diced ingredients and stir-fry for 2-3 minutes, add the seasoning ingredients and mix well. Stir this into the rice.

Place one-sixth of the rice mixture on the underside of each lotus leaf and fold into a square package to completely enclose the filling. Arrange the parcels side by side on a rack in a wok or in a steamer, cover and steam over simmering water for about 20 minutes. Use scissors to cut a cross in the top of each parcel to expose the contents before serving. The fragrance of the lotus leaf will thoroughly penetrate the rice, giving it a unique and tantalising taste.

## Guangzhou 广州

# RADISH PUDDING

*Radish pudding is a traditional Guangdong snack, and is made in most households in early winter, when radishes appear in the markets. It is always enjoyed during the Chinese New Year celebrations.*

250 g (8 oz) rice flour
875 g (1¾ lb) giant white radish (Japanese daikon or
    icicle radish)
1½ tablespoons sugar
½ teaspoon white pepper
2 Chinese sausages, steamed for 5 minutes
3-4 dried black mushrooms, soaked for 25 minutes
3 tablespoons dried shrimps, soaked for 25 minutes
1 slice Yunnan or other well-salted ham
3 spring onions (shallots/scallions)
2 tablespoons chopped fresh coriander
2 tablespoons lard
light soy sauce

Place the rice flour in a large mixing bowl and add enough cold water to make the flour evenly damp. Grate the radish and add to the rice flour paste with the sugar and pepper.

❋Finely dice the remaining ingredients, except the coriander and lard. Stir-fry in hot lard for 2-3 minutes, then add to the radish paste with the coriander. Mix well.

❋Line a deep 25 cm (10 in) square or round cake tin with a piece of greaseproof paper. Thickly grease the paper and the sides of the tin with lard. Pour in the radish mixture and smooth the top. Place on a rack in a large covered wok, or in a steamer, cover and steam for about 1½ hours, until the pudding feels firm on top and a chopstick inserted into the centre comes out clean.

❋Invert the pudding onto a plate, but do not remove the tin until almost cool. Cut into slices and then into large squares when cold.

❋Cook on a hot griddle plate with a very little oil or lard until slightly crisp and golden on the surface. Serve with soy sauce.

RADISH PUDDING

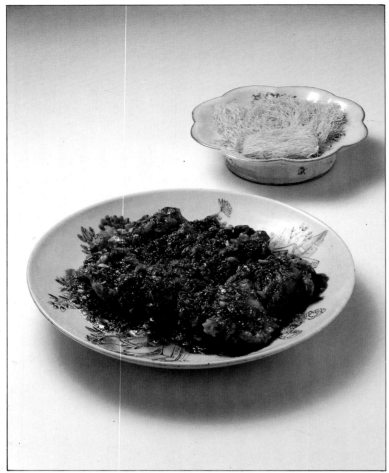

continue to knead until the dough feels elastic and is very smooth. Cover with a damp cloth and leave for 20 minutes.
❋ Roll out as thinly as possible, then roll the sheet up into a cylinder and cut into very narrow strips. Toss in flour, then set aside.
❋ Scale, clean and fillet the fish. Cut each fillet in half lengthways to give four long strips. Mix the cornflour with cold water to make a thick batter and coat the fish.
❋ Heat the oil in a wok to smoking point, then reduce the heat slightly. Deep-fry the fish, two pieces at a time, until cooked through and lightly browned on the surface. Lift out and keep warm on a serving plate.
❋ Reheat the oil to smoking point, reduce the heat and deep-fry the noodles in several batches until crisp and golden. Lift out and arrange on another serving dish.
❋ In another wok heat the oil for the sauce and add the sugar. Cook until it turns to caramel, then add the remaining pre-mixed sauce ingredients, boiling until the sauce thickens and turns clear. Pour over the fish and serve.

*\*2-3 cakes of pre-prepared egg noodles can be used in place of these home-made noodles. They should be softened in water first, then drained well and allowed to partially dry before deep-frying.*

SWEET AND SOUR FISH WITH NOODLES

Beijing 北京

# SWEET AND SOUR FISH WITH NOODLES

*The story behind this dish concerns the Empress Dowager Cixi who was fleeing from a foreign aggressor and took refuge in Xian. On her return to Beijing, she passed through the Kai Feng Fu, one of China's ancient capitals in Henan Province.*

*Realising that the Empress was fond of sweet and sour dishes, a local cook prepared sweet and sour fish with noodles for her. The Empress thought the dish delicious, it became popular and was handed down through the generations.*

1 x 625 g (1¼ lb) fresh carp or other meaty white fish
1 cup (125 g/4 oz) cornflour (cornstarch)
oil for deep-frying

SWEET AND SOUR SAUCE

2 tablespoons vegetable oil
½ cup (125 g/4 oz) sugar
½ cup (125 mL/4 fl oz) brown vinegar
1 tablespoon dark soy sauce
3 tablespoons superior or other light soy sauce
¾ cup (175 mL/6 fl oz) chicken stock (broth)
4 cloves garlic, chopped
1-2 pickled or fresh red chillies, chopped
1 spring onion (shallot/scallion), finely chopped
2½ teaspoons cornflour (cornstarch)

NOODLES*

2 small eggs
2 tablespoons cold water
3 cups (375 g/12 oz) flour

To make the noodles, break the eggs into a large bowl and beat well. Add the water and one-quarter of the flour and beat this mixture until very smooth.
❋ Gradually work in the remaining flour, kneading it with your hands, then turn out onto a lightly floured surface and

Beijing 北京

# RICE WITH PINEAPPLE AND ASSORTED FRUIT

2 cups (375 g/12 oz) raw, short-grain white rice
3 rings fresh pineapple
½ apple
1 Chinese pear or firm, unripe pear
2 tablespoons raisins
2 tablespoons chopped, candied melon
2 tablespoons chopped walnuts
2 tablespoons chopped glacé cherries
2 tablespoons lard
3 tablespoons sugar

Cook the rice with 3 cups (750 mL/24 fl oz) of cold water over very gentle heat until the rice is tender and the liquid completely absorbed.
❋ Cut the pineapple into small fan shapes, peel, core and dice the apple and pear.
❋ Heat a wok and add the lard, stir-fry the rice until each grain is coated with the fat. Add the nuts and fruit except the pineapple and continue to stir-fry for another minute. Sprinkle with sugar and stir-fry a further 2 minutes until the ingredients are tender and well mixed.
❋ Arrange the pineapple around the edge of a serving plate and pile the rice in the centre.

RICE WITH PINEAPPLE AND ASSORTED FRUIT

## Guangzhou 广州

# GOLDEN RICE WITH PIGEON EGGS

*In China there are many ways to cook rice dishes, but this one is unique, and was originally known as Palace Golden Rice. In feudal China, Imperial chefs continually had to create new dishes to satisfy demanding empresses. One chef, Fang Shi, was said to have had the ability to turn things into gold, and as this recipe demonstrates, in the hands of a capable chef, plain white rice can, in fact, be transformed into "gold fragments".*

4 cups (500 g/16 oz) freshly cooked white rice (about
   1½ cups [250 g/8 oz] raw rice)
3 cloves garlic
90 g (3 oz) prawn (shrimp) meat
2 chicken livers
5 medium-sized chicken eggs
½ cup (125 mL/4 fl oz) vegetable oil
6 pigeon or quail eggs
1 teaspoon sesame oil
6 stalks choy sum, or other Chinese green vegetable

SEASONING

2 tablespoons superior or other light soy sauce
1 teaspoon salt
1 teaspoon sugar
⅓ teaspoon white pepper

Spread the cooked rice on a tray to cool. Very finely chop the garlic, then dice the prawn meat and chicken livers. Beat the chicken eggs lightly in a small bowl, adding 1 tablespoon of water and a pinch of salt.

※ Heat half the vegetable oil in a wok and stir-fry the garlic for 30 seconds. Add the prawns and chicken livers and stir-fry until they change colour and are beginning to firm up. Add the rice and stir-fry until the rice has warmed through. Add the seasoning ingredients and mix in well. Pour in the beaten eggs and continue to stir-fry over low heat until the eggs have mixed well with the rice. The eggs should still be quite moist and only half cooked.

※ Pile onto a heatproof plate and shape into a flat mound. Make six small depressions in the top and break a pigeon egg into each.

※ Heat the remaining vegetable oil in the wok and add the sesame oil. Put in the choy sum and stir-fry briefly, then add ½ cup (125 mL/4 fl oz) water, cover and cook until the vegetables are almost tender.

※ Arrange around the rice dish, place the whole dish in a steamer, or on a rack in a wok, and steam over simmering water until the pigeon eggs are just cooked.

213

云南
Yunnan

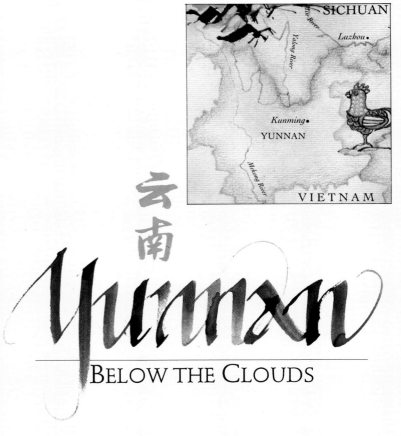

# 云南 Yunnan
## BELOW THE CLOUDS

Possibly the most beautiful corner in all China is the southwest. It is also possibly the least known, a great pity because Yunnan and neighbouring Guizhou and western Guangxi are among the most fascinating as well as the most scenic areas in the land. The ravines are steep, the mountains covered in jungle, the rivers rush in fast turbulence towards the Gulf of Tonkin and the mighty Mekong slashes through Yunnan. Southeast Asia lies over the next hill; Yunnan borders Burma, Laos and Vietnam, and culinary ties are close.

A rich racial stew makes up the people of the three southwesterly provinces; minorities are probably a majority in Yunnan itself where dozens of different peoples inhabit the valleys. Some of them are tiny remnants of once-mighty tribes; peoples like the Achang, who now count themselves as only twenty thousand; the fifty-eight thousand Bulong and their cousins, the four thousand remaining Dulong; ten thousand Jinuo people and twenty-three thousand Nu. But there are also sizeable communities like the Bai (over a million); the Hani and the Yao (one million each) and hundreds of thousands of Tibetans. A million Miao live in Guizhou. Thais, too, who stayed behind when their forefathers left to form Thailand, remain in the hills. Five million Yi and fourteen million Zhuang are scattered through all three provinces. Every one of these races has its own culture and cuisine. All are mixed in with what is generally considered to be Chinese cooking to give a gastronomic treat that can be found nowhere else.

Yunnan means Below the Clouds, and the name signifies the remoteness of the land. The clouds referred to are those that eternally shroud the mountains that fringe Sichuan. In the past nobody knew what lay on the far side of the forbidding mountains that marked the limits of Chinese civilisation, so they just referred to it as "Below the Clouds". This lack of knowledge bred legends and myths of a fabulous land, a kind of Chinese El Dorado. Although the Yuan Dynasty deposed the

CROSSING THE RICE PADDIES
LEO MEIER

*(previous page)*
AUTUMNAL FIELDS IN NORTHERN YUNNAN
GREGORY HEISLER

A BAI GRANDMOTHER IN HER KITCHEN
GREGORY HEISLER

WATER BUFFALOES, ESSENTIAL TO TRADITIONAL FARMING LIFE
GREGORY HEISLER

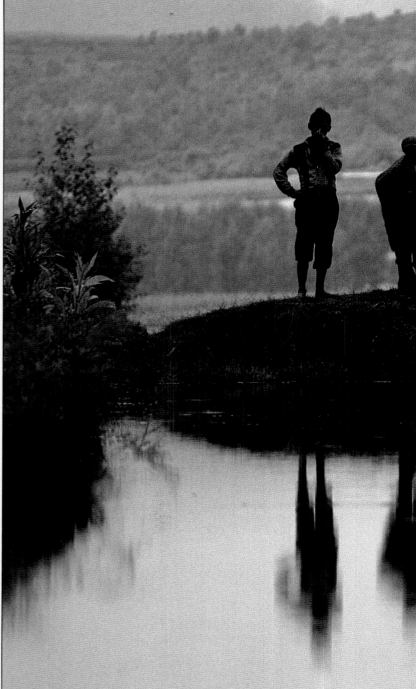

Thai kings of Yunnan in the thirteenth century, the province still lay outside the pale of knowledge, wracked by ceaseless Muslim uprisings which were put down by successive dynasties with a bloodthirstiness outstanding even for the Manchus. Then in the early years of the twentieth century the great mineral wealth of Yunnan was discovered and the myth of an El Dorado in the misty hills turned out to be true.

The many races of the southwest provinces have borrowed freely from each others' kitchens. The culinary result is a splendid smorgasbord from hill tribes and hunters, farmers and fishermen, and the sophisticated gastronomy of Nanning, the capital of Guangxi and a city which can boast of a long and unique cuisine of its own. Kunming, Yunnan's capital, claims China's most perfect climate and is known as the city of perpetual spring. Its restaurants also have a well-deserved reputation for exotic dishes which carry the tangy flavour of Vietnamese herbs, steamed carp and perch from the cool waters of the high-country lakes, and noodles served with green peppers. The red peppers of Sichuan make guest appearances in many Yunnan dishes and one of the gifts of the Kunming kitchen is steamed chicken in a Yunnan pot which is the Chinese version of a French pot-au-feu.

Into the regional cooking pot go many influences. The various minorities who make up the colourful anthropological map of the southwest make their contribution. The largest recognised minority in China is the Zhuang who live in their own sprawling autonomous region occupying half of southern Guangxi Province. A happy, amiable people, the Zhuang have developed a rich and nutritious diet based on the abundance of the fertile southern coast and mountains. One specialty that features in their feasts is a giant pyramid-shaped dumpling stuffed with rice and ground pork. These dumplings are said to be the biggest in China and cook for many hours in sealed pottery jars over the embers of a slow fire.

PUPILS AT THE LI JIANG NATIONAL SCHOOL, YUNNAN PROVINCE                    GREGORY HEISLER

China also has minorities within minorities, adding further colourful confusion to its gastronomic map. During the Yuan Dynasty (1206-1368 AD), the Mongols determined to bring the entire country under their central rule. The best way to do so was to establish colonies in the outer reaches of the empire. This they did, but as in later years their empire in China shrivelled the outposts were abandoned, leaving racial enclaves like the one on the shores of Lake Lugu, which lies like a spectacular pearl in the highlands on the Yunnan-Sichuan border. There today, Mosuo minority people still proudly claim Mongol origin and on feast days celebrate with dishes like stewed lamb. The descendants of the Mongols in Yunnan – Muslim colonists transplanted to take Yuan rule to the area – are the only sizeable group in south China who today appreciate lamb.

Other ingredients and ideas come from the bordering lands. Indian culture, including Buddhism, seeped into China through Yunnan and has left an underlying influence, and the Han Chinese have brought with them their own many cuisines. The results are a many-splendoured table. One dinner can include tribal, Islamic, Vietnamese, Sichuan and other dishes.

The cooking of Guizhou likewise reflects trends from neighbouring provinces – the red pepper of Hunan is a notable feature. For generations Guizhou was the

YOUNG BUDDHIST ACOLYTES                                          LEONG KA TAI

EVERY FERTILE PIECE OF ARABLE LAND IS UTILISED

MARY ELLEN MARK

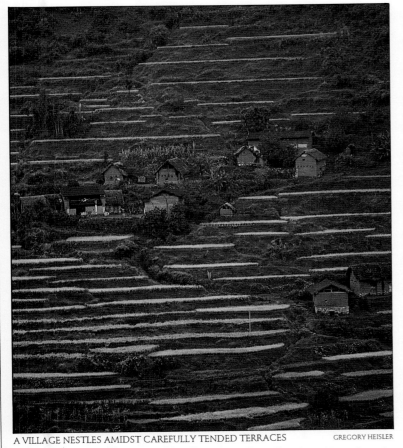

A VILLAGE NESTLES AMIDST CAREFULLY TENDED TERRACES          GREGORY HEISLER

poor, backward relation of southern China. It was said there was not one piece of flat land in the entire province, an exaggerated claim unhappily based on fact. The rice grows vertically in Guizhou, it is said, and seeing the terraces that have been adzed with agony out of the steep hillsides, each as small as a garden and built with enormous labour, one is prepared to believe it. But the rivers are rich, the woods provide game and the province has a selection of mushrooms and fungi second to none.

For generations landlocked, poor Guizhou was also desperately short of salt. There was none to be mined as in other inland provinces, and most people were too poor to buy the salt imported from the distant ports of the South China Sea. Salt was a luxury, and when it could be afforded a block of salt took pride of place in the centre of the table. Family and important guests would gather, take a piece of meat or vegetable in their chopsticks and rub it over the salt before eating the morsel. The exotic taste of salt was a rare and valued treat. Other provinces may cook sweet and sour, but Guizhou is known for its unique contribution of salt and sour cooking. Such a recipe calls for a fish to be rubbed inside and out with salt, then to be stuffed with strongly salted pickle and fried. When it is served it comes with yet more salt and pepper. Guizhou diners of today are making up for the salt their forebears could not afford.

A VILLAGE COOK

GREGORY HEISLER

221

蔬
果
Vegetables
&
Fruit

蔬
果

# Vegetables & Fruit

HARALD SUND

FRUIT AND VEGETABLE SELLERS AT SHIMIAN MARKET, SICHUAN PROVINCE

THE daily food of the Chinese is among the healthiest in the world, due mainly to the preponderance of vegetables. Although no longer the incredible luxury it once was, the rarity of meat for most of the population over many centuries has helped to make a tradition in which vegetables play a vital culinary role at the centre of the gastronomic stage.

In any city or hamlet, seasonal vegetables can be seen for sale in busy street markets. Like a culinary kaleidoscope ceaselessly in motion, the colours, variety and types of vegetables on sale change with the locality and the season as new crops are harvested and reach the marketplace. Foreigners will recognise many familiar vegetables on sale, because for thousands of years the Chinese farmer has enthusiastically adopted plants brought back by returning traders and adventurers, and chefs have just as keenly adapted these newcomers to existing recipes. Vegetables from every continent grow in China today, but so do many others which have seldom made the gastronomic trip abroad.

With the economic reorganisation of recent years under which China's eight hundred million peasants have been encouraged to grow and sell their own private crops after meeting state quotas, the range of vegetables on sale has notably increased. Nowhere is this more evident than in the verdant south where a warm sub-tropical climate helps the diligent market gardeners coax a fresh vegetable crop from their tiny plots every two months. It is a very different story in the north. Any autumn visitor to Beijing can see loads of Tianjin cabbages – the big, elongated vegetables known as Chinese cabbages – trucked into the city from the state farms of Hebei Province. The cabbage is stored in every home to eke out the chill winter months when fresh vegetables do not grow, and ones that are on sale are expensive imports to the capital from more temperate zones. The hardy cabbages keep for months in the cold winters, and although the outer layers may become yellowish and dry, the inside remains tender and juicy until spring returns. Along with turnips and a vast variety of pickles, the humble cabbage plays a vital role in the daily diet of millions of northern Chinese for six months of the year.

One of the gastronomic tragedies of China's culinary history is that so many of the delightful regional specialties are unknown elsewhere. The blue turnip of Tianjin, for example, is still unknown to most people outside Hebei and Shandong. Similarly, some of the crunchy and deliciously fresh winter-garden crops of the south never make it to the northern markets where they would bring joy to the monotony of Manchurian tables in the long winter months. With the exception of the wealthy and the privileged, people have always had to make do with what is produced close at hand. This is, however, slowly changing with improvements in transport.

The Chinese chef in every regional kitchen insists, wherever possible on the freshest vegetables, preferably straight from the garden, but if that is impossible certainly direct from the market. This fastidiousness can be seen in any Chinese market where buyers prod, poke and peer at the goods on display to ensure they have not passed their peak. Many newcomers to a Chinese table may think they are eating some exotic new plant when they are merely enjoying an unfamiliar part of an old favourite. The leaves of the pea plant, for example, are generally discarded in the West, but are a prized delight in Guangzhou. Another example is the spinach root, usually unknown in Europe, but as eagerly cooked and eaten in China as the green leaves. For the uninitiated, China has a vast, baffling array of vegetables. This is because over the centuries China has borrowed with willing enthusiasm from every continent to add to its own rich garden heritage, and a nation of gardeners lets no small corner of ground go to waste – gourds, squashes and melons grow on vines covering storehouses in the fields; the bamboos that line village lanes provide food as well as building materials; seaweed gives a free, mineral-rich crop, while inland the prized water chestnut and valuable lotus grow in ponds which are home for duck and carp alike.

Vegetables in the Chinese cuisine have played an important role for four major reasons: religion, poverty, health and farm economics. Those who follow Buddhist teachings choose to avoid eating meat (though not necessarily fish), and vegetable dishes have been raised to glorious heights to provide a vibrant, exciting meatless cuisine. On the other hand, millions of peasants have traditionally been unable to afford meat – famine, in-vasion, immigration or political instability have often caused culinary chaos making meat and fish too expensive for any but the wealthy or privileged.

Even in the good times there have been many cooks in the kitchens of China who prefer the healthy vitality of vegetables. Ancient herbalists have long recognised (although not always aware of the scientific and dietary reasons) that vegetables play a vital part in maintaining good health, and insisted that a variety of fresh garden foods should be on the menu at every meal. The growth of China's huge population has put immense pressure on the patient, ancient agricultural practices, and simple economics has dictated the intensive farming practices in use today; one field of carefully tended vegetables can keep many more people alive than if the same area is used to graze a couple of sheep or a cow. Hence the absence of grazing stock in most parts of the country: plants are more efficient people-feeders than animals.

A STRIKING SELECTION OF CHINESE VEGETABLES

SHUFUNOTOMO

## Guangzhou 广州

# STUFFED WINTER MELON SOUP

*This is a traditional banquet delicacy to serve during summer and autumn. The melon takes on a jade colour, appears crystal-like and is translucent, the ingredients within the melon being half visible.*

1 kg (2 lb) rounded end of a winter melon*
1 chicken carcass
125 g (4 oz) fresh prawn (shrimp) meat
125 g (4 oz) boneless frog or chicken meat
125 g (4 oz) duck meat
125 g (4 oz) lean pork
125 g (4 oz) lean ham
125 g (4 oz) fresh or canned straw mushrooms
125 g (4 oz) angled luffa or stalks of broccoli
6 cups (1½L/48 fl oz) superior stock (*see page 124*) or chicken stock (broth)

SEASONING

1 teaspoon sesame oil
2 teaspoons salt
⅓ teaspoon white pepper
1 teaspoon sugar

Thinly skin the end of the melon, then scoop out the seeds and fibrous centre. Place in a large pot with the chicken carcass inside and add boiling water to cover. Simmer gently for about 20 minutes. Discard the chicken bones and the water and set the melon aside.

※ Cut the meat and vegetables into small dice. Place in a large casserole and add the seasoning ingredients. Carefully turn over the melon so that it covers the diced ingredients, forming a dome in the casserole. Pour the stock into the casserole, then set it on a rack in a wok or in a steamer, cover and simmer over gentle heat for about 1 hour until the diced ingredients and the melon are completely tender and full of flavour. Garnish the melon top with coriander leaves or designs cut from melon or cucumber skin. Skilled chefs often cut the design directly onto the melon before cooking.

*Substitute a hollowed water melon shell and add chopped choko (chayote) as a vegetable.*

## Sichuan 四川

# STUFFED PEA SPROUT SOUP

*Pea sprouts, in actual fact, are not sprouts at all but the tender round leaves of the sweet pea plant. They are bright green and have a delicate taste. Served as a vegetable accompaniment, pea sprouts are simply stir-fried, but in this interesting and unusual recipe, small balls of finely minced chicken are pressed onto the pea leaves to make a delicious and subtly flavoured soup. Giving the impression of a bouquet of white flowers, this dish is a favourite at springtime banquets.*

125 g (4 oz) chicken breasts
1 small egg white
2-3 teaspoons cornflour (cornstarch)
500 g (1 lb) pea leaves
5 cups (1¼L/40 fl oz) clear chicken stock (broth)
1 tomato
salt

Very finely mince (grind) the chicken breasts with a cleaver or in a food processor. Add the lightly beaten egg white and the cornflour and mix to a paste.

※ Rinse the pea leaves in cold water, sorting out any tough stems and discoloured leaves. Drain well and wipe the larger leaves with a cloth to dry. Press a small ball of the chicken paste onto as many leaves as possible.

※ Bring the stock to the boil, then reduce the heat and put in the pea leaves. Simmer for about 5 minutes, until the vegetable is tender and the chicken white, then add salt to taste. Do not overcook, or the leaves will turn yellow and become bitter.

※ Drop the tomato into a saucepan of boiling water, remove and peel, cut it into wedges, then trim away the pulp and seeds leaving petal shapes. Arrange these on the top of the soup and serve at once.

## Guangzhou 广州

# HAINAN COCONUT POTAGE

*Coconut trees are abundant in tropical China, particularly on Hainan Island where this dish originated. There are many stories about coconuts; one concerns Emperor Cheng Di who, in about 20 BC, chose Zhao Feiyan as his Empress. Her sister wove a mat with coconut leaves and sent it to her as a present to congratulate her, wishing her to be a mother to many sons, just like the fruitful coconut tree.*

2 coconuts
30 g (1 oz) fresh mushrooms
125 g (4 oz) chicken breast meat
60 g (2 oz) lean ham
coconut or peanut oil
½ cup (125 mL/4 fl oz) coconut cream
3 cups (750 mL/24 fl oz) water or chicken stock (broth)
¾ teaspoon salt
fresh coriander

Saw the tops off the coconuts and use the liquid as a refreshing drink.

❋Cut the mushrooms, chicken and ham into small dice. Sauté briefly in a wok with a little coconut or peanut oil and place in a saucepan with the coconut cream, water and salt. Bring to the boil and simmer for about 5 minutes, then divide the soup between the two coconut shells, place the tops of the shells in position and set on a rack in a wok or in a steamer. Cover and steam for about 30 minutes until the soup has thoroughly absorbed the flavour of the coconut.

❋Garnish with chopped coriander and serve.

HAINAN COCONUT POTAGE

THICK JADEITE SOUP

## Beijing 北京

# THICK JADEITE SOUP

*There is a touching story behind the creation of this dish concerning a beautiful young girl who was about to be married to a handsome prince when their tribe was invaded by foreigners. Before he departed to lead his army into battle, the prince gave the girl a piece of jade as a token of his love.*

*The girl gazed at the piece of jade night and day, thinking of her prince and could not eat or sleep. Her worried mother made this nutritious soup in which the bright green of spinach contrasted with the white of the chicken to represent the piece of jade she so coveted. She ate, regained her health and married the triumphant prince.*

SPINACH SOUP

250 g (8 oz) fresh spinach leaves, finely chopped
1 teaspoon rice wine or dry sherry
1 teaspoon sugar
1½ tablespoons lard or vegetable oil
1½ cups (375 mL/12 fl oz) chicken stock (broth)
1 tablespoon cornflour (cornstarch)

CHICKEN SOUP

280 g (9 oz) chicken breast meat
1 teaspoon rice wine or dry sherry
½ teaspoon sugar
¾ teaspoon salt
2 teaspoons ginger juice
3 egg whites
1½ cups (375 mL/12 fl oz) chicken stock (broth)
1 tablespoon cornflour (cornstarch)
1 tablespoon lard or vegetable oil
cherry tomatoes (garnish)

Stir-fry the spinach in a wok with rice wine, sugar and lard until softened, then add the stock and cover. Simmer gently for about 7 minutes until the spinach is tender. Mix the cornflour with a little cold water or stock, stir into the soup and simmer, stirring, until thickened.

❋To prepare the chicken soup, very finely mince (grind) the chicken meat and season with the rice wine, sugar, salt and ginger juice. Beat in the egg whites, stirring until the mixture is very thick and smooth. Add the chicken stock and cornflour and beat again thoroughly.

❋Heat the wok and add the lard. Pour in the chicken mixture and simmer, stirring, for about 6 minutes over moderate heat until the chicken has cooked through and is very white.

❋Pour the chicken soup into a deep serving dish, keeping it as much to one side of the dish as possible. Reheat the spinach soup and carefully pour into the other side of the dish, using a wide spatula to push the chicken soup to the side, so that the two colours are clearly separated. Garnish with cherry tomatoes and serve.

WINTER MELON CUP WITH LOTUS SEEDS

# Beijing 北京

# WINTER MELON CUP
# WITH LOTUS SEEDS

*The giant white winter melon is a common Chinese vegetable, very juicy and rich in vitamins, though rather plain in taste. It is said to clean the system, reduce swelling, stop pain and make the skin smooth, soft and moist. In this recipe the soup ingredients are simmered in the scooped-out melon skin.*

1 x 4 kg (8 lb) winter melon*
chicken stock (broth)
30 g (1 oz) dried lotus seeds, soaked for 1 hour
90 g (3 oz) duck breast meat
2 dried black mushrooms, soaked for 25 minutes
90 g (3 oz) lean ham
90 g (3 oz) lean pork
1 dried scallop, soaked for 25 minutes
1 tablespoon rice wine or dry sherry
2 slices fresh (root) ginger
1 egg white, well beaten
1 tablespoon cornflour (cornstarch)
45 g (1½ oz) fresh or canned crab meat

Select the most attractive end of the melon, wipe it with a damp cloth and scoop out the seeds and the fibrous centre. Carve a decorative motif on the skin around the sides, and use a sharp knife to make zig-zag cuts around the rim.

🌸 Fill the melon with boiling stock and add a large pinch of salt. Stand upright in a heatproof dish and place on a rack in a wok or steamer. Cover and steam over briskly boiling water for about 20 minutes.

🌸 Skin the lotus seeds and use a toothpick to push out the bitter centre core. Finely dice the duck meat, mushroom caps, ham and pork, and shred the scallop. Place in a saucepan adding the lotus seeds and wine. Ladle the stock from the melon over the ingredients and bring to the boil. Cook until the lotus seeds are tender, then return to the melon.

🌸 Add the ginger, egg white and cornflour mixed with a little cold water and return to the steamer. Steam for 30-35 minutes, then remove the ginger and stir in the crab meat just before serving.

*Substitute a hollowed water melon shell and add chopped choko (chayote) as a vegetable.*

231

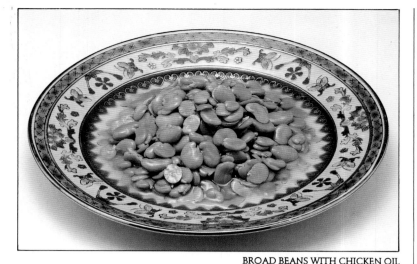

FRENCH BEANS WITH CHICKEN OIL

BROAD BEANS WITH CHICKEN OIL

## Shanghai 上海

# FRENCH BEANS WITH CHICKEN OIL

*Rendered chicken fat is used to add a gloss and a deliciously rich flavour to many dishes, particularly fresh vegetables. It is sometimes used as cooking oil, but is usually heated up and poured over the finished dish.*

315 g (10 oz) fresh French (green) beans ·
1 tablespoon vegetable oil
¾ teaspoon salt
½ cup (125 mL/4 fl oz) chicken stock (broth)
1 teaspoon cornflour (cornstarch)
2 teaspoons rendered chicken fat, melted

Rinse the beans, drain well, and cut off both ends.
※ Heat the oil in a wok and stir-fry the beans for 2 minutes. Add about 1 tablespoon of water, cover and cook for another minute until tender, but still crisp. Add the salt and the chicken stock mixed with cornflour and simmer, stirring until the sauce thickens. Stir in the chicken fat before serving.

## Shanghai 上海

# BROAD BEANS WITH CHICKEN OIL

315 g (10 oz) fresh broad beans, shelled
1 teaspoon salt
2 cups (500 mL/16 fl oz) chicken stock (broth)
2 teaspoons cornflour (cornstarch)
1 tablespoon rendered chicken fat, melted

Shell the beans, scald in boiling water, then drain and immerse in cold water until cool. This brightens the colour. Drain and peel off the outer skin. Place the beans, salt and chicken stock in a wok, bring to the boil and simmer until the beans are tender. Remove with a slotted spoon and set aside.
※ Boil the liquid briskly until reduced to about ½ cup (125 mL/4 fl oz). Mix the cornflour with a little cold water and stir into the sauce to thicken, return the beans and stir until warmed through. Mix in the chicken fat and serve.

## Sichuan 四川

# "CHICKEN" AND DRIED LILY FLOWERS

*"Golden needles" are the dried flower buds of the tiger lily. These lilies grow in the south and north of China, but are especially abundant in Sichuan. The flower is picked while still in bud, and usually sold in the dried form, the best quality being bright yellow. Nutritious and delicious, dried lily buds impart a subtle muskiness to a dish. In this recipe they are artistically presented in small knotted bundles with cubes of vegetarian chicken.*

60 g (2 oz) dried lily flowers (golden needles)
375 g (12 oz) vegetarian chicken*
1 whole bamboo shoot, cooked fresh or canned
3 tablespoons oil for frying
1 teaspoon sesame oil

SEASONING/SAUCE

1½ cups (375 mL/12 fl oz) chicken stock (broth)
1 tablespoon rice wine or dry sherry
1 tablespoon light soy sauce
3-4 slices fresh (root) ginger
¾ teaspoon salt
1 teaspoon sugar
pinch of white pepper
2-3 teaspoons cornflour (cornstarch)

Soak the lily flowers in hot water for about 30 minutes to soften. Cut off the hard ends and tie together in pairs, knotting in the centre. Drain and squeeze out excess water.
※ Cut the "chicken" into bite-sized pieces. Cut the bamboo shoot into thin slices, using only the open-structured point of the shoot. Heat the oil in a wok, stir-fry the lily flowers briefly and push to one side. Add the "chicken" and bamboo shoot and stir-fry until they are crisp and lightly coloured on the surface.
※ Add the pre-mixed seasoning/sauce ingredients except the cornflour, and bring to the boil. Simmer, covered, over gentle heat for about 30 minutes until the "chicken" is tender and the lily buds have imparted their unique flavour to the dish.
※ Mix the cornflour with a little cold water and stir into the sauce, simmering until thickened. Add the sesame oil and serve at once.

*Vegetarian chicken is made from layers of beancurd skins seasoned with soy sauce, compressed to a rectangular shape and steamed. It can sometimes be purchased from Chinese food stores. Chicken breasts can be used as a substitute and cooked in the same way.*

"CHICKEN" AND DRIED LILY FLOWERS

SPRING BAMBOO SHOOTS WITH SALTED VEGETABLES

## Shanghai 上海

# SPRING BAMBOO SHOOTS WITH SALTED VEGETABLES

*Bamboo grows abundantly south of the Yellow River in China. The shoots are a valued ingredient in Chinese cooking and differ according to the time of harvest. Spring bamboo shoots have a faint scent and a clear colour. Winter bamboo shoots are plump, short and crisp with a distinct taste and can be easily stored for use throughout the year. Bamboo shoots gathered in the summer and autumn are called whip bamboo shoots and only the tender parts at the top are eaten.*

500 g (1 lb) fresh or canned spring bamboo shoots
30 g (1 oz) salted mustard greens, shredded*
1 teaspoon cornflour (cornstarch)
½ teaspoon sesame oil

SEASONING/STOCK

1 cup (250 mL/8 fl oz) chicken stock (broth)
2 tablespoons lard
1 teaspoon salt
½ teaspoon sugar

Trim the bamboo shoots and cut them into wedge-shaped slices about 2.5 cm (1 in) long.

✖In a wok heat the seasoning/stock ingredients to boiling point, add the bamboo shoots and cover. Simmer until tender but still crisp – for about 6 minutes. Add the mustard greens and stir in evenly, then add the cornflour mixed with a little cold water and stir until the sauce thickens. Adjust the seasoning and stir in the sesame oil before serving.

*Available as a preserve in Chinese food stores.*

## Sichuan 四川

# SICHUAN PICKLED VEGETABLES

Pickled vegetables are very popular in Sichuan and are prepared by almost every family in the towns and villages. They refresh the taste buds, removing greasiness and helping fats break down in the system. They have a stimulating saltiness, coupled with the sharp taste of vinegar and chilli, and have a warming effect on the body. Pickling preserves vegetables, making them available at all seasons, even during mid-winter, when fresh vegetables are in limited supply in China.

Pickles are served and used in many ways. They may be eaten uncooked, as a side dish, stir-fried in a number of different dishes, or added to pot dishes and soups to increase flavour.

Pickles are made throughout the year as the vegetables come into season. Typical Sichuan pickled vegetables include cabbage, kale, turnip, giant white radish, carrot, gourd, chilli capsicum (bell pepper), long (snake) beans, celery, young ginger and the local long thin cucumbers similar to those used in Japanese cooking.

The method used and the degree of saltiness or hotness required will dictate the fermenting time, and is a matter of personal choice. Pickled vegetables, usually packed in large stone jars, last for many months and generally do not require refrigeration.

Family recipes for pickles, and those created by restaurant chefs, are usually closely guarded secrets. The seasoning ingredients comprise salt, dried chillies, rice wine and other liquor and brown sugar. But other spices and condiments including those that make up the famed Chinese five spice mixture – cassia, fennel, pepper, licorice or anise and cinnamon – are often used for flavour and aroma.

SICHUAN PICKLED VEGETABLES

SWEET AND SOUR VEGETARIAN SPARE RIBS

## Beijing 北京

# SWEET AND SOUR VEGETARIAN SPARE RIBS

*This tasty vegetarian dish was created by a famous Beijing chef who fashioned typical vegetarian ingredients – yam and winter bamboo shoots – into the shape of spare ribs. Crisp outside and tender inside, this dish is well known and much appreciated among the many Chinese vegetarians who hold the yam to have important nutritional and medicinal value.*

1½ kg (3 lb) yams or taro
1 teaspoon salt
½ cup (60 g/2 oz) cornflour (cornstarch)
220 g (7 oz) fresh or canned winter bamboo shoots
2 teaspoons sesame oil
3 tablespoons peanut oil

SAUCE

1 tablespoon sesame oil
1 tablespoon finely chopped fresh (root) ginger
1 tablespoon dark soy sauce
2 teaspoons brown vinegar
½ cup (125 mL/4 fl oz) chicken stock (broth)
1 tablespoon sugar
2½ teaspoons cornflour (cornstarch)
salt and pepper

Peel the yams and cut into cubes. Place on a rack in a wok or a steamer, cover and steam until very tender, then mash while still warm, adding the salt and cornflour. Mix until smooth and set aside.

✻ Peel the fresh bamboo shoots and cut off the tough bases. Cut shoots lengthways into quarters about 5 cm (2 in) long. Cut away the corrugated inner part of each piece to produce a smooth strip resembling a spare rib bone.

✻ Press a portion of the mashed yam around each "bone" to give the appearance of a spare rib, leaving both ends of the "bone" exposed.

✻ In a large wok heat the 2 teaspoons of sesame oil and the peanut oil until very hot. Carefully fry the "spare ribs" in several batches until golden brown. Drain and pile on a serving plate.

✻ Rinse the wok, add 1 tablespoon of sesame oil and stir-fry the chopped ginger for about 30 seconds. Mix the remaining sauce ingredients in a dish and pour into the wok. Bring to the boil and simmer, stirring, until thickened. Return the "spare ribs" and stir gently in the sauce until well coated. Remove and sprinkle with a little extra sesame oil before serving.

BAMBOO SHOOTS STUFFED WITH PRAWNS

## Shanghai 上海

# BAMBOO SHOOTS STUFFED WITH PRAWNS

90 g (3 oz) peeled fresh prawns (shrimps)
90 g (3 oz) white fish fillet
90 g (3 oz) pork fat
500 g (1 lb) fresh or canned spring bamboo shoots
2 egg whites, beaten
1 cup (125 g/4 oz) cornflour (cornstarch)
500 g (1 lb) lard
1 tablespoon rendered chicken fat, melted

SAUCE

¾ cup (175 mL/6 fl oz) chicken stock
2 teaspoons rice wine or dry sherry
½ teaspoon salt
1½ teaspoons cornflour (cornstarch)

Pound the prawns, fish and pork fat until smooth and mix together thoroughly.

✻ Simmer the fresh bamboo shoots until partially cooked, and drain well. Make two lengthways slits from the centre to the tip and fill with the stuffing, squeezing the bamboo shoots back into their conical shape. Dip into the egg white and coat with cornflour.

✻ Heat the lard in a wok and fry the stuffed bamboo shoots over moderate heat for about 3 minutes, then remove and drain well.

✻ Mix sauce ingredients together, bring to the boil, return the bamboo shoots and cook quickly over high heat for 2-3 minutes, sprinkle on the chicken fat and serve at once.

STIR-FRIED PEAS WITH BROWN BEAN SAUCE

## *Beijing* 北京

# STIR-FRIED PEAS WITH BROWN BEAN SAUCE

125 g (4 oz) lean pork
250 g (8 oz) fresh peas, shelled
2 tablespoons lard
2 spring onions (shallots/scallions), chopped
3 slices fresh (root) ginger, chopped
1 tablespoon brown bean sauce
2 teaspoons light soy sauce
1 teaspoon rice wine or dry sherry
2 tablespoons chicken stock (broth)
½ teaspoon sesame oil

Dice the pork to the size of peas. Boil the peas until just tender and drain well, then cover with cold water and set aside.
※ Stir-fry the diced pork in the lard in a wok over high heat until it turns white, then add the spring onions, ginger and brown bean sauce. Stir-fry for about 1 minute until fragrant, then add the peas with the rice wine, stock and sesame oil, stir-fry together briefly and serve.

## *Beijing* 北京

# STIR-FRIED CUCUMBER

125 g (4 oz) lean pork
1 large cucumber
1 teaspoon salt
1 tablespoon lard
1 spring onion (shallot/scallion), chopped
1 slice fresh (root) ginger, chopped
3 teaspoons brown bean sauce
2 teaspoons light soy sauce
1 teaspoon rice wine or dry sherry
1½ tablespoons chicken stock (broth)
½ teaspoon sesame oil

Cut the pork into small dice. Peel and dice the cucumber, discarding the seed core. Sprinkle with salt, leave for 10 minutes, then rinse well in cold water and drain thoroughly.
※ Stir-fry the pork in the lard in a wok over high heat until it turns white. Add the spring onion, ginger and brown bean sauce and stir-fry for about 1½ minutes until fragrant. Add the cucumber, soy sauce, wine and stock and stir-fry together for another minute, then add the sesame oil and serve.

STIR-FRIED CUCUMBER

## *Guangzhou*

# DEEP-FRIED MASHED POTATO IN PEAR SHAPES

*The imitation of a pear is almost perfect in this innovative dish. The flavour is delicate, soft and smooth. After tasting several other courses and some wine at a banquet, the Chinese like to serve an imitation dish to match the cheerful atmosphere.*

750 g (1½ lb) peeled potatoes
2 tablespoons cornflour (cornstarch)
1 small slice ham
2 eggs, well beaten
1 cup (125 g/4 oz) dry breadcrumbs

FILLING

45 g (1½ oz) chicken hearts
45 g (1½ oz) lean pork
30 g (1 oz) fresh prawn (shrimp) meat
3 fresh or dried mushrooms, soaked for 25 minutes
1 tablespoon lard

SEASONING

½ teaspoon salt
pinch of white pepper
½ teaspoon sugar
1 teaspoon rice wine or dry sherry
⅓ teaspoon sesame oil

Cut the potatoes into cubes and boil in salted water until very tender. Drain thoroughly and leave to dry for about 1 hour, then mash smoothly, adding the cornflour and set aside.
※ To prepare the filling, finely dice the chicken hearts, pork, prawns and mushrooms and mix with the seasoning ingredients. Heat the lard in a wok and sauté the filling for about 2 minutes over moderate heat until it is cooked. Remove and leave to cool.
※ Divide the potato mixture into 10 portions and form each into a flat, round shape. Place a spoonful of the filling in the centre of each, and working with well oiled hands, form each into a pear-shape, ensuring that the filling is totally enclosed. Cut the ham into slivers and use as the "stems".
※ Heat the oil in a wok to moderate, coat each potato "pear" with beaten egg and breadcrumbs and deep-fry until golden. Lift out carefully, drain well and serve at once.

STIR-FRIED HAZELNUTS WITH PORK AND BROWN BEAN SAUCE

BROAD BEANS AND BAMBOO SHOOTS

## Beijing 北京

# STIR-FRIED HAZELNUTS WITH PORK AND BROWN BEAN SAUCE

90 g (3 oz) lean pork
125 g (4 oz) hazelnuts
2 cups (500 mL/16 fl oz) peanut oil
2 spring onions (shallots/scallions), chopped
2 slices fresh (root) ginger, shredded
3 teaspoons brown bean sauce
1 teaspoon light soy sauce
1 teaspoon rice wine or dry sherry
2 tablespoons chicken stock (broth)
½ teaspoon sesame oil

Cut the pork into small dice. Toast the hazelnuts or blanch in boiling water until the skins loosen, then rub off.
❋ Heat the peanut oil in a wok and fry the hazelnuts until lightly coloured, remove and set aside.
❋ Pour off all but 2 tablespoons of the oil and stir-fry the pork until it turns white. Add the spring onion, ginger and brown bean sauce and stir-fry together for 1½ minutes.
❋ Add the hazelnuts, the soy sauce, rice wine and stock. Simmer for 2 minutes, then sprinkle with the sesame oil and serve at once.

## Sichuan 四川

# BROAD BEANS AND BAMBOO SHOOTS

125 g (4 oz) fresh or frozen broad beans
185 g (6 oz) fresh spring bamboo tips, or sliced canned bamboo shoots
1 tablespoon lard
1 tablespoon rendered chicken fat, melted
1 cup (250 mL/8 fl oz) chicken stock (broth)
1 teaspoon salt
1 teaspoon soy bean powder or cornflour (cornstarch)

Drop the broad beans into boiling water and simmer briefly until the skins loosen, then drain and peel off the skins to reveal the jade green beans.
❋ Heat the lard in a wok and stir-fry the broad beans and bamboo shoots together over moderate heat for about 1½ minutes. Then pour in the stock, retaining a little to mix with the thickening agent, and add the salt. Cover and simmer until

tender but still crisp. Mix the soy bean powder or cornflour with the retained stock, pour into the wok and simmer gently, stirring, until thickened.
❋ Spoon onto a serving plate and carefully stir in the chicken fat. Serve hot or cold.

## Shanghai 上海

# GREEN VEGETABLE HEARTS WITH CREAM SAUCE

750 g (1½ lb) green vegetable hearts, or young bok choy or broccoli
2 tablespoons oil for frying
2 teaspoons cornflour (cornstarch)
1 tablespoon cream

SEASONING/SAUCE

½ cup (125 mL/4 fl oz) chicken stock (broth)
1 teaspoon salt
½ teaspoon pepper

Remove the outer leaves of the vegetables, wash thoroughly, and drain well. Scald in boiling water for a few seconds, drain and rinse in cold water to retain the bright green of the leaves.
❋ Heat the oil in a wok and stir-fry the vegetables quickly until partially cooked, then add the seasoning/sauce ingredients, cover and simmer until the vegetables are tender.
❋ Stir the cornflour into the cream and pour into the wok, stirring until the sauce thickens. If the sauce in the wok has evaporated, add a splash of cold water to give a good quantity of creamy sauce.
❋ Check the seasoning, then lift onto a serving plate and serve at once.

GREEN VEGETABLE HEARTS WITH CREAM SAUCE

TOMATOES STUFFED WITH EIGHT DELICACIES

MUSHROOMS AND STUFFED RAPE HEARTS

## Beijing 北京

# TOMATOES STUFFED WITH EIGHT DELICACIES

*The number eight is considered to be lucky in China. The old city of Beijing, for example, is said to have been built like the body of an eight-armed warrior, and had eight gates. The lucky number eight also features in Chinese cooking where eight different ingredients are often used in the stuffing, as in this dish.*

6 large ripe tomatoes
hard boiled eggs (garnish)
button mushrooms (garnish)

FILLING

60 g (2 oz) white fish meat
60 g (2 oz) chicken breast meat
4 fresh or canned button mushrooms
4 fresh or canned straw mushrooms
4 dried black mushrooms, soaked for 25 minutes
2 small stalks Chinese kale (gai larn) or broccoli
45 g (1½ oz) fresh or canned bamboo shoots
5 cm (2 in) piece cucumber

SEASONING

2 teaspoons rice wine or dry sherry
¾ teaspoon salt
1 slice fresh (root) ginger, finely chopped
1 tablespoon rendered chicken fat, melted

SAUCE

¾ cup (175 mL/6 fl oz) chicken stock (broth)
1 teaspoon rice wine or dry sherry
½ teaspoon salt
1½ teaspoons cornflour (cornstarch)

Drop the tomatoes into a pot of boiling water for about 8 seconds, then remove and peel carefully. Slice the tops off and retain, then scoop out the seeds and soft inner flesh and set aside.

To prepare the filling, place the fish and chicken with the fresh and the dried black mushrooms on a rack in a wok or steamer, cover and steam until tender. Boil the vegetable stalks to soften. Chop all the filling ingredients into very small dice, add the seasoning ingredients and mix well. Stuff the tomatoes with this filling and put the lids in place.

Arrange in a heatproof dish and steam for about 15 minutes, then drain off the liquid which has accumulated in the dish. Garnish with hard-boiled eggs and button mushrooms.

Boil the sauce ingredients in the wok, stirring until thickened, and pour over the tomatoes before serving.

## Beijing 北京

# MUSHROOMS AND STUFFED RAPE HEARTS

12 young rape or bok choy hearts
90 g (3 oz) white fish fillet
cornflour (cornstarch)
1 teaspoon dried shrimp eggs (roe) or 1 small carrot
24 small fresh or canned button mushrooms
½ cup (125 mL/4 fl oz) chicken stock (broth)
salt
1 tablespoon rendered chicken fat, melted

SEASONING

2 teaspoons Shaoxing rice wine or dry sherry
⅓ teaspoon salt
2 teaspoons melted lard
1 tablespoon finely chopped spring onion (shallot/scallion)
1 teaspoon ginger juice
1 egg white, well beaten

Wash the rape hearts and cut in halves lengthways, then trim the root section so that the leaves are just holding together at the bottom. Scald in boiling water, then rinse in cold water to retain the colour. Drain well, coat the root section on the inside with cornflour and set aside.

Mince (grind) the fish very finely and mix with the seasoning ingredients. Beat the mixture until it is smooth and white and place a spoonful of it into the root section of each piece of vegetable.

Finely shred the carrot, if used, and sprinkle over the fish stuffing, or add a few shrimp eggs.

Turn each mushroom cap between your fingers, and using a sharp knife held at an angle to the cap, make a series of curving cuts following the natural shape of the cap from centre top to the edge. Remove narrow strips of mushroom flesh so that the finished cap has a pinwheel effect when viewed from the top. Sprinkle with salt and arrange in the centre of a heatproof plate.

Place the stuffed rape hearts around the edge of the dish, filling outwards, and set on a rack in a wok or steamer. Cover and steam for about 15 minutes until the vegetables and mushrooms are both tender.

Pour the chicken stock into a wok with the liquid from the plate, add ½ teaspoon salt and bring to the boil. Simmer until slightly reduced, then add the chicken fat and pour over the vegetables before serving.

239

GREEN CAPSICUMS WITH PRAWN FILLING

DRY STEWED WINTER BAMBOO SHOOTS WITH MUSHROOMS

## Guangzhou 广州

# GREEN CAPSICUMS WITH PRAWN FILLING

*Green capsicums originated in the South American tropics, and were introduced into China during the Ming Dynasty (1368-1644 AD). The Guangdong variety have rounded, ridged shapes resembling lanterns and are called either lantern or bell peppers.*

6 green capsicums (bell peppers)
185 g (6 oz) fat pork
185 g (6 oz) fresh prawn (shrimp) meat
3 tablespoons cornflour (cornstarch)
oil for frying

SEASONING

½ teaspoon salt
½ teaspoon sugar
pinch of bicarbonate of soda (baking soda)
pinch of white pepper

SAUCE

1 tablespoon fermented black beans
2 spring onions (shallots/scallions)
1 teaspoon grated fresh (root) ginger
1 teaspoon finely chopped garlic
½ cup (125 mL/4 fl oz) chicken stock (broth)
2 teaspoons rice wine or dry sherry
2 teaspoons superior or other light soy sauce
⅓ teaspoon sesame oil
1 teaspoon sugar
pinch each of salt and pepper

Cut the capsicums into quarters, trimming away the stems, seeds and internal ribs. Coarsely mince (grind) the pork and prawn meat and mix to a paste with the seasoning ingredients. Dust the inside of the capsicums with cornflour, then fill each with a portion of filling, smoothing the top. Coat the filling lightly with cornflour.

❈ Heat the oil and fry the stuffed capsicums, filling side down, for about 2 minutes, then turn and fry the other side for a further 2-3 minutes. The capsicums should soften, but retain a certain crispness. Drain and arrange on a serving plate.

❈ Finely chop the black beans and the white parts of the spring onions. Drain off the oil from the wok and return about 1½ tablespoons. Stir-fry the black beans, spring onions, ginger and garlic for 1½ minutes, add the remaining sauce ingredients and bring to the boil. Simmer for about 1 minute, then add a little cornflour mixed with cold water to thicken. Pour over the capsicums just before serving.

## Beijing 北京

# DRY STEWED WINTER BAMBOO SHOOTS WITH MUSHROOMS

*This recipe involves two cooking methods – stewing and deep-frying. The former tenderises and flavours, the latter gives a crisp finish.*

185 g (6 oz) fresh or canned winter bamboo shoots
  (peeled weight)
125 g (4 oz) fresh or canned champignons
1 cup (250 mL/8 fl oz) chicken stock (broth)
2 tablespoons light soy sauce
1½ teaspoons sugar
oil for deep-frying
1 tablespoon rice wine or dry sherry
1 teaspoon sesame oil

Wash the bamboo shoots and slice lengthways into narrow strips. Use a sharp knife to cut a cross in the top of each mushroom cap. Place the bamboo shoots and mushrooms in a saucepan and cover with boiling water. Simmer for 6 minutes, then drain well.

❈ Transfer to a pottery casserole and add the stock, soy sauce and sugar. Bring to the boil, then reduce heat and simmer gently, uncovered, until the liquid has evaporated. Stir from time to time so the ingredients are evenly cooked and absorb the seasoning.

❈ Heat the oil in a wok until smoking. Dry the bamboo shoots and mushrooms on paper towels and deep-fry in a frying-basket for 1-1½ minutes until thoroughly crisp on the surface, but do not overcook or they will taste dry and bitter.

❈ In another wok, stir-fry the bamboo shoots and mushrooms with the rice wine and sesame oil. If desired, sprinkle with 1 teaspoon sugar before serving.

## Beijing 北京

# FRIED "YELLOW CROAKER"

*One may be astonished to find yellow croaker fish featuring on the menu of a Chinese vegetarian restaurant, but although the dish looks almost exactly like its aquatic counterpart, it is in fact made from only vegetarian ingredients, wrapped in beancurd skin and moulded into a fish shape. A garnish of colourful and tasty ingredients gives it an attractive appearance as well as a salty, hot and sweet taste.*

3 dried black mushrooms, soaked for 25 minutes
250 g (8 oz) cooked or canned and chopped winter bamboo
  shoots
2 teaspoons rice wine or dry sherry
½ teaspoon salt
125 g (4 oz) peeled yam or taro
2 tablespoons peanut oil
2 dried beancurd skins
1 tablespoon flour
2 teaspoons cornflour (cornstarch)
oil for frying

SAUCE

¼ red capsicum (bell pepper)
¼ green capsicum (bell pepper)
30 g (1 oz) canned bamboo shoots
2 spring onions (shallots/scallions)
2 dried red chillies, finely chopped, or 1 tablespoon chilli bean
  sauce
½ teaspoon finely chopped fresh (root) ginger
1 tablespoon light soy sauce
1 tablespoon red vinegar
2 teaspoons rice wine or dry sherry
1 tablespoon sugar
½ cup (125 mL/4 fl oz) chicken or vegetable stock (broth)
1 teaspoon sesame oil

Drain the mushrooms and squeeze out as much water as possible, remove stalks and dice the caps finely. Mix with the bamboo shoots and season with wine and salt, then set aside.

※ Cube the yam and steam over briskly simmering water until tender, then drain and mash while still warm. Heat the peanut oil in a wok and stir-fry the bamboo shoots and mushrooms for 1 minute, then mix in the yam and set aside.

※ Wipe the beancurd skins with a wet cloth to soften. Place one on top of the other and spoon the filling along the centre of the top one. Wrap the top skin around the filling, in a narrow rectangular shape, then wrap the other skin around this, working it into the shape of a fish.

※ Mix the flour and cornflour with a little cold water and brush thickly over the "fish".

※ Shallow-fry the "fish" in a wok on both sides until golden brown, lift out carefully, using two spatulas, and place on a serving plate. Keep warm.

※ To prepare the sauce, dice the capsicums finely, discarding inner ribs, seeds and stem. Dice the bamboo shoots and spring onions. Heat 3 tablespoons of the frying oil and stir-fry the vegetables for 1½ minutes until softened. Add the chillies or chilli bean sauce and fry briefly, then add the remaining sauce ingredients and bring to the boil. Simmer briskly until the sauce has reduced slightly and pour over the "fish". Serve immediately.

FRIED "YELLOW CROAKER"

VEGETABLE AND CHICKEN ROLLS

## Beijing 北京

# VEGETABLE AND CHICKEN ROLLS

185 g (6 oz) chicken breast meat
18 rape hearts, or hearts of other fresh young Chinese green
    vegetable
2 fresh red chillies or ½ red capsicum (bell pepper)
2 egg whites
3 tablespoons cornflour (cornstarch)
large pinch of salt
3 tablespoons lard or vegetable oil

### SEASONING/SAUCE

¾ cup (175 mL/6 fl oz) chicken stock (broth)
1 spring onion (shallot/scallion), finely chopped
2 slices fresh (root) ginger, shredded
2 teaspoons rice wine or dry sherry
½ teaspoon salt
1½ teaspoons cornflour (cornstarch)

Cut the chicken meat into 18 thin long slices and set aside. Trim and thoroughly wash the vegetables and drain well. Cook in boiling water until half done, then drain. Cut the chilli or capsicum into thin slivers.

Mix the egg whites with cornflour and salt to a paste. Spread some of this paste over each piece of chicken and wrap around the centre of each vegetable heart. Spread the remaining cornflour paste over the top of the chicken and tie a strip of red chilli or capsicum around the centre of each to hold the bundles in place.

Heat the lard or vegetable oil in a wok and gently fry half the vegetable rolls, turning several times carefully, until the chicken is white and the vegetable cooked through. Remove, cook the remaining rolls and set aside.

Reheat the wok, pour in the pre-mixed sauce ingredients, bring to the boil, then carefully slide in the rolls and turn in the sauce until evenly coated. Lift onto a serving plate and serve immediately.

STEWED MUSHROOM SOUP

## Guangzhou 广州

# STEWED MUSHROOM SOUP

*Several types of mushrooms grow in different seasons in Guangdong. Gill fungus grows during periods of excessive rainfall and is of poorer quality with slightly inferior fragrance to the large winter mushrooms with a thick cap and strong scent. This type is called "dong gu", and the variegated ones are the most outstanding, with a cracked surface and excellent colour and fragrance.*

*This kind of mushroom soup is traditionally simmered in a clay or "sand" pot covered with a piece of tissue paper tied on with string.*

24 dried black mushrooms, soaked for 25 minutes
6 slices fresh ginger
2 spring onions (shallots/scallions)
6 cups (1½ L/48 fl oz) superior stock (*see page 124*)
2 tablespoons rendered chicken fat (optional)

### SEASONING

2 teaspoons rice wine or dry sherry
1¾ teaspoons salt
1 teaspoon sugar

Drain the mushrooms and trim the stems close to the caps. Place in a saucepan with half the ginger and spring onions, add a pinch of salt and cover with cold water. Bring to the boil, simmer for 3 minutes and drain.

Return the mushrooms to the saucepan, adding the remaining ginger and spring onions, the seasoning ingredients, stock, and chicken fat, if used. Bring just to the boil, cover and simmer very gently for about 30 minutes. The liquid should be kept just below the boil so that the soup remains clear. Skim off the chicken fat and serve.

## Beijing 北京

# BRAISED BAMBOO SHOOTS

375 g (12 oz) fresh or canned bamboo shoots
½ cup (60 g/2 oz) cornflour (cornstarch)
2 cups (500 mL/16 fl oz) oil for frying
3 slices fresh (root) ginger
¼ small red capsicum (bell pepper)
¼ small green capsicum (bell pepper)
½ teaspoon sesame oil

### SEASONING/SAUCE

¾ cup (175 mL/6 fl oz) clear stock*
1 tablespoon dark soy sauce
1 teaspoon rice wine or dry sherry
1 teaspoon sugar

Wash fresh bamboo shoots and boil for about 8 minutes until half cooked. Drain canned bamboo shoots. Cut into long

BRAISED BAMBOO SHOOTS

STIR-FRIED DICED CARROTS

slices, make a short slit along the centre of each slice and pull one end through the centre slit so that the slice of bamboo shoot forms a curl. Coat with cornflour and fry in hot oil until the coating is lightly coloured. Lift out and drain.

※ In another wok heat 1½ tablespoons oil and fry the ginger slices for 30 seconds, then discard. Add the bamboo shoots and pour in the seasoning/sauce ingredients. Simmer until the bamboo shoots are tender.

※ Shred the capsicum finely and add to the pan. Heat until softened, then sprinkle with the sesame oil and serve.

*To prepare the clear stock, stir-fry a handful of beans sprouts in a wok, then add 2 cups (500 mL/16 fl oz) of water and simmer briefly until reduced by half. Separate the vegetables from the resultant stock and use for other purposes.*

## Beijing 北京

# STIR-FRIED DICED CARROTS

*This side dish originated in the days of the Manchurian invasion. During the battle the soldiers had no time to cook, so they would just roast over an open fire whatever meat or vegetables they could find, then add some brown bean sauce to enhance the flavour. Even after the establishment of the Qing Dynasty (1644-1911 AD) this style of cooking remained popular, although the imperial chefs improved the flavour by stir-frying and these dishes became daily side dishes at the imperial court.*

125 g (4 oz) lean pork
250 g (8 oz) fresh young carrots
1 tablespoon sesame oil
2 cubes dried beancurd, soaked for 10 minutes
1 tablespoon dried shrimps, soaked for 25 minutes
2 tablespoons lard
2 spring onions (shallots/scallions), chopped
2 slices fresh (root) ginger, chopped
1 tablespoon brown bean sauce
1 tablespoon light soy sauce
2 teaspoons rice wine or dry sherry
⅓ cup (75 mL/2½ fl oz) chicken stock (broth)
1 teaspoon cornflour (cornstarch)

Dice the pork and carrots and sauté the carrots in the sesame oil in a wok for about 2 minutes until they turn red, then set aside. Squeeze the water from the dried beancurd and cut into small dice. Drain the shrimp.

※ In a wok, stir-fry the pork in the lard over high heat until it turns white, then add the spring onions, ginger and brown bean sauce and stir-fry for another minute.

※ Add the carrots, beancurd and dried shrimps and continue to stir-fry until the carrot is tender. Add the soy sauce and rice wine and fry again briefly, then add the stock mixed with the cornflour and stir-fry together until the sauce thickens. Add about 1 teaspoon of the sesame oil, used to stir-fry the carrots, and serve at once.

## Beijing 北京

# FRIED WINTER BAMBOO SHOOTS

*Winter bamboo shoots are the very young shoots of a particular type of hairy bamboo. They have a distinct flavour and are considered to be tastier than other winter vegetables. In this dish they are combined with crisply fried lobe-leaf seaweed.*

500 g (1 lb) fresh or canned winter bamboo shoots
¾ teaspoon salt
2 tablespoons rice wine or dry sherry
30 g (1 oz) lobe-leaf seaweed (wakame)
oil for deep-frying

Peel the coarse outer leaves from the fresh bamboo shoots and cut off their tough bases. Cut each shoot lengthways into quarters, place in a dish and season with the salt and wine.

※ Soak the seaweed in warm water to soften, then drain well and cut out the hard spine and any tough ribs. Rinse again in cold water, cut into small pieces and drain.

※ Heat the wok and add about ½ cup (125 mL/4 fl oz) of oil. When very hot, stir-fry the bamboo shoots until the edges are crisp, then remove with a slotted spoon and set aside.

※ Add another cup (250 mL/8 fl oz) of oil and heat to smoking point. Deep-fry the seaweed until crisp and bright green. Do not overcook or it will turn brown and taste bitter. Remove from the oil, mix with the bamboo shoots and serve immediately.

FRIED WINTER BAMBOO SHOOTS

TWO KINDS OF MUSHROOMS WITH GREEN VEGETABLES

MUSHROOM AND PORK PATTIES

## Shanghai 上海

# TWO KINDS OF MUSHROOMS WITH GREEN VEGETABLES

2 hearts of young Chinese cabbage (bok choy)
peanut or vegetable oil
250 g (8 oz) fresh button mushrooms
12 dried black mushrooms, soaked for 25 minutes

### SAUCE A

1 cup (250 mL/8 fl oz) liquid from the soaked dried mushrooms
1 tablespoon dark soy sauce
1 teaspoon sugar
1 teaspoon cornflour (cornstarch)

### SAUCE B

½ cup (125 mL/4 fl oz) chicken stock (broth)
¼ teaspoon salt
½ teaspoon sugar
1 teaspoon cornflour (cornstarch)
1 tablespoon milk or cream
½ teaspoon sesame oil

Cut the vegetable hearts in halves lengthways, remove the ends of the stems and discard any wilting or loose leaves. Rinse well in cold water, then shake out as much water as possible.

Stir-fry the cabbage in a wok with 1 tablespoon of oil for 1 minute, add 3 tablespoons water, cover and braise until tender. Lift out, drain and keep warm.

Trim the fresh button mushrooms and rinse with cold water, then dry well. Drain the black mushrooms, squeeze the water out and cut off the stems.

Heat about 2 tablespoons of oil in a wok and stir-fry the black mushrooms for 1 minute. Mix the sauce A ingredients together and pour into the wok. Simmer for about 3 minutes until the liquid is well reduced and the mushrooms are tender. Spoon onto one end of an oval serving plate and arrange the green vegetables across the centre.

Rinse out the wok and heat 2 tablespoons of oil. Stir-fry the button mushrooms quickly, add the sauce B ingredients and simmer until softened. Check the seasoning, dish onto the other end of the serving plate and serve at once.

## Beijing 北京

# MUSHROOM AND PORK PATTIES

*Black mushrooms are considered to be the queen of the mushrooms, not only because of their exceptional taste, but also because of their high nutritional and medicinal value. People who work with black mushrooms are said never to suffer from influenza because they are constantly inhaling the powder from the dried mushrooms.*

24 medium-sized dried black mushrooms
185 g (6 oz) lean pork, preferably fillet/tenderloin
1 tablespoon cornflour (cornstarch)
1 cup (250 mL/8 fl oz) oil or lard for frying
3-4 slices canned, or fresh and cooked bamboo shoot

### SEASONING

2 teaspoons ginger juice
½ teaspoon salt
1 egg white

### SAUCE

¾ cup (175 mL/6 fl oz) reserved mushroom liquid or chicken stock (broth)
1 tablespoon rice wine or dry sherry
1 tablespoon light soy sauce
1½ teaspoons sugar
1-2 teaspoons oyster sauce
2½ teaspoons cornflour (cornstarch)

Place the mushrooms in a heatproof dish and cover with warm water, leave to soak for at least 25 minutes until soft, then place the dish on a rack in a wok or steamer, cover and steam for 10 minutes. Remove and drain well, then cut off the stems, squeeze the excess liquid from the caps and set aside.

Very finely mince (grind) the pork, add the seasoning ingredients and stir the mixture in one direction only until smooth. Dust the inside of the mushroom caps lightly with cornflour and fill with a portion of the pork paste, smoothing the tops with a wet spoon.

Heat the oil or lard in a wok and fry the mushrooms, filling downwards, for about 1½ minutes, then remove and drain well.

Pour off the oil, add the pre-mixed sauce ingredients except the cornflour to the wok and bring to the boil. Slide in the mushrooms and simmer for about 4 minutes, then transfer to a serving plate and garnish with the bamboo shoot slices.

Mix the cornflour with a little cold water and stir into the sauce. Stir over moderate heat until thickened, then pour over the mushroom patties and serve at once.

CANDIED APPLE

# Beijing 北京

# CANDIED APPLE

*This northern-style dessert has become popular in Beijing restaurants around the world, and consists of slivers of apple coated with piping-hot sugar toffee. They are dipped into a dish of iced water before eating so that the outer coating of toffee is crisp, while the apple is tender and sweet inside.*

3-4 ripe apples
½ cup (60 g/2 oz) flour
3 tablespoons cornflour (cornstarch)
1 egg white, lightly beaten
oil for deep-frying
1-2 teaspoons sesame oil
iced water

TOFFEE

2 tablespoons water
1 tablespoon lard
½ cup (125 g/4 oz) sugar

Peel and core the apples, then cut into wedges. Place the flour in a plastic bag, add the apple wedges, close the top and shake vigorously to coat the apple evenly with flour. Remove the apple and mix the remaining flour with the cornflour and egg white to make a thick batter, adding a little cold water as needed.

Heat the oil in a wok until almost smoking and add the sesame oil. Dip each piece of apple into the batter and deep-fry in several batches until golden, turning once or twice. Drain well.

Spread a little sesame oil over a serving plate and pour the iced water into a bowl.

Drain the wok and add the toffee ingredients. Cook over moderate heat without stirring until the sugar has turned a caramel colour, then quickly turn off the heat.

Dip each piece of apple into the toffee using wooden chopsticks, and place on the oiled plate. Serve immediately, dipping into the iced water before eating.

247

## Sichuan 四川

# STUFFED PEARS

*The snow pear from Sichuan has a crisp firm texture, is very sweet and juicy, and is thought to be beneficial for the lungs and throat. The unique dish described in this recipe is often served as dessert at winter banquets.*

8 snow pears or other ripe fresh pears
1 tablespoon glutinous rice
1 tablespoon pearl barley
8 lotus seeds, fresh, dried or canned
8 fox nuts
4 dates
16 glacé cherries
1½ tablespoons chopped candied melon or pineapple
½ cup (125 g/4 oz) crushed rock sugar

Peel and core the pears, and remove the stems. Rinse the rice, barley, lotus seeds and fox nuts, place in a heatproof dish on a rack in a wok or steamer, cover and steam until cooked.
Wash the dates, stone and chop them with the glacé cherries and melon. Add to the cooked ingredients and stuff the filling into the prepared pears.
Stand upright on a heatproof plate and steam for about 15 minutes, or until the pears are tender. Decorate each with a cherry.
Melt the rock sugar in a wok, adding 1 tablespoon of water. Cook gently until golden, then pour over the pears and serve.

## Sichuan 四川

# LOQUAT JELLY

*The serving of dried and fresh fruits at banquets goes back some two thousand years in China. We can find such terms as "Bian Shi" in ancient books. "Bian" indicates a kind of food basket made of split bamboo, which was used to hold fruit or dried meat at banquets and when offering sacrifices to gods or ancestors.*

*Although actual desserts made a late appearance in Chinese menus, many varieties of jellied fruit desserts became popular once the gelatinous seaweed extract agar agar became available. This recipe can be adapted for seasonal availability of fruits, loquats being a refreshing summer dessert.*

24 fresh loquats
15 g (½ oz) agar agar strips or powder*
3 cups (750 mL/24 fl oz) cold water
½ cup (125 g/4 oz) sugar
glacé cherries

Skin the loquats and remove the seeds, then place one each in the bottom of 24 Chinese teacups or other small dishes.
Place the agar agar in a wok or saucepan, add the water and slowly bring to the boil, stirring constantly. Simmer for 2-3 minutes, then add the sugar and stir slowly until dissolved and simmer for another 2-3 minutes.
Strain through a fine mesh strainer over the loquats. Allow to cool, then chill in the refrigerator.
Unmould the jellies onto a serving plate and decorate the dish with glacé cherries. Serve cold.

*Strip agar agar may require more time to dissolve than powdered types. Jellies made with agar agar do not require refrigeration once they have set.*

#  Glossary

**ABALONE** The king of the molluscs in Chinese cuisine. Canned or dried, it is widely available but, like most other ingredients in any Chinese recipe, the fresher the better.

**AGAR AGAR** Sheets of dried, pressed seaweed that feature in some Chinese and Manchurian dishes. It is used like gelatin, which can act as a substitute. Can be bought in sheets or powdered form.

**BALSAM PEAR (CHINESE BITTER MELON)** A small and wrinkled, cucumber-like vegetable with soft flesh and a central seed core. It adds a tart taste to stews and braised dishes, and is sold fresh or canned. Cucumber is a pleasant alternative.

**BAMBOO SHOOTS** These look like the horn of a small water buffalo. Different species vary in size, texture and taste. Originally, the shoot was used in northern and western cuisines but in recent years has also appeared on the Guangdong table. They can be bought in cans in Chinese stores. Celery hearts make a passable substitute.

**BEANCURD** The processed extract of the soy bean which comes in the form of jelly, custard, and dried, fried, hard or soft cakes of all shapes and sizes. Takes on the taste and aroma of whatever it is cooked with.

*Beancurd sheets* come in dry layers and are used to wrap other ingredients, usually for stews. When slowly cooked, the sheets dissolve and produce a rich broth of soy milk in which the vegetables and meat are cooked. Soak or dampen before use.

*Preserved* or *fermented beancurd* comes in tough-skinned squares in a pickle of chilli and brine. Known as Chinese cheese, the taste often seems offensive to Western palates, in the same way as dairy cheeses are often unpleasant in taste and odour to the Chinese.

**BEAN PASTE** There are many varieties made from different ingredients added to a basic fermented paste usually made from soy beans. Pastes can be found in cans and jars in every Chinese food shop. Even if the colourful labels are in Chinese only, the pictures give a good indication of what the contents will taste like.

*Hot bean paste* is served with every Sichuan and Hunan meal. It is made from the basic soy paste with hot red peppers crushed and fried in oil. Salty and palate-jarringly hot, it gives Sichuan food its distinctive taste.

*Hot black bean paste* is one of the most tasty of all the seasonings, and a marvellous accompaniment to crab. This fermented sauce comes in many brands and styles. All are delicious.

*Sweet bean paste* is a rich, salty, sweet sauce made from soy beans fermented with salt, sugar and seasonings. Used in marinades, as a seasoning and as a dip.

*Yellow bean paste* comes from the yellow soy bean and is very salty. Used sparingly it is delicious, but too much can kill rather than complement other tastes.

**BEAN PASTE, SWEETENED RED** This is a thick sweet mixture made from red beans. Used as a filling for cakes, dumplings and buns.

**BEAN SAUCES** *Brown bean sauce* is a more liquid version of the fermented bean paste, being quite salty in taste but mildly flavoured. *Hot bean sauce* is a mixture of fermented soy bean and chilli preserved in salt.

**BEAN SPROUTS** Available fresh or canned. The fresh ones will last at least a week in a sealed plastic bag or box, and are vastly superior to the canned variety.

To grow them at home, soak a handful of dried soy or mung beans. Put dampened cheese cloth in a colander, place the beans on top, put another layer of cloth over that and pour on a cup of warm water. Suspend the colander in a large saucepan and place in a warm cupboard. Give the beans another soaking through the cloth four times a day for five days, by which time you should have a nice crop of beans ready for the pot or wok.

**BEAN THREAD NOODLES** Made from the flour of the mung bean. The light, translucent threads are used to thicken stews and hotpots or as the base for a meal of vegetables.

**BOK CHOY** Choy means vegetables in Chinese and bok means white. The chef in the Chinese kitchen has an enormous range from which to choose. Generally, the generous southern gardens provide the widest selection of fresh greens and the further north one goes the narrower becomes the range. The Chinese "white cabbage" is a small, white-stemmed cabbage with deep-green leaves, a favourite of the Guangdong kitchen and a staple green accompaniment for many a meat or beancurd dish. There are hundreds of different varieties of cabbage, scores of assorted types of bok choy. Some cousins of this family are as small as 10cm (4in) long, others grow three times as large. It should be cooked as swiftly as possible, no more than two or three minutes, and served immediately to keep the succulent taste and goodness of the leaves.

**CABBAGE** Comes in a great variety from tiny delicate bok choy to the solid northern Tianjin cabbage. It is an essential and delicious part of many meals. Any cabbage can be used with magnificent effect in its place.

**CAMPHOR** Woodchips used to smoke poultry, particularly chicken for Jiangsu, Henan and Anhui dishes. Black tea leaves do the job equally well.

**CASSIA** A variety of cinnamon found in southern China.

**CHICKEN FAT** The rendered fat of a chicken, reduced during fast boiling in a double boiler. Used for stir-frying and to add flavour and shine to sauces and finished dishes. Duck fat is treated in the same way.

**CHILLI OIL** Used in spicy dishes, it is made by heating ½ cup (125 mL/4 fl oz) of good quality sesame or vegetable oil and adding 2½ tablespoons of chilli powder, flakes or, best of all, whole chillies. The oil is then allowed to cool and strained. It keeps indefinitely in a jar.

**CHILLI PASTE** Can be added to the food when cooking or placed in a side dish into which diners can dip their chopsticks to make their food as hot as they can take it.

**CHOY SUM** A sparsely leafed, green vegetable with small yellow flowerheads and a slightly bitter flavour.

**CHRYSANTHEMUM** The fresh petals of white chrysanthemum flowers are used as a garnish and for their delicate flavour in some dishes.

**CLOUD EAR FUNGUS** One of the countless varieties of dried fungi, this one is a tiny, crinkled, dry fungus which turns gelatinous in soups and stews. Another variety is called wood ear fungus. Soak to soften.

**CORIANDER** Also called Chinese parsley, it is much stronger than the Western variety, which can be used as a poor substitute. Coriander will grow like a weed in a windowbox or garden, and every serious amateur chef should have some growing.

**FEN LIQUOR** A strong spirit used mainly in marinades. Vodka, white rum or brandy can be used instead with little cost to taste.

**FERMENTED BLACK BEANS** Soft, dried, salted black beans used as a flavouring.

**FERMENTED GLUTINOUS RICE JUICE** The result of cooked glutinous rice being treated with brewer's yeast to produce a fermentation with a strong brewed flavour.

**FISH SAUCE** More familiar in the Vietnamese kitchen, but originally Chinese and still used in many country recipes. The pale brown, light sauce can be used to cook (sparingly) or as a condiment in which to dip vegetables.

**FIVE-SPICE POWDER** Made from cinnamon, brown Sichuan peppercorns, cloves, fennel and anise. Different chefs call for different proportions of the mixture and trial and error is the best way to find a suitable blend. It is available commercially.

**FUNGI** Countless varieties of dried fungi are available, including *cloud ear fungus* and *wood ear fungus*. Soak to soften.

**GALANGAL** The aromatic rootstock of certain plants of the ginger family.

**GINGER** One of the major ingredients in Chinese cuisine. Its taste is as pleasing as the appearance of the knobbly, gnarled root is ugly. With meat, fowl, fish and vegetable dishes, steamed, stir-fried or stewed, finely chopped ginger is an indispensable essential for almost every Chinese meal. It can be stored for weeks in a refrigerator, but use it fresh wherever possible. Make sure all skin is peeled off before use.

**GINGER JUICE** Made by squeezing slices of fresh (root) ginger in a garlic crusher.

**GINGKO NUTS** Small, oval nuts, sometimes called white nuts. Used mainly in vegetarian dishes, stuffings, soups, or as a garnish. Sold fresh, canned or dried, the bitter core must be removed before use.

**GLUTINOUS RICE** Available as long or short grain varieties, it has a cloudy, white appearance, unlike the usual pearly, white rice. When cooked it forms a sticky mass, and is often used in sweets and cakes.

**GOLDEN NEEDLES** The dried flower buds of the tiger lily. Used in simmered winter dishes and stir-fried to both give and take flavour from other ingredients. Usually knotted before being added to the dish.

**HOISIN SAUCE** Made from soy beans and chillies with sugar and salt added to give it a sweet but biting taste. A delicious partner for meat and poultry dishes.

**LARD** Rendered pork fat used for stir-frying and for sweets and pastry making.

**LOQUATS** Look like apricots but taste like peaches.

**LOTUS** The floating leaves of the lotus, immortalised in Chinese paintings, are only the most obvious part of the plant. The seeds, pale yellow when they are dried, are used for decorating desserts or for casual nibbling. The root looks like a string of plump, firm sausages, the sweet flesh inside something like a ripe cucumber. The delicacy can be braised, stir-fried or boiled and at festivals is sold as a candied sweet.

**LOTUS SEED PASTE** Boiled and mashed with oil and sugar, a dry but rich paste.

**LUFFA** A long, green gourd halfway between a skinny pumpkin and an okra. It can be distinguished in markets by the heavy ridges running along the skin. It is sometimes known as angled luffa because of the angles made by these ridges. The squash-like flesh, with little taste of its own, is usually stir-fried with other vegetables or meat.

**LYCHEES** Justly famed as one of the best ways to finish a feast. The rough red skin peels off to reveal the ripe, plump, juicy pulp. Also available canned.

**MAO TAI** A potent (some might say lethal) clear spirit with an overwhelming odour and a memorable after effect. Not for nothing is it known as White Lightning. Mao Tai is a common accompaniment for a Chinese banquet, along with wines of the Shaoxing sort and some of China's excellent beers. Newcomers to the table should beware of overindulgence in Mao Tai and similar spirits such as the equally fearsome Kaoliang.

**MELONS** Come in all shapes and sizes, but the most commonly used are the globe-shaped, light green *winter melons*. The white, juicy flesh can be cut out and cooked as the main ingredient in the famed Winter Melon Soup, then served on the table in the original gourd which has been carved into a superb dining top decoration. Substitute hollowed water melon for the shell and chokos (chayotes) for the flesh.

**MONOSODIUM GLUTAMATE (MSG)** You either swear by it or curse it. Many professional Chinese chefs call MSG "the master" because a handful of the composition allows them to serve just about anything and make it taste good. But in recent years there has been a wide backlash against the use of the substance and many people doubt its value from a culinary angle and fear its side effects from the point of view of health. Originally made from wheat gluten which had been dried and fermented, MSG has for decades been made chemically. Overuse of it causes various effects in diners such as headaches, hot flushes, dryness and tiredness. Many discriminating chefs and experienced cooks refuse to use MSG and in such culinary capitals as Hong Kong there is a move in a number of leading Chinese restaurants to ban its use. Some of these establishments proudly boast that they do not use MSG; the result is that they attract hordes of knowledgeable gourmets who want to savour real tastes instead of chemicals.

**MUSHROOMS** These come in infinite varieties. Every province has its prize varieties, but *dried black mushrooms* are universal. They can be purchased in most Chinese food stores and must be soaked to soften before use. Any type of mushroom makes a palatable and acceptable alternative in home cooking, although European varieties have a foreign flavour. The most common Chinese types are the *button mushrooms, yellow straw mushrooms,* the *golden needle mushrooms,* the *black forest* and the large *umbrella mushrooms* of Hunan.

**MUSTARD** The green leaves, which come in a number of versions, mostly dark green and sometimes pickled, are used in stir-fried dishes and some stews. The thick stem/root section needs to be shredded or diced before use.

**NOODLES** Fat, thin, long, short, broad, slender – take your pick because they come in all shapes and sizes. They can be made of mung bean flour like the delicate, transparent vermicelli, from wheat flour or from rice. Home cooks in non-Asian countries can use Italian pastas in place of noodles in most Chinese recipes.

**OIL FOR STIR-FRYING** Almost invariably vegetable oil. It can be flavoured with chilli (*see* chilli oil) or, more rarely, with onion, ginger or five spices.

**ORANGE PEEL** Is used to add a dash of sweetness to spicy Hunan and Sichuan dishes. You can buy it dried or canned, or make your own.

**OYSTER SAUCE** A delicious and classic accompaniment to swiftly stir-fried greens. The rich flavouring comes from steamed oysters judiciously blended with soy sauce and salt.

**PEA LEAVES** The small, bright green leaves from the sweet pea plant. Young spinach will do instead.

**PEPPER** The black and white varieties were introduced during the Tang Dynasty (618-907 AD), when pepper was called for in almost every dish at the tables of the wealthy.

**PEPPER, SICHUAN** The brown peppercorn of western China – the flower pepper of Sichuan – is still favoured above the "barbarian" pepper, and the whole peppercorn is often cooked rather than being ground. It is in fact the seed of the prickly ash tree (*Xanthoxylum pipertum*). Also known as Fagara pepper, and sold under the Japanese name Sansho.

**PEPPERCORN SALT** A mixture of ground Sichuan brown peppercorns and salt. Used as a seasoning and condiment.

**PICKLES** Served at the start of a meal or to add a pungent, salty flavour to Chinese cooking, they differ depending on the region and the season. There are countless varieties of vegetables and solutions but among the most popular are cabbages, mustard greens and roots, radishes, turnips and cucumbers. Chillies are often added to the brine to give a spicy taste.

**PLUM SAUCE** Tart and sweet at the same time, has a taste that seems heaven-made to go with roast goose or duck. It also contains apricots, chilli and vinegar, which explains the exciting reddish brown tone.

**PORK FAT NET (CAUL LINING)** A large sheet of pork fat, used to wrap food to form rolls or to prevent dryness. It holds the food together while frying but eventually melts away unless coated with batter or flour, when it makes a crisp crust. Available from Chinese food stores.

**PRAWN CRACKERS** Also called "krupuk", they are compressed slivers of prawn and flour paste. They expand into large translucent crisps when deep-fried.

**PRAWNS (SHRIMPS)** The heads and tails are generally left on to add flavour and colour to the dish. To devein prawns, hold with the back curling upwards, push a toothpick into the centre back and gently hook out the dark vein. You can also cut along the back with a sharp knife and pull out the vein.

Cooked prawns are easily peeled by sliding the shell off. To peel uncooked prawns, cut the shell along the underside between the rows of legs and remove the whole shell.

**PRESERVED VEGETABLES** Used to give a pungent, salty flavour to Chinese dishes. They are sold by weight in Chinese food stores, and are also known as spiced vegetables. Preserved mustard is the most common. Mustard greens are the leaves, and mustard root the stem or root, and must be shredded or diced before use.

**QUAIL EGGS** Readily available hard-boiled in cans. Substitute very small chicken eggs.

**RAPE** The plant of the Brassica group, the leaves of which are used in some Chinese cooking. *Rapeseed oil* has been used in China as a fine cooking oil for many centuries.

**RED FERMENTED RICE (WINE LEES)** A mash of red rice and wine. Called for in some strong, regional recipes and virtually impossible to obtain in a non-Chinese society. Japanese miso paste can be used instead, but should be first diluted with water.

**RICE WINE** Many varieties are available, but *Shaoxing rice wine* is possibly the most famous in China and essential to many Shanghai and Yangtze Valley recipes. Available in most Chinese food stores worldwide, any shopowner will be delighted to chat about the different wines he stocks. As a drink to accompany food, it should be served warm from a teapot-like container in small cups without handles. Dry sherry can be used as a substitute in cooking.

**SCALLION OIL** Used to give extra flavour when stir-frying. It is made by frying roughly chopped spring onions (shallots/scallions) in oil until they are light-brown. Use 4 spring onions to 3 tablespoons of oil, and remove with a slotted spoon before using the oil. Peanut oil is preferred by Guangzhou cooks, although other vegetable oil is suitable.

**SEA CUCUMBER (BÊCHE-DE-MER)** A delicacy among southern gourmets who prize its rubbery texture. Known also as sea bear (because of its resemblance to bear's paw) it is the basis of expensive specialty dishes in some of the world's top Chinese restaurants. Soak, remove stomach, then pre-cook for one to several hours, depending on cooking time of final dish.

**SEAWEEDS** Mostly used in conjunction with other vegetables in soups. They must be soaked before use, preferably overnight, and should be rinsed thoroughly before and after soaking.

**SESAME OIL** Comes from the crushed and roasted seeds of the sesame plant. This treatment gives the oil its rich, nutty taste. It is used mainly as an aromatic garnish, and occasionally for cooking.

**SESAME PASTE (TAHINA)** A thick yellow paste made from ground sesame seeds. Peanut butter is a rather poor substitute for the aromatic, thick richness of sesame.

**SHARKS' FINS** Can be bought from well-stocked Chinese stores, but they are extremely expensive and daunting to prepare.

**SHRIMP PASTE** Is sold dried and should be cooked before being eaten. It has an unpleasant smell before being cooked but adds a distinctive flavour to certain dishes. Anchovy concentrate can be used instead if necessary.

**SILVER SPROUTS** Mung bean sprouts with the roots and seed pods removed. They are silvery when cooked.

**SOY SAUCE** Makes a Chinese meal. It is hard to imagine picking up your chopsticks without this familiar friend at your elbow. Salty, pungent and essential for cooking and as a garnish, it is absolutely indispensable for enjoyment of Chinese food. *Light soy sauce* is thinner and lighter in flavour than *black soy sauce* which is used mainly in stews. *Sweet soy sauce* is thick, black and sweet.

STAR ANISE   Comes from a shrub that is cousin to the magnolia. It gets its name from the star-like splay of its pod. Western anise, although not from the same botanical family, can be used as a substitute.

STOCKS   Vary from region to region, and are made by boiling meat, bones, poultry or vegetables in water for hours, skimming and filtering. Stock cubes are a poor substitute. Clear stock is made by simply frying a handful of bean sprouts and then boiling them in 1 or 2 cups (250-500 mL/8-16 fl oz) of water.

VERMICELLI   Usually a transparent bean thread pasta made from mung bean flour; can also be made from rice flour. Sold dried, in bundles. Both types can be deep-fried, or used in soups and stews.

VINEGAR   Plays an important, often overlooked role in every regional kitchen. Each province prides itself on the quality and clarity of its vinegar. *Rice vinegar,* light and clear with a sharp taste, is the most common. Any good quality vinegar is an acceptable alternative.

Several other types of vinegar are used in Chinese cooking. Distilled from fermented rice, the range includes *red vinegar,* which is mildly flavoured and used in sauces and dips; *brown* or *black vinegar,* stronger in taste and colour, and with a slight sweetness and fine aroma; *sweet black vinegar* is an especially sweetened dark rice vinegar used only occasionally.

WATER CHESTNUTS   Really the bulb of wild rushes. Very expensive and a lot of trouble to prepare, but now available in cans. The powdered flour called for in some exotic recipes is also available outside China.

WHITE RADISH   A popular cold starter, sliced thinly and eaten either raw with chilli or pickled. Its sharp taste turns sweet when cooked. Sweet white turnip can be substituted in cooked dishes.

YUNNAN HAM   Reputedly the finest in China. There is nothing quite the same, but you can substitute another well-salted ham.

WAGUO INN, NEAR SHIMIAN VILLAGE, SICHUAN PROVINCE

HARALD SUND

# Index

## POULTRY

## SEAFOOD

# Acknowledgments

The author and publisher would like to thank the proprietors and staff of the following restaurants for their co-operation and assistance in the production of *China the Beautiful Cookbook*. In particular we would like to thank the chefs who shared the original recipe for each dish with us.

## BEIJING

Quanjude Roast Beijing Duck Restaurant, Pianyifang Roast Beijing Duck Restaurant, Donglaishun Restaurant, Kaorouji Restaurant, Kangle Restaurant, Douyichu Shaomai Restaurant, Nanlaishun Xiaochi Restaurant, Tongheju Restaurant, Henan Restaurant, Jinyang Restaurant, Hongbinlou Restaurant, Yanbinlou Restaurant, Chunyanlou Restaurant, Fangshan Restaurant, Tingliguan Restaurant, Fengzeyuan Restaurant, Cuihualou Restaurant, Shaguoji Restaurant, Beijing Vegetarian Restaurant, Beijing Hotel, Xinqiao Hotel.

## SHANGHAI

Shanghai Old Restaurant, Laozhengxing Restaurant, Renmin Restaurant, Dafugui Restaurant, Yangzhou Restaurant, Yufoshi Vegetarian Restaurant, Lüyangcun Restaurant, Dongfeng Restaurant, Lübolang Restaurant, Zhiweiguan Hangzhou-style Restaurant, Ningbo Restaurant, Dahongyun Restaurant, Meilongzhen Restaurant, Xinya Cantonese-style Restaurant, Meiweizai Restaurant, Chenghuangmiao Food Centre, Qiaojiazha Dianxin House, Qiaojiazha Restaurant, Wufangzai Dianxin House, Dahuchun Dianxin House, Experimental Restaurant of Shanghai Food and Beverage School, Dianxin House of 1st Food and Beverage Corporation of Huangbu in Shanghai.

## GUANGDONG

Panxi Restaurant, Nanyuan Restaurant, Likoufu Sea Food Restaurant, Dasanyuan Restaurant, Dongjiang Restaurant, Snake Restaurant, Shahe Restaurant, Beiyuan Restaurant, Guangzhou Restaurant, Datong Restaurant, Beixiu Restaurant, Daijiang Caotang Restaurant, Quanwailou Restaurant, Shaocheng Restaurant, Tianfu Restaurant.

## SICHUAN

Chengdu Restaurant, Furong Restaurant, Xiaodongtian Restaurant, Chen Mapo Bean Curd House, Gongcun Restaurant, Xingfu Restaurant, Yudong Restaurant, Huixian Restaurant, Rongleyuan Restaurant, Laosichuan Restaurant, Jingchengyuan Restaurant, Shangqingsi Restaurant, Yuyuan Restaurant, Yeweixiang Restaurant, Caigengxiang Vegetarian Restaurant.

錦

銀杏蓮子青香

水煮青元桥

枇杷麵

銀耳枇杷花蓮